Data Response
for Economics

DATA RESPONSE
FOR ECONOMICS

G. Walker

CHECKMATE
GOLD

© G. WALKER 1988

First published in Great Britain 1988 by Checkmate Gold Publications,
P.O. Box 36, Ellesmere Port, South Wirral. L66 7PB.

British Library Cataloguing in Publication Data
Walker, G.
Data response for economics examinations
1. Economics — Examinations, questions, etc.
I. Title
330'.076   HB171.5

ISBN 1 85313 005 2

All rights reserved. No part of this publication may be reproduced, stored in a retrieval system, or transmitted in any form or by any means, electronic, photocopying, recording, or otherwise, without prior permission of Checkmate Gold at P.O. Box 36, Ellesmere Port, South Wirral. L66 7PB.

Text set in 10/12 pt Times
by Merseyside Graphics Ltd., 130 The Parade, Meols, Wirral L47 5AZ
Printed by Billing & Sons Limited, Hylton Road, Worcester WR2 5JU.

Cover design by Merseyside Graphics Ltd.

PREFACE AND ACKNOWLEDGEMENTS etc.

The aim of this book is threefold. Firstly it provides a range of past examination questions in data response so that students can appreciate what to expect in the examination. Secondly the answers, hopefully, will help students to relate their knowledge of Economics gained in classroom lectures to real world problems and thus aid the revision process. Lastly the book can be used as an Advanced Level Course workbook which can complement the textbook and enable the student to learn and understand both principles and application of economics.

ACKNOWLEDGEMENTS

I am grateful to the following for permission to reproduce copyright material:— (all sources are indicated in the text).

THE TIMES for extracts from "The Price of Tea" by M. Prest, 4th Jan. 1984, "Takeovers, Who Benefits?" by E. Palamountain, 21st Nov. 1986, "Cadbury-Schweppes & United Biscuits", 22nd Nov. 1986, "The Problem of Floating Exchange Rates", 16th Nov. 1983, "Foreign Exchange and Money Markets Selected Rates, 24th April 1986, "Alcohol Sales", 10th May 1983.

THE SUNDAY TIMES for the table "U.K. Interest Rates", 8th March 1981.

THE INVESTORS CHRONICLE for extracts from "West End Regains Momentum, 7th Nov. 1986 and "U.K. Cement Industry Restrained by Imports", 28th Jan. 1983.

THE FINANCIAL TIMES for "Why Gold Still Glitters" by S. Brittain, 30th Sept. 1979.

THE ECONOMIST for the table from "Too Equal", 1st Nov. 1986 and Figs. 1, 2, 3 from "U.K. Consumers' Expenditure on Alcohol 1971-84", 13th Sept. 1984.

THE GUARDIAN for the extracts which appeared in the editions of 4th August 1982, 5th May 1981; sources and authorship indicated in the text.

PENGUIN BOOKS for the extract from "The New Industrial State" by J.K. Galbraith.

WEIDENFELD & NICHOLSON LTD. for the table from "The U.K. Economy" 10th Ed. by A.R. Prest, E.D.J. Coppock, Eds.

THE BOOKSELLER for the extract from "The U.K. Book Publishing Industry" 8th Oct. 1983.

BBC ENTERPRISES LTD. for the extract from "Whatever Happened to Britain", by John Eatwell, 1983.

CAMBRIDGE UNIV. PRESS for the table on Economies of Scale in the Motor Car Industry reproduced from C.F. Pratten "Economies of Scale in Manufacturing Industry" 1971, page 142 table 14.4.

BANK INFORMATION SYSTEM for the extract from "Guide to International Financial Systems", 1984.

MIDLAND BANK for numerous charts, articles, etc. from "Midland Bank Review" sources listed.

OXFORD UNIVERSITY PRESS for "Male Unemployment by Duration 1970-85", chart, reproduced from "How we can Beat Unemployment" by R. Layard, 1986 and for the extract from "Privatisation" in British Economic Survey, Autumn 1983.

THE BRITISH RAIL BOARD for Annual Report 1978.

C.S.O., H.M.S.O. for various tables, charts, graphs from Social Trends, Economic Progress Report, U.K. National Accounts, Economic Trends, U.K. Census of Production, White Paper on Transport, U.K. Balance of Payments, Financial Statistics, Family Expenditure Surveys, Annual Abstract of Statistics, sources and editions as listed.

LLOYDS BANK for extracts and tables, etc. from "The British Economy in Figures, 1986" and "Lloyds Bank Economic Bulletin", "Lloyds Bank Review", "An Economic Profile of Britain 1986". Sources indicated.

NATIONAL WESTMINSTER BANK for the extracts and tables from "National Westminster Bank Quarterly Review". Sources listed.

BRITISH TELECOM for "Your Guide to Telephone Charges", Nov. 1986.

THE UNITED NATIONS for World Development Report 1981/2, The World Bank and World Bank and Demographic Yearbook, 1981.

THE ROYAL BANK OF SCOTLAND for "The Royal Bank of Scotland Review" extracts and tables, etc., sources listed.

THE BUILDING SOCIETIES ASSOCIATION for the "B.S.A. Bulletin" of Jan. 1986, for the chart.

I would also like to thank the following Examination Boards for permission to use past 'A' Level Examination questions. The specimen answers are entirely the work of the author and do not in any way represent the Boards' opinions, model answers or marking schemes. In particular, the University of London School Examination Board accept no responsibility whatever for the accuracy or method of working in the answers given.

Examination Boards

S.U.J.B.	Southern Universities Schools Examination Board.
A.E.B.	Associated Examining Board for the G.C.E.
London	University of London School Examination Board.
R.I.C.S.	Royal Institute of Chartered Surveyors.
C.A.C.A.	Chartered Association of Certified Accountants.
Oxford	Oxford Delegacy of Local Examinations.
I.O.B.	Institute of Bankers.

Finally, I would like to thank my wife, Rosemary, for all her hard work in the typing of the manuscript. **Graham Walker, 1987**

"Orthodoxy is my doxy; heterodoxy is another man's doxy"
(Bishop Warburton 1698-1779)

CONTENTS

			Page
Section 1			
Chapter	1	Introduction and Points to Remember	1
Section 2			
Chapter	2	Averages	5
	3	Graphs and Charts	9
	4	Time Series Graphs	17
	5	Index Numbers	20
	6	Graphs and Equations	25
	7	Demand and Supply Elasticity	27
	8	Compounding and Discounting, Investment Analysis	32
Section 3 QUESTIONS			
Chapter	9	Micro-Economics — Basic Concepts	36
	10	Market Analysis	43
	11	Distribution of Income	50
	12	Supply–Theory of the Firm	64
	13	Structure of Industry, Scale and Location	75
	14	International Trade–Development Economics	94
	15	Money and Banking	107
	16	Macro-Economics, National Income Accounts	114
	17	Public Finance	128
Section 4 ANSWERS			
Chapter	18	Micro-Economics — Basic Concepts	132
	19	Market Analysis	139
	20	Distribution of Income	150
	21	Supply–Theory of the Firm	166
	22	Structure of Industry, Scale and Location	180
	23	International Trade–Development Economics	199
	24	Money and Banking	214
	25	Macro-Economics, National Income Accounts	225
	26	Public Finance	245

SECTION 1

Chapter 1
INTRODUCTION AND POINTS TO REMEMBER

Why Data Response?
Data Response questions are increasingly used as a form of assessment in Economics examinations. They are now established as a reliable form of assessment because they enable economic theories to be applied to real world situations and in so doing students are able to relate their knowledge to current economic problems and events, i.e. Economics has some practical value. This means the data response approach to economics allows for the new activity centred philosophy to learning stressed in the new educational assessment initiatives, e.g. G.C.S.E. At the same time educational research has shown how data response scores are a more reliable indicator of overall examination performance than either the essay or multiple choice form. In short the data response approach allows the candidate and student to apply economic theory, and in so doing they are able to select relevant principles and hence discriminate between arguments and policies. Economic theories are also being applied and evaluated so the candidate must know and be able to use a range of economic and numerical skills before getting down to writing a structured and cogent response. Data response balances the theoretical academic deductive approach, which was the hallmark of the earlier forms of assessment, with the more inductive or empirical real world approach. This means that whilst the deductive or theoretical aspect stresses an analytic framework, often using unrealistic assumptions, data response with its emphasis on evidence and observation allows the student to question principles and develop a more sensible and pragmatic grasp of the economic environment. Whatever the educational philosophy underlying data response questions, Advanced level Exam. Boards, the new G.C.S.E. syllabus, B.T.E.C. and other professional and degree awarding institutions have all incorporated this form of assessment within their overall testing packages. Educationally Data Response questions test the candidate in the higher order of skills, namely the ability to analyse, synthesise, evaluate and apply principles. These skills account for around 30% of the total examination marks, though individual examination boards vary in the actual marks awarded for the Data Response questions.

Data Response Questions
There is no standard format or type of data response question. Questions are often structured from simple definitions or calculations to a discussion and evaluation of principles involved. On the other hand, questions can be unstructured. For example "Discuss the economic significance of the above

information" etc. Furthermore, the type of question can range from the hypothetical to the factual and prose comprehension though currently there is no common practice amongst the main Advanced level Examination Boards. The A.E.B., London, and S.U.J.B. tend to offer a choice and structure their questions over all three types of questions. The Cambridge Board and Cambridge and Oxford Boards use numerical or statistical data together with short response questions. Oxford Delegacy incorporate the data response question within the Essay paper and the J.M.B. tend to go for one large passage, e.g. a newspaper article, often with a table, and structured questions. Nevertheless, for all this disparity it may be useful to briefly outline the three main question types and provide simple guidance points.

a) **Hypothetical Type**
A favourite with London, A.E.B. and S.U.J.B. whereby hypothetical data are presented usually on the firm, supply or demand, National Income, etc. The question can incorporate definitions, calculations and a discussion on the economic principles involved and candidates are left in no doubt regarding which economic ideas are being tested. These questions are similar to multiple choice questions and so the answers should follow the structure of the question and candidates should show all calculations or workings. In the main, be brief and to the point in your answer and relate and explain your ideas to the Data. It is useful with this type of question to make a rough plan of your answer beforehand.

b) **Factual Type**
These questions use real data in the form of a table, chart, diagram or news-cutting, etc. They are selected from the Press, Government publications, Treasury Report, Bank Review etc. The data are not specifically designed for examination purposes so the student should carefully read, often more than once, to grasp its economic significance and relevance. Underline any important points or statistical information, and you may have to discriminate and disregard much of the passage. This does not matter and in itself is a test of your ability to select only that material relevant to the question. Examiners' Reports regularly stress that the failing of students with this type of question is their inability to understand the statistical presentation, technique or concept. This means, for example, candidates should be able to understand time and cross sectional data. They should also be able to understand:— index numbers, "real" and current prices, trends and seasonal variations, logarithmic and normal scales. Also they should recognise a simple equation, a pie chart or histogram etc., and generally understand the significance and relationship between a passage and the accompanying table, chart or diagram. This means those who have studied mathematics or statistics will be able to cope better than those from a non-numerate background. See the Statistical Chapters.

(c) Prose Comprehension Type

These are specifically selected textual passages again from a newspaper, book or Government publication etc. The questions are structured to incorporate definitions and interpretation of basic economic principles. The more difficult questions concern the usefulness, or evaluation, of the theories with regard to the data. These questions are often difficult because there is usually more than one answer and the passage can cover a wide range of principles and syllabus areas. In this type of question, search for the likely major principles being tested and note how they are being applied. There may be other minor ideas which can be used but the importance of these can often be seen by the way the question is structured.

Sometimes a passage relates to only one economic problem but there are usually underlying assumptions which have to be made explicit and discussed. The source of the passage can often be a clue as to why it was selected. To gain practice for this question type get into the habit of continually reading good quality newspapers and try to relate economic ideas you are familiar with to the relevant financial or economic article. This enables you to develop a critical approach and encourages sensible comment and evaluation of the main arguments.

Some Summary Points to Remember

(i) Know and understand basic economic theory thoroughly.
(ii) Continually practice relating economic theory to the real world by looking at suitable tables, passages etc. in newspapers and other sources.
(iii) Obtain past Examination Reports and Questions and practice doing the Data Response problems within the time allowed. Note the marks allowed where these are printed and allocate time accordingly.
(iv) Develop a good background knowledge of current commercial, economic and political events.
(v) Know and be able to work with basic statistical concepts and key economic formula (see Statistical Chapters).
(vi) Appreciate why examiners use Data Response questions. Are you able to apply theory to real or hypothetical data?
(vii) Check instructions regarding the Data Response questions and allocate time on the basis of the number of questions to be attempted and the marks awarded. Structure your answer on the basis of the question and appreciate that the latter parts of a question often use the answer you obtained in the first part of the question.
(viii) Write legibly, logically and try to be neat when drawing up a chart, table or diagram. Slang must be avoided — write in textbook English.
(ix) In conclusion, Examiners Reports stress the following "Data Response questions are frequently open-ended, permitting a variety of

approaches and material. In assessing answers, examiners, whilst requiring theoretical and factual correctness, take answers on their merits. Each exposes the candidate's intellectual and educational standard, as well as technical grasp and skill. Examination centres would do well to consider how far their study of economics is part of an educational process: the former being an instrument of the latter. Above all, Data Response questions can be so varied that a questioning approach to the subject is important. The relevant theory to provide a structure needs to be selected and applied. Its appropriateness to the situation needs to be considered and a reasoned discussion presented. In the ideal case, applied economics requires the selective use of theory and a synthesis with the facts of the situation. In this respect they discriminate in favour of those who have been *educated* in their subject."

Source: London. 1982 'A' Economics Examiners Report.

SECTION 2 USING STATISTICS

Chapters 2 to 8 provide a selection of simple statistical and quantitative concepts which may be useful when answering data response questions. They do **not** provide a comprehensive treatment and students are advised to refer to the standard texts on statistics and mathematics.

Chapter 2
AVERAGES

1. AVERAGES:— THE MEAN

TABLE 1
Schools and Costs 1986/87

Authority	Pupil : Teacher Ratio Secondary Schools	Secondary School Unit Cost per Pupil (£)
1. Barnet	19.9	1305.5
2. Brent	11.2	1807.9
3. Enfield	14.9	1220.9
4. Hertfordshire	15.0	1213.1

Source: T.E.S., 31/10/86.

Most people use the "mean" when they calculate an average. This is calculated by dividing, as in the case of unit cost per secondary school pupil, the total costs by the number of pupils. Again the pupil : teacher ratio is calculated in the same way; by dividing the total number of teachers in an authority by the total number of secondary school children. It is simple to work out and easy to understand. In economics it is used to calculate average cost and average revenue etc.

Question on Table 1. Comment on the cost-effectiveness of secondary school education between the four authorities.

2. AVERAGES:— MEDIAN AND MODE AND FREQUENCY DISTRIBUTIONS

Often the mean is used in Income analysis to calculate average or "per-capita" income in a country. However, as with all mean average figures, it fails to take account of the overall distribution of income, so this average can sometimes be misleading and unrealistic. In order to give a better indication of average incomes the "median" can be used. The median is the value of the middle item between the lowest and highest value and would therefore indicate more accurately, for example, the representative income in the country. The mode is another measure of the average and is the most common or most frequently occurring value in the distribution.

FREQUENCY DISTRIBUTIONS show the overall behaviour of the variable and indicates whether the pattern is "skewed" or "normal" in its behaviour.

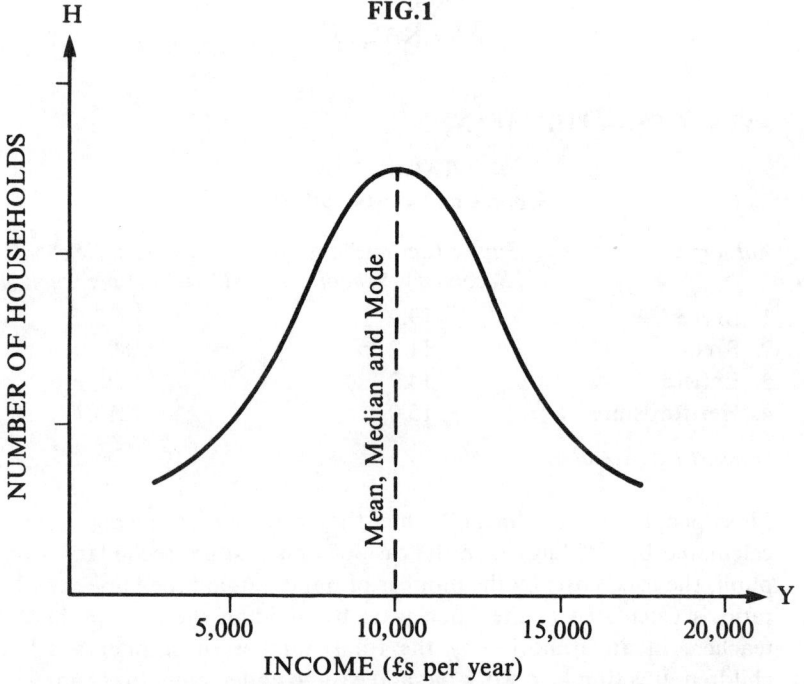

A perfectly normal distribution of income; the mean, median and mode coincide.

In a perfectly normal distribution of income, see Fig. 1, referred to as a "bell" curve the mean, median and mode would be the same, i.e. £10,000 and if everyone earned the same, i.e. £10,000, the distribution would be a single line perpendicular to £10,000 on the Y axis. However, in the real world, income distribution is usually lopsided and in the case of Fig. 2 the U.K. distribution in 1979 indicates a 'skewed' distribution with each average different. Again Fig. 3 shows the frequency distributions, in percentage terms, for manual male and female G.B. employees in 1984 which indicate different overall income distributions.

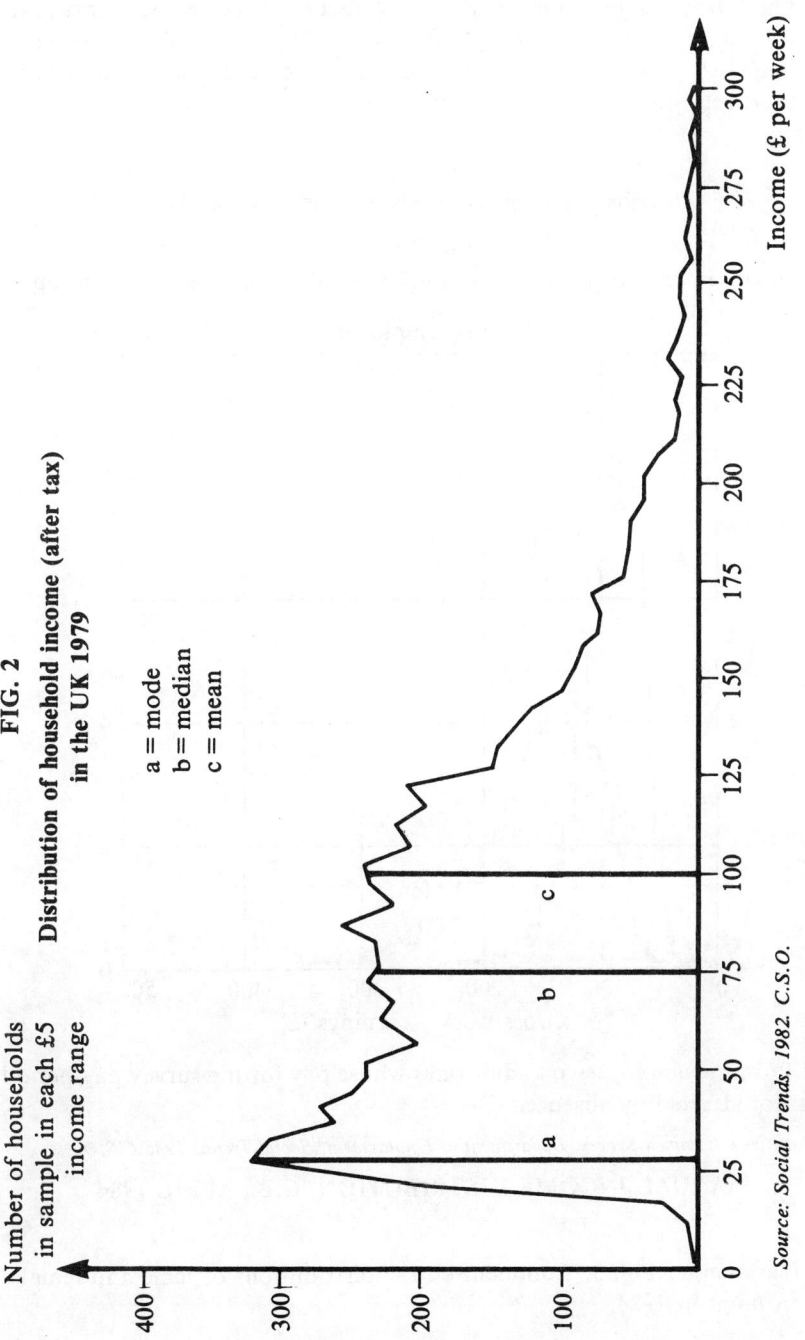

Fig. 2. In this positively skewed distribution of income, each average is different.

8 Averages

Fig. 3 below shows the frequency distribution in percentage terms, for manual employees, male and female, in 1984. This illustrates how frequency distributions can vary and in both cases the distributions are positively skewed with most workers earning low wages.

FIG. 3
Distribution of gross weekly earnings[1], April 1984

Great Britain

Estimated percentage with gross weekly earnings in £5 earnings groups

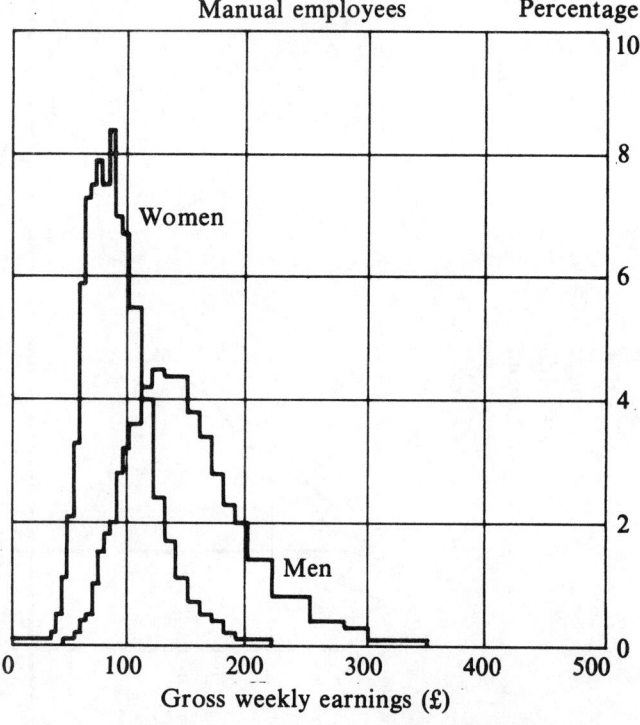

[1] Of full-time employees on adult rates whose pay for the survey pay-period was not affected by absence.

Source: New Earnings Survey, Department of Employment, Social Trends 1986 C.S.O.

MANUAL INCOME DISTRIBUTION, G.B., APRIL 1984

Question on Fig. 3. Comment on the distributions of male and female earnings in 1984.

Chapter 3
GRAPHS AND CHARTS

Graphs and charts are simple devices which help illustrate economic theory, data, and findings. A familiarity with the main types are essential when answering data response questions.

(i) Histograms

These relate the value of discrete or grouped data, along the horizontal axis, to the number of observations or frequency, along the vertical axis. A typical example is the "Population Pyramids" of Figs. 4a and 4b below, where frequency is along the horizontal axis and the variable (age) is along the vertical axis. Also, the income distributions in Figs. 1 and 2 are frequency distributions showing the continuous behaviour of a variable (Income). They have all been derived from histograms of grouped income data.

Population: by sex, age and marital status, 1971 and 1981[1]

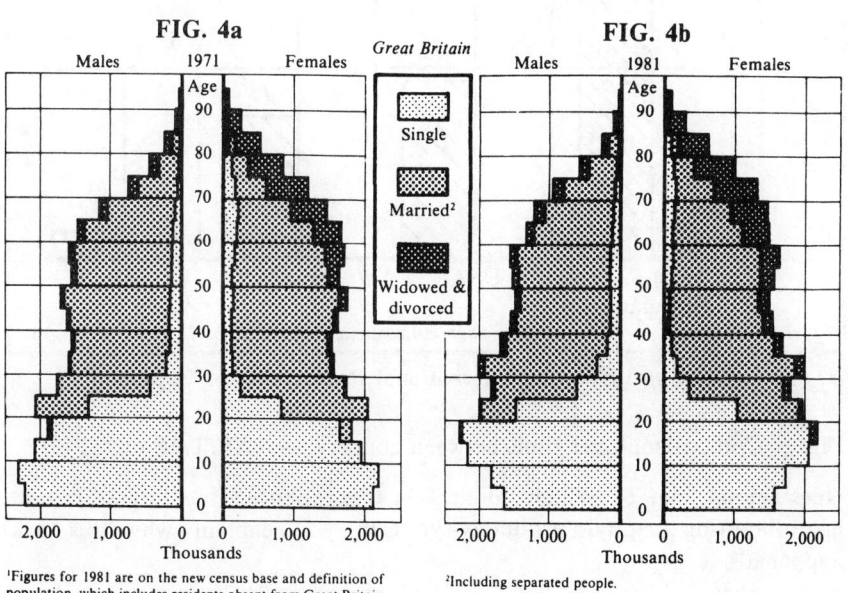

[1]Figures for 1981 are on the new census base and definition of population, which includes residents absent from Great Britain and excludes overseas visitors. The reverse was the case in 1971.
Source: Social Trends, 1986. C.S.O.

[2]Including separated people.
*Source: Population Census, 1971 and 1981.
Office of Population Censuses and Surveys.*

Frequency Distribution of GB Population
Note: Frequency or numbers are along horizontal axis and class intervals are on vertical axis.

10 Graphs and Charts

Question on Figs. 4a/4b. Comment on the changing structure of the GB population between 1971 and 1981. Discuss their economic significance.

(ii) Bar Charts

Bar charts represent data by a series of bars which visually indicate the scale of the variables. Figs. 5, 6 and 7 illustrate their use in economics.

FIG. 5

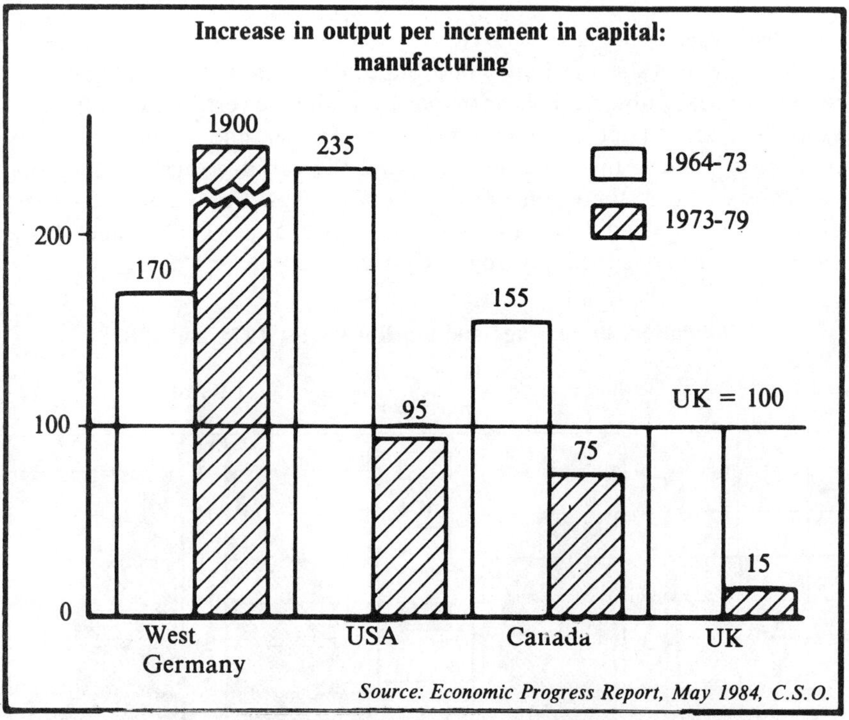

Increase in output per increment in capital: manufacturing

[Bar chart showing values: West Germany 170 (1964-73), 1900 (1973-79); USA 235 (1964-73), 95 (1973-79); Canada 155 (1964-73), 75 (1973-79); UK = 100, 15 (1973-79)]

Source: Economic Progress Report, May 1984, C.S.O.

Bar Chart Showing International Productivity of Capital

Fig. 5. Comparison over time/between country — CAPITAL OUTPUT.

Question on Fig. 5. Which country has experienced the largest fall in manufacturing capital productivity? Can you explain why this has happened?

FIG. 6
People in households[1]: by type of household and family in which they live

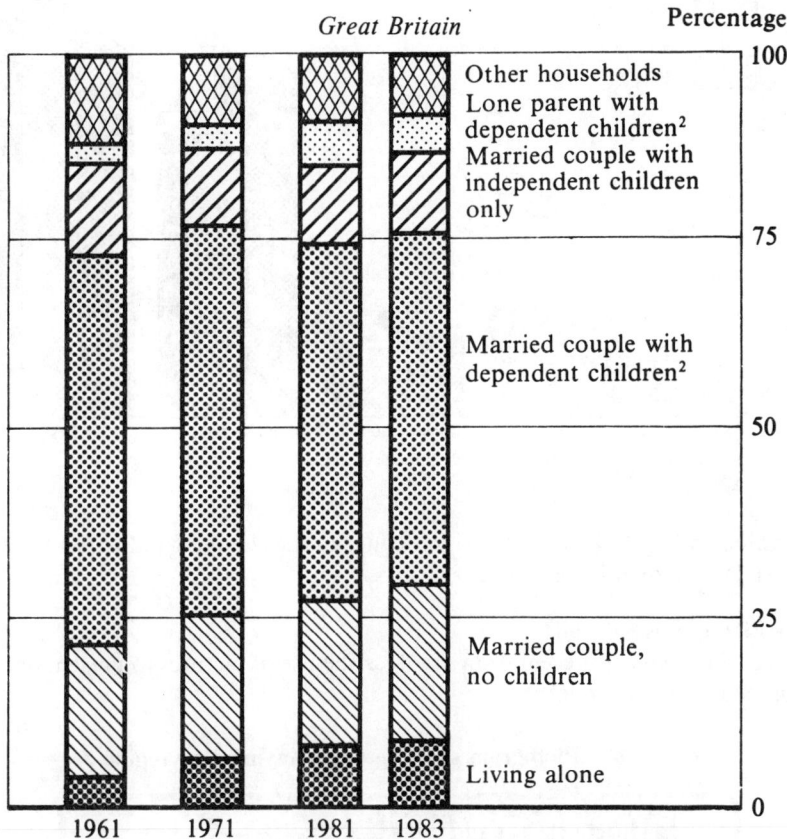

[1] The data for 1961, 1971, and 1981 are taken from the Population Censuses for those years; the 1983 data are from the General Household Survey.
[2] These family types may also include independent children.

Source: Office of Population Censuses and Surveys, C.S.O.

Question on Fig. 6. Describe how the household unit has changed in GB from 1961 to 1983. What are the economic implications of these changes?

12 Graphs and Charts

FIG. 7 Comparison of sector shares of GDP over time

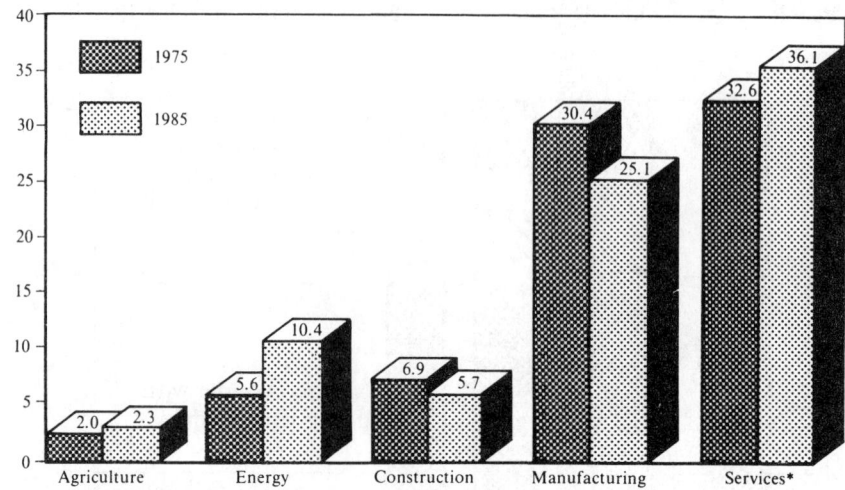

*Excluding national and local government, education and health
Source: UK National Accounts, HMSO and CSO data.

Question on Fig. 7. Discuss the significance of the changing industrial shares of GDP as shown in the bar chart.

(iii) Pictograms
This form of visual presentation involves the use of pictures to present data. Figs. 8 and 9 illustrate.

FIG. 8 Pictogram showing unemployment by region

Graphs and Charts 13

Question on Fig. 8. Comment on regional variations in UK unemployment.

FIG. 9
Growth in import penetration in the UK car market

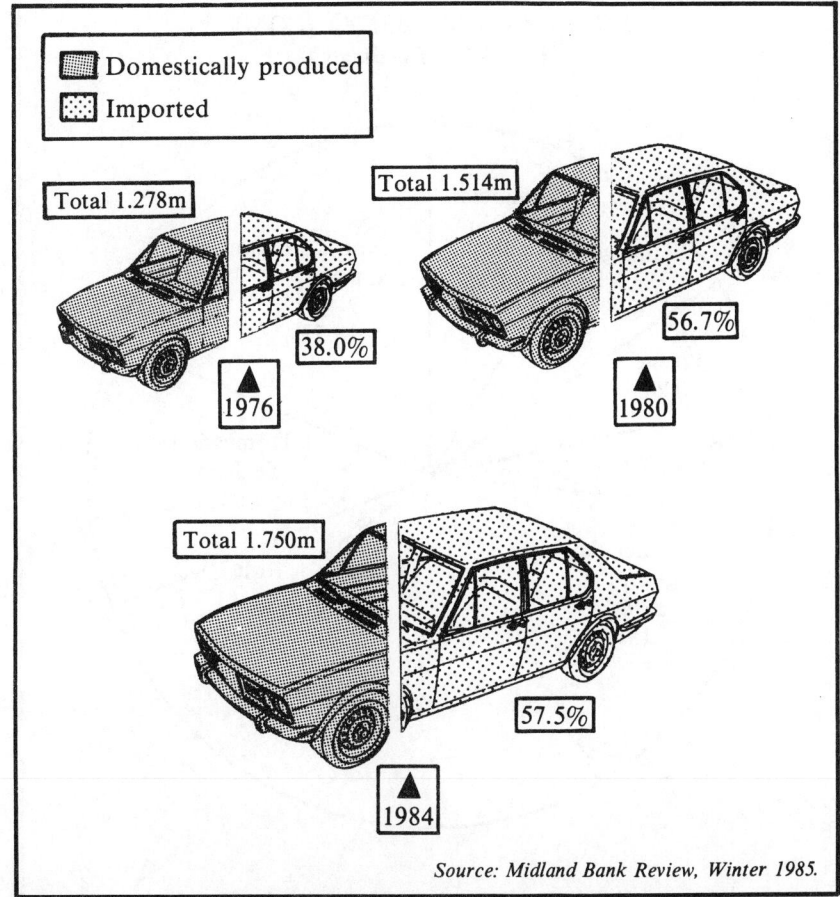

Source: Midland Bank Review, Winter 1985.

FIG. 9. PICTOGRAM SHOWING IMPORT PENETRATION IN UK CAR MARKET (NEW CARS)

Question on Fig. 9. Describe and comment on the UK new car market between 1976 and 1984.

(iv) Pie Charts
This is a circle, divided by radial lines, into sections, so that each one is proportional to the size of the figure represented. It therefore shows the sizes of component figures in proportion to each other and to the overall total. Figures 10 and 11 illustrate.

14 Graphs and Charts

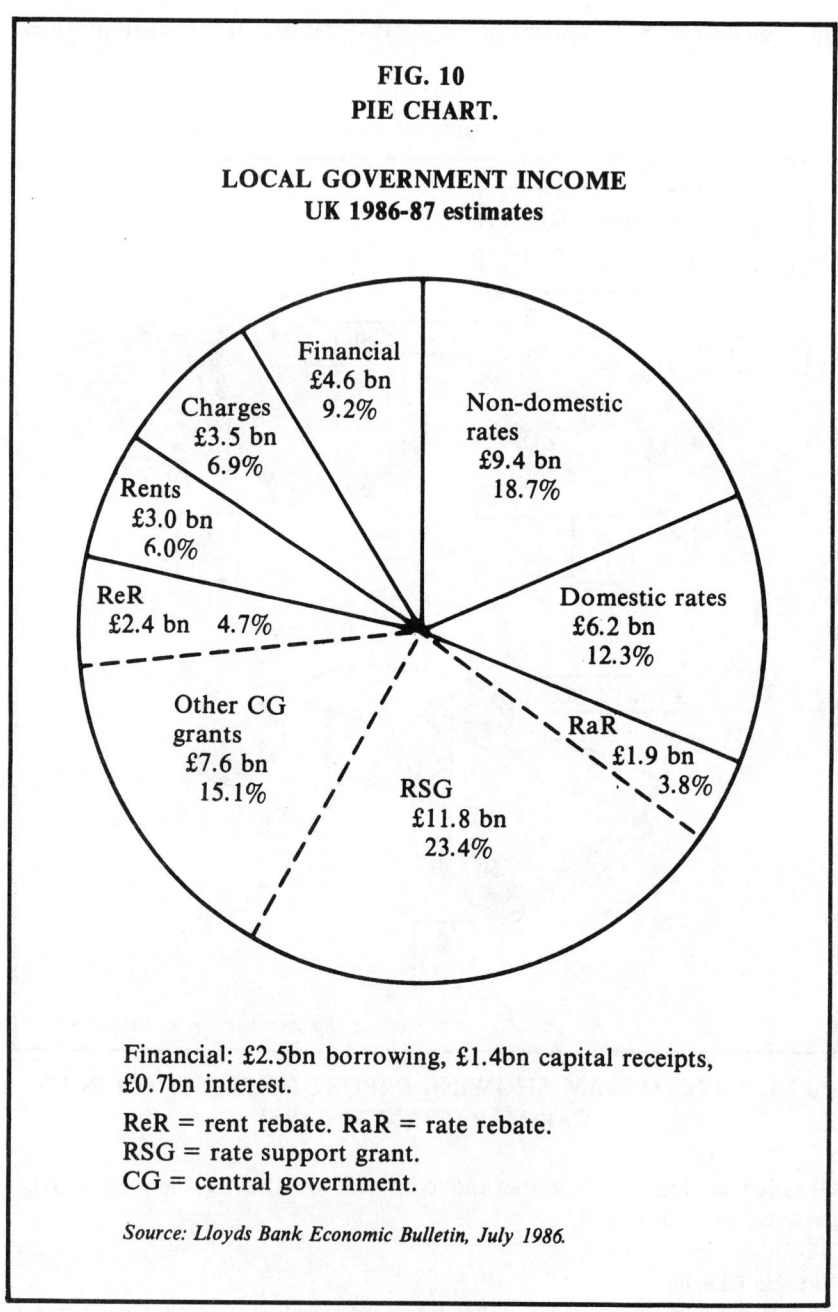

FIG. 10
PIE CHART.

LOCAL GOVERNMENT INCOME
UK 1986-87 estimates

Financial: £2.5bn borrowing, £1.4bn capital receipts, £0.7bn interest.

ReR = rent rebate. RaR = rate rebate.
RSG = rate support grant.
CG = central government.

Source: Lloyds Bank Economic Bulletin, July 1986.

Question on Fig. 10. Explain the components of local government income and comment.

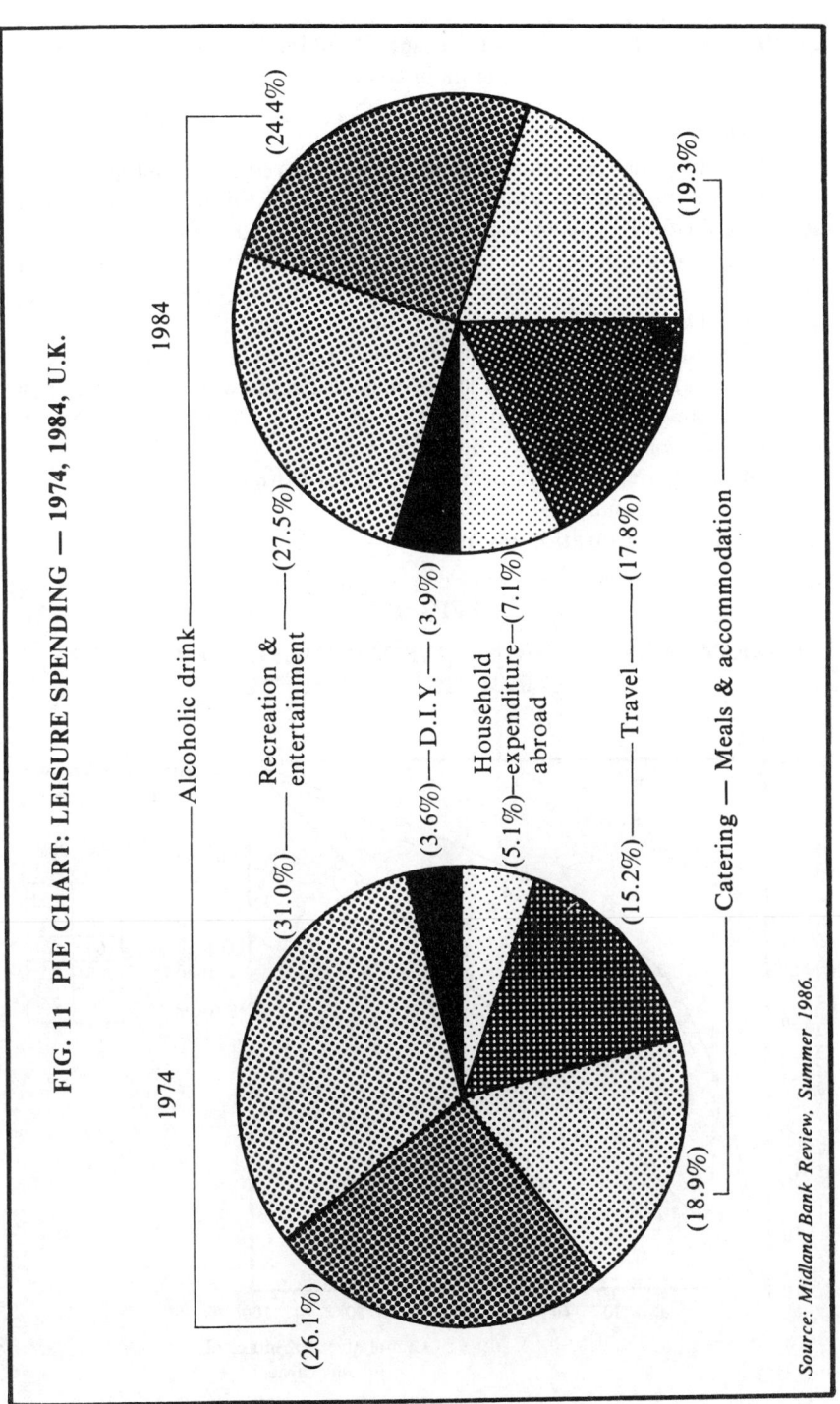

FIG. 11 PIE CHART: LEISURE SPENDING — 1974, 1984, U.K.

Source: *Midland Bank Review, Summer 1986.*

16 Graphs and Charts

Question on Fig. 11. Describe how leisure spending has changed and outline the economic importance of the main trends.

(v) **Lorenz Curves**

The derivation of frequency distributions is based upon actual income received by householders. Another way of presenting this information is by a LORENZ CURVE. This indicates how far the actual distribution of income etc. deviates from a perfectly equal distribution. It is derived by calculating, in percentage terms, the cumulative change in both income and frequency variables. The further the curve is from the centre line the greater the inequality and vice versa. In the hypothetical Lorenz Curve, Fig. 12, around 10% of pre-tax income earners receive 40% of income which illustrates how unequal income distribution often is. Lorenz Curves can be used to illustrate inequalities in other areas of economics, e.g.
(i) Industrial concentration of output etc., over time etc.
(ii) Industrial output and costs (efficiency).
(iii) The impact of taxation on incomes — see Fig. 12.

FIG. 12

LORENZ CURVE SHOWING HYPOTHETICAL PRE & POST TAX DISTRIBUTION OF INCOME

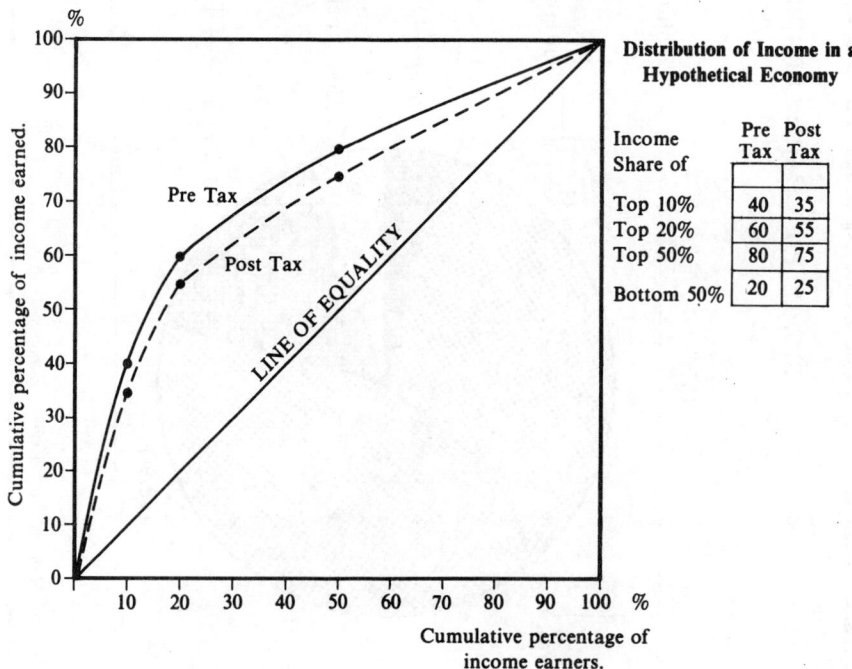

Chapter 4
TIME SERIES GRAPHS

Whilst it is possible to present time series data in a table it is normally easier to identify the main findings in a graphical form. Much of economics is concerned with analysing behaviour over time and so these graphics are used in demand, output, income, distribution and trade cycle analysis etc. Time Series graphs can be used with index numbers to show up "real" changes — Fig. 13 illustrates and shows three components of a time series graph, in 'real' terms.

FIG. 13
Real changes in motor vehicle expenditure and total consumers' expenditure

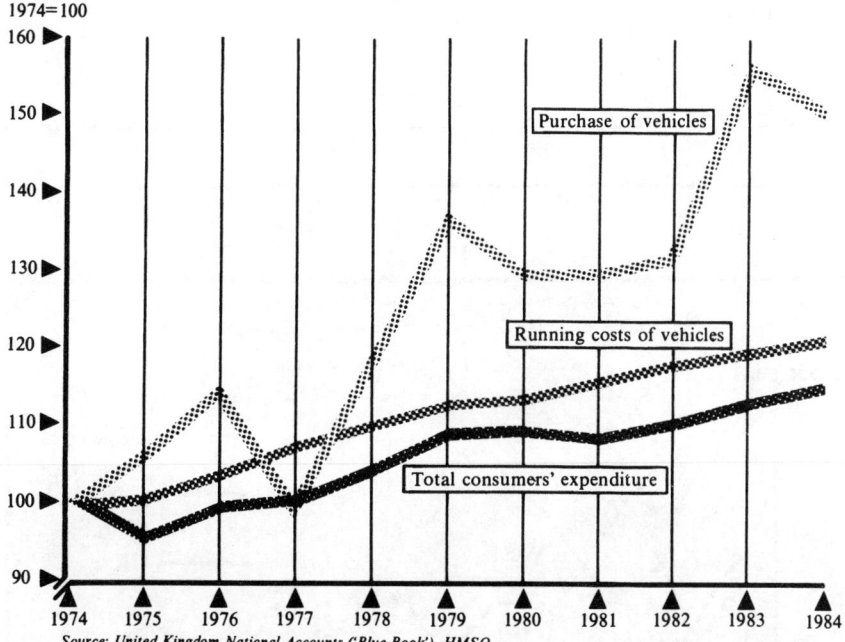

Source: United Kingdom National Accounts ('Blue Book'), HMSO.

TIME SERIES GRAPHS. MOTOR VEHICLE EXPENDITURE (INDEX NUMBERS)

Time Series graphs can indicate the overall trend within the series and other graphs can break total values into component items or show comparisons between countries etc. See Figs. 14, 15 and 16.

Question on Fig. 13. Comment upon the behaviour of the three variables illustrated in fig. 13. What is the significance of 1974=100?

FIG. 14

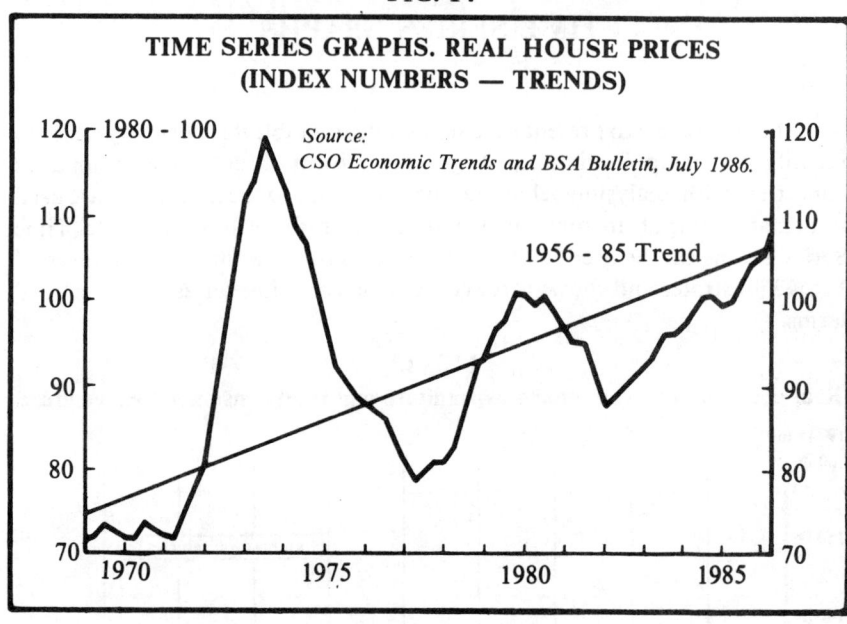

FIG. 15

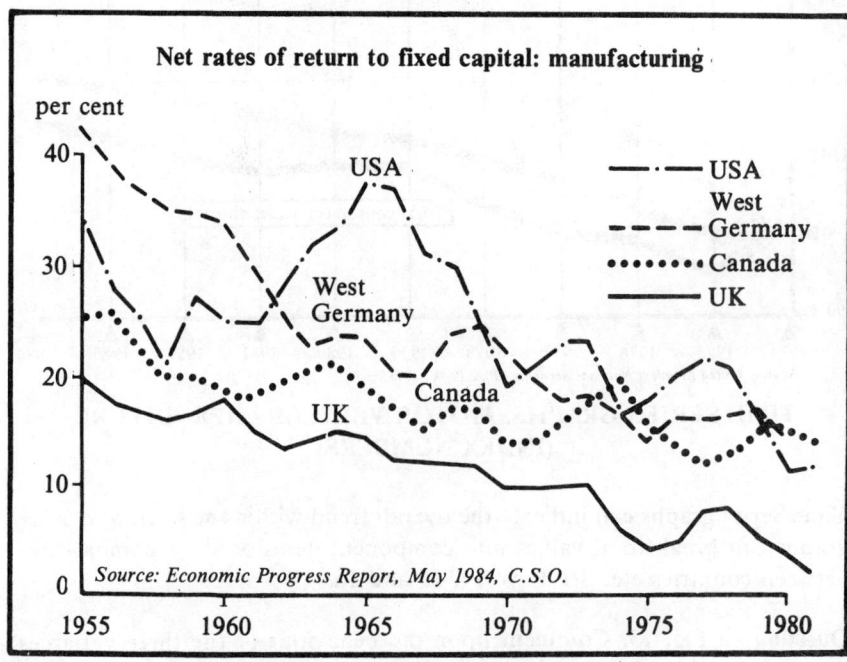

FIG. 15 TIME SERIES — INTERNATIONAL CAPITAL RETURNS

Fig. 14 also uses the notion of index numbers to obtain a "real" trend line which helps show up cyclical or seasonal variation over time. This trend could then be 'extrapolated' or projected into the future so that predictions could be made. Interpolation is when a trend is predicted **between** known values. Fig. 15 shows four separate trends on one diagram.

Question to Fig. 14. Describe and account for the 1956-85 trend in real house prices.

Question to Fig. 15. Explain the term "net rates of return" and describe and comment on the overall trend shown.

Lastly, Fig. 16 shows how time series graphs can be used to show the components of an overall trend; in this case passenger transport. However, the same idea could be used to compare components of aggregate demand such as consumer spending (C), investment spending (I) etc.

FIG. 16
Passenger transport by mode 1954:1984

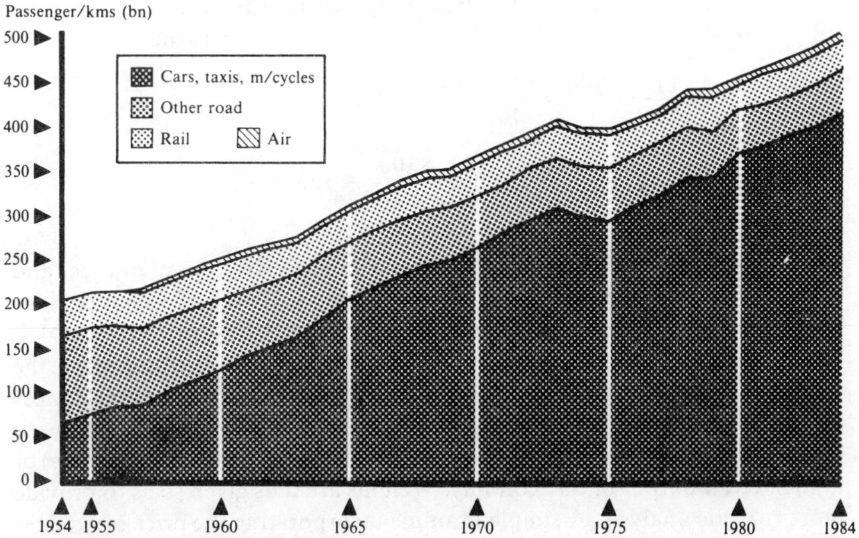

Passenger/kms (bn)
500
450
400
350
300
250
200
150
100
50
0
Cars, taxis, m/cycles
Other road
Rail
Air
1954
1955
1960
1965
1970
1975
1980
1984

Source: Midland Bank Review, Winter 1985.

FIG. 16 TIME SERIES — PASSENGER TRANSPORT

Question to Fig. 16. Comment on the changing passenger modes of transport 1954-84.

Finally, many time series graphs are **"seasonally adjusted"**. All this means is that where regular, predictable, seasonable variations exist, then these can be calculated and eliminated from actual figures to give the overall trend figure.

Chapter 5
INDEX NUMBERS

Index Numbers are simple and easy to understand numbers which attempt to relate the change in a number of variables through one number called the base year number and represented by 100. In Table 2 the price of oranges (current money prices) is reduced to a simple price relative and shown as an index of price compared to the original year 1, i.e. the base year. See (a).

TABLE 2

Years	Output of Oranges	Price of Oranges	Index of output	(Price Relative) Index of Prices
1	10,000	10	111	100
2	12,000	11	133	110
3	9,000	15	100	150

(a) Price Index — Year 1 = 100 Base weighted (Laspeyres)
(b) Output Index — Year 3 = 100 Current weighted (Paasche)

e.g. (a) $\dfrac{\text{Price Yr.2} \times 100}{\text{Price Yr.1}} = \dfrac{11 \times 100}{10} = 110,$

(b) $\dfrac{\text{Output Yr.2} \times 100}{\text{Output Yr.3}} = \dfrac{133 \times 100}{100} = 133$

Table 2 also shows a current (Yr.3) weighted index of output of oranges and economic data often show "base" weighted and/or "current" weighted price and output indices, so carefully note which one is used — see APPENDIX. Table 2 indicates at a glance the overall behaviour of price and output, i.e. the Trend. Whilst this analysis is sufficient when using one product, **overall** prices or output calculations have to incorporate appropriate "weights" in order to reflect the significance of say oranges within the household budget (prices) or in the **overall** output of an economy. Weights are thus given so as to provide more realistic analysis. A simple example incorporating the price of oranges and apples in Year 1 and 2 gives a weighted fruit price index, using the base year 1. See table 3.

TABLE 3

Product	Price Yr.1	Price Yr.2	Weight =	Yr.1	Yr.2
Oranges	10	11	×4	40	44
Apples	6	12	×6	36	72
Yr.1 =100	16	23	10	76	116

Unweighted Fruit Index (Base Yr.1 = 100) (Laspeyres)
$$\frac{\text{Price of Oranges} + \text{Apples Yr.2}}{\text{Price of Oranges} + \text{Apples Yr.1}} \times 100 = \frac{23}{16} \times 100 = 144$$

Weighted Fruit Index (Base Yr.1 = 100) (Laspeyres)
$$\frac{\text{Weighted Price of Oranges/Apples Yr.2}}{\text{Weighted Price of Oranges/Apples Yr.1}} \times 100 = \frac{116}{76} \times 100 = 153$$

Table 4a and 4b show how index numbers can be used to indicate the extent of inflation and purchasing power. In table 4a the base years are periodically changed, e.g. 1885=100, 1900=100 etc., so realistic and representative baskets of goods are updated. The table thus indicates the changing purchasing power of the £ over the short and long term.

TABLE 4a
Purchasing power of the £ UK
taking value as equivalent to 100p in various years

Year													
1885	100													
1900	107½	100												
1913	93	86½	100											
1925	52½	49	56½	100										
1938	59½	55½	64	113	100									
1946	45½	42½	49	86½	76½	100								
1955	30½	28½	33	58	51½	67½	100							
1965	22½	21	24½	43	38	49½	74	100						
1975	10	9	10½	18½	16½	21½	32	43½	100					
1980	5	4½	5½	9½	8½	11	16½	22	51	100				
1981	4½	4	5	8½	7½	10	14½	20	45½	89½	100			
1982	4	4	4½	8	7	9	13½	18	42	82½	92	100		
1983	4	3½	4	7½	6½	8½	13	17½	40	78½	88	95½	100	
1984	4	3½	4	7	6½	8	12½	16½	38½	75	84	91	95½	100
1985	3½	3½	4	6½	6	8	11½	15½	36	70½	79	86	90	94½	100

Note: Moving Base Years.

TABLE 4b
Note: Base Year 1975=100

	1975	1980	1985
Price indices			
Retail prices	100	195.6	276.9
of which food	100	192.0	252.3
Input prices (8)	100	182.1	250.8
Average price of new dwellings on mortgage	100	213.7	290.6
Import prices	100	172.4	250.3
Export prices	100	196.5	281.9
Terms of trade (9)	100	114.0	112.8
Actual prices (end year)			
Milk — pint	8.5p	17p	23p
Tea — 125g	10.5p	27p	43p
Quarterly rail season ticket — Woking-Waterloo	£74.70	£182.50	£246.00
Petrol — one gallon of four-star	76p	131p	191p
British Leyland Mini — 1,000cc	£1,374	£2,796	£3,447
Newspaper — Daily Mail	6p	12p	20p

Source: The UK Economy in Figures 1986 – Lloyds Bank 1986.

22 Index Numbers

Question on Table 4a. Identify periods in the UK when the purchasing power of the £ **rose** and **fell** most rapidly.

Table 4b shows actual prices and price indices for a number of items. Price indices are 1975=100 and allow quick and simple comparisons of inflation rates to be made. Actual prices can be changed to indices form using base prices, e.g. 1975=100 (Laspeyres) or current prices, e.g. 1985=100 (Paasche). This is a useful exercise and so a price index based on milk prices for 1975=100 would be for 1980 = $\frac{17p}{8.5p} \times 100 = 200$.

Task. Work out base and current price indices for tea between 1975 and 1985.

Finally, table 5 over uses index numbers in a sophisticated TABULAR form to show international productivity comparisons for 1981. It is accompanied by a number of comments which serve to illustrate how the table can be interpreted in economic terms.

Note: in the case of table 5, the UK serves as the standard yardstick, i.e. Britain=100.

Economic Comments on Table 5

"British labour productivity is often compared unfavourably with our competitors'. But the inefficiency with which we misuse labour bears no comparison with the horrendous way in which we waste our capital stock.

Comparisons between countries are hampered by the lack of a common unit of measurement. American output is naturally measured in dollars and British in pounds. But when exchange rates are used to convert different currencies to the same base, one gets bogus results. Exchange rates reflect relative prices only of traded goods. They do this very badly because they are also affected by capital flows. They are, moreover, extremely volatile. If, for instance, the US dollar appreciates 10 per cent against the pound, this does not mean that the value of Britain's output has fallen 10 per cent compared with American. But that is what the use of current exchange rates would tell you.

Fortunately the OECD has come up with a better way of comparing output between countries. It has taken a set of average international prices for physical units — tonnes of steel, yards of cloth, etc — and recalculated each country's national output from scratch using these standard prices in all cases. The results are shown in Table 5.

In 1981 American output was between six and seven times Britain's. Japan's was $2\frac{1}{2}$ to $3\frac{3}{4}$ times (depending upon which bits of each economy are compared, the whole GDP, industry or just manufacturing): Germany's output was $1\frac{1}{2}$ to 2 times Britain's; and French output was one sixth to one half larger.

TABLE 5
Index Numbers and Tabular Information
— International Comparisons 1981 —

Use of labour and capital

Britain 100

Resources used: (1) Labour employed in producing

	Gross Domestic Product	Industrial Output	Manufacturing Output
USA	449	341	334
Japan	249	257	239
Germany	108	137	142
France	89	87	82

Resources used: (2) Net Capital Stock used in producing –

	GDP	Industrial output	Manufacturing output
USA	—	608	235
Germany	130	57	60
France	—	85	86

Resources used: (3) Capital per worker:

	Whole economy	Industry	Manufacturing
USA	—	178	70
Germany	120	66	73
France	—	62	61

Output produced:

	GDP	Industrial	Manufacturing
USA	626	615	696
Japan	243	288	374
Germany	138	157	219
France	116	117	145

Labour productivity – output per worker

	Whole economy	Industry	Manufacturing
USA	140	179	141
Japan	98	112	127
Germany	128	115	133
France	131	134	143

Capital productivity – output per unit capital   Note: Britain=100

	Whole economy	Industry	Manufacturing
USA	—	100	297
Germany	106	194	243
France	—	204	254

Source: O.E.C.D. 1982.

Surprisingly, Britain's labour productivity, for the economy as a whole (GDP), was marginally greater than Japan's. But Japan is backward in agriculture, services and distribution. The average German, Frenchman and American produced overall some 30 per cent to 40 per cent more than the average Brit.

All our competitors produced between a quarter and a half as much again of manufactured goods per worker as we did.

It is often supposed that Britain's poor labour productivity is because we don't invest enough — that the average British worker has fewer and older machines at his elbow. This is only true compared with American industry. The US industrial worker has 80 per cent more capital equipment per head and produces 80 per cent more output with it — they use more capital than we do, but just as wastefully. In French and German industry (and manufacturing everywhere) our competitors employ only two-thirds as much capital per head but produce two to three times as much output from each unit of it.

American, German and French labour productivity is greater than British, because they make better use of fewer but better and newer machines.

British investment has demonstrably been pushed too far. We have invested too well in quantity, while others have invested more wisely in quality.

Source: Investors Chronicle, 16 December 1983.

Finally, Fig. 16 shows a time series of the real value of student grants with 1962=100

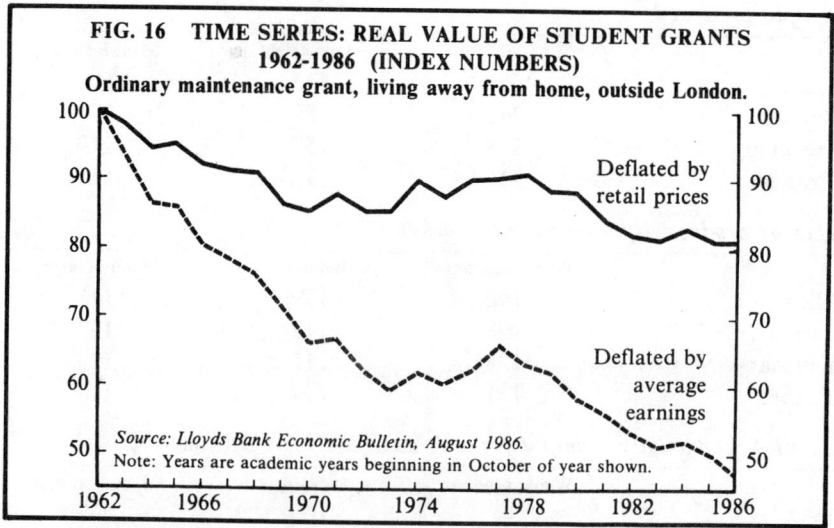

Question on Fig. 16. Explain and comment on the two methods of price deflation in Fig. 16.

Chapter 6
GRAPHS AND EQUATIONS

GRAPHS AND EQUATIONS

Graphs can be also used to show the mathematical relationship of one variable to another. On the horizontal (x) axis is one variable and on the vertical axis (y) is the other variable. It is then possible, if observations (data) are plotted, to relate x and y by means of a simple linear equation of the form $y = a + bx$. **Note:** Non-Linear Equations are not usually required for other than Degree level Economics courses. In the equation a is the constant and b is the coefficient, the rate by which x changes to y, and thus is either increasing (+) or decreasing (-). Here are some simple examples:—

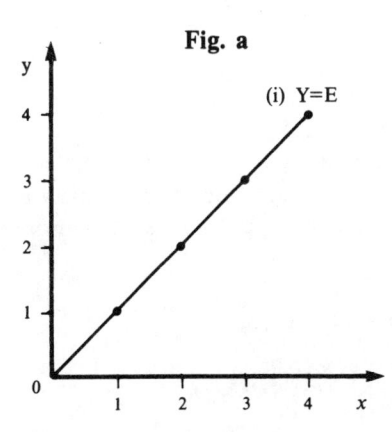

Fig. a

(i) Y=E

(i) $y = x \quad \begin{pmatrix} a = 0 \\ b = 1 \end{pmatrix}$

e.g. Consumption Function; income equals consumption (45°) line

i.e. MPC = 1. (No saving) the multiplier = $\dfrac{1}{\text{MPS}} = \dfrac{1}{0} = \infty$

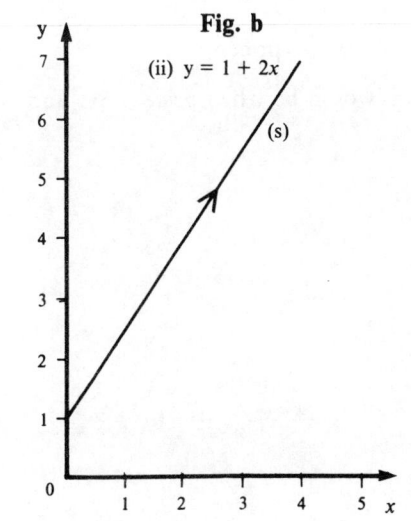

Fig. b

(ii) $y = 1 + 2x$

(s)

(ii) $y = 1 + 2x \quad \begin{pmatrix} a = 1 \\ b = 2 \end{pmatrix}$

e.g. supply schedule

Fig. c

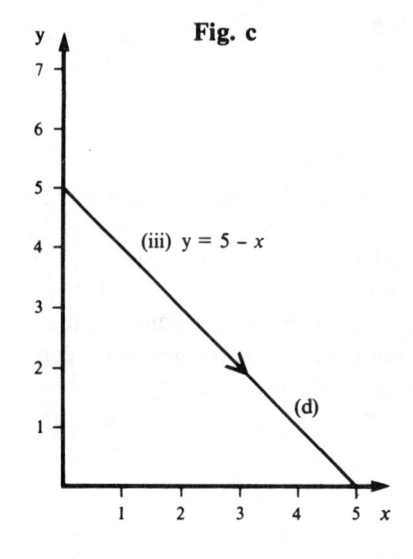

(iii) $y = 5 - x$ $\begin{pmatrix} a = 5 \\ b = -1 \end{pmatrix}$

e.g. demand schedule

(iii) $y = 5 - x$

(d)

Note: See Regression formula in APPENDIX for value of a and b

Problem Solving — MARKET ANALYSIS

If Figs. b and c were the supply and demand conditions it is possible to solve the equation and hence obtain the equilibrium price and quantity in the market. So in equilibrium demand equals supply and so equations (ii) = (iii)

So $\quad y = 1 + 2x = 5 - x$
and $\quad 1 + 2x = 5 - x \quad$ solving
$\quad x = 1\frac{1}{3}$

Equilibrium output = $1\frac{1}{3}$.
To obtain the price insert the value of x into (iii)

So $\quad y = 5 - (1\frac{1}{3}) = 3\frac{2}{3}$ = price.

So in the competitive market, equilibrium would be when price = $3\frac{2}{3}$ and output = $1\frac{1}{3}$.

Chapter 7
ESSENTIAL NOTES ON DEMAND/SUPPLY ELASTICITY

(a) **PRICE ELASTICITY OF DEMAND (P.E.D.)**
The formula which is most commonly used to measure P.E.D. is:—

$$\frac{\text{PERCENTAGE OR PROPORTIONATE CHANGE IN QUANTITY DEMANDED}}{\text{PERCENTAGE OR PROPORTIONATE CHANGE IN PRICE}}$$

This measures the degree of change in quantity demanded to a small change in price over a small area on a demand curve; and either percentage or proportionate changes can be used. Diagram 1 and Table 1 illustrate how it is calculated.

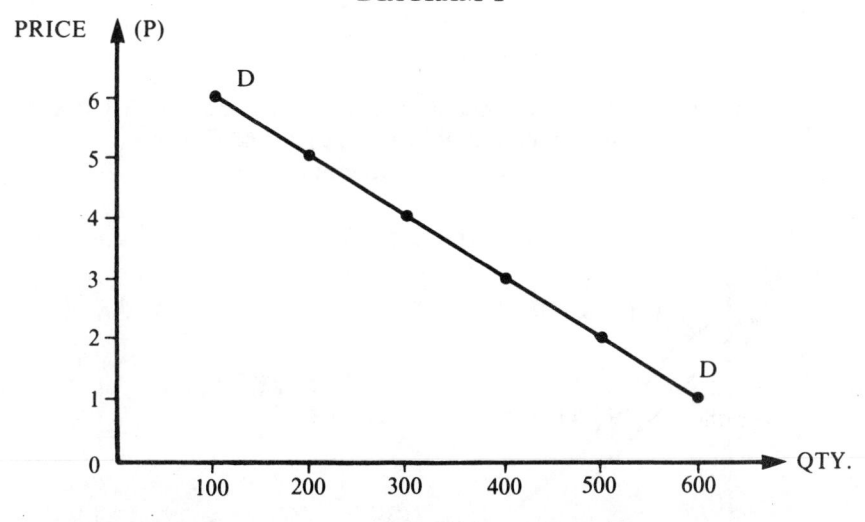

DIAGRAM 1

TABLE 1

Price (P)	Quantity
6	100
5	200
4	300
3	400
2	500
1	600

The resulting coefficient gives a measure of the degree of elasticity **around a**

point on the demand curve. If it is < 1 demand is inelastic, > 1 demand is elastic, = 1 demand is unitary or 0 demand is totally inelastic.
Table 1 is a simple demand schedule and diagram 1 is its demand curve.

Using the formula to obtain an estimate of P.E.D. for a price reduction from 5p to 4p we have

$$\text{P.E.D.} = \frac{\%\ \Delta Q}{\%\ \Delta P} = \frac{\frac{100}{200} \times 100}{\frac{1}{5} \times 100} = \frac{50\%}{20\%} = -2.5$$

which represents a high degree of elasticity.

For a price reduction from 2p to 1p we have

$$= \frac{\frac{100}{500} \times 100}{\frac{1}{2} \times 100} = \frac{20\%}{50\%} = -.4$$

which represents an inelastic demand. This illustrates the fact that P.E.D. varies along a demand curve, and along a straight line demand curve will vary from 0 to ∞ (zero to infinity). See Diagram 2.

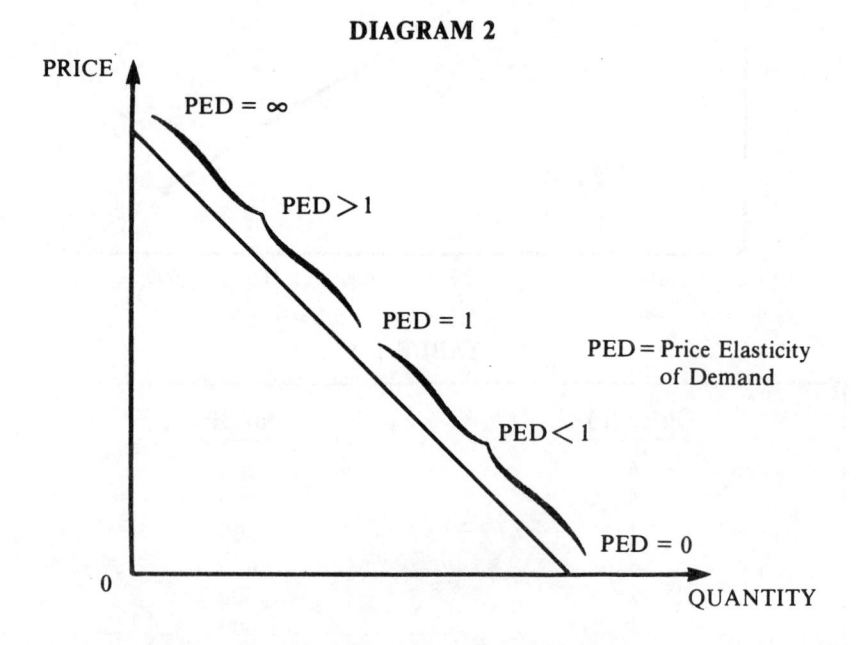

DIAGRAM 2

PRICE
PED = ∞
PED > 1
PED = 1
PED = Price Elasticity of Demand
PED < 1
PED = 0
0
QUANTITY

(b) INCOME ELASTICITY OF DEMAND (I.E.D.) measures the responsive of demand for a good to changes in income. Measured as

$$\text{I.E.D.} = \frac{\text{PERCENTAGE CHANGE IN QUANTITY DEMANDED}}{\text{PERCENTAGE CHANGE IN INCOME}} = \begin{array}{l} = 1 \text{ unit elasticity (B)} \\ > 1 \text{ elastic (+) (A)} \\ < 1 \text{ inelastic (+) (C)} \\ (-) \text{negative, i.e. "inferior" (D)} \end{array}$$

Diagram 3 shows how income elasticity of demand varies graphically.

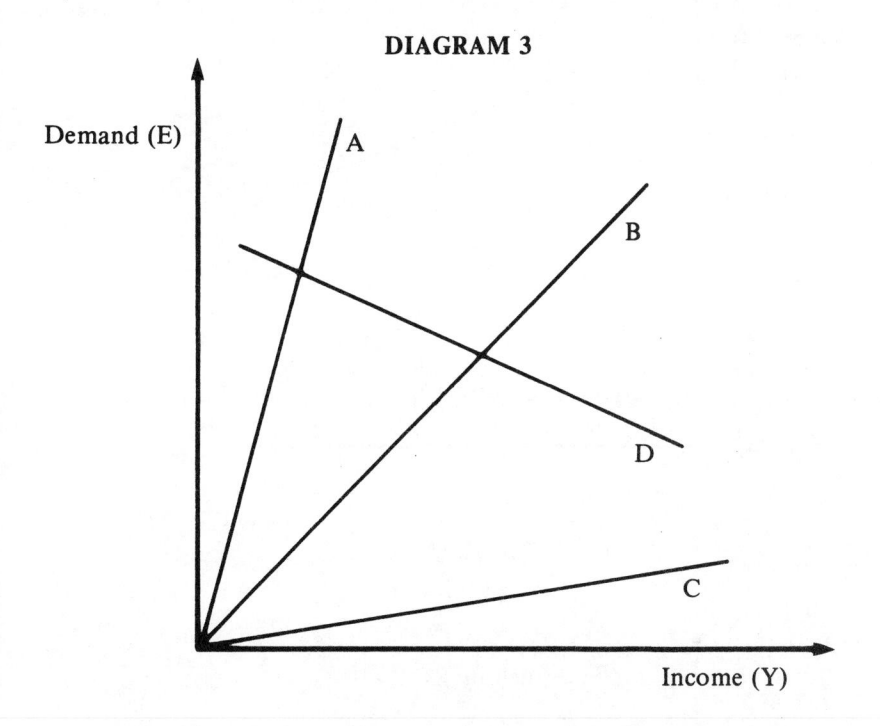

DIAGRAM 3

[Graph with Demand (E) on vertical axis and Income (Y) on horizontal axis, showing curves labelled A, B, C, and D]

Income elasticity of demand can be used as a quantitative measure over time, between income groups, products or regions etc.

(c) **CROSS ELASTICITY OF DEMAND** measures the responsive of the quantity demanded of one good to the change in the price of another good. Where goods are close substitutes or complements, cross elasticity is high, i.e. elastic. Measured as

Cross Elasticity of Demand for X with respect to Y =

$$\frac{\text{Percentage change in Quantity Demanded of Good X}}{\text{Percentage change in the price of Good Y}} = \begin{array}{l} + \text{ substitutes } \begin{array}{l} >1 \\ <1 \end{array} \\ - \text{ Complements} = 1 \end{array}$$

30 Essential Notes on Demand/Supply Elasticity

Diagrams 4 and 5 show the relationship between substitutes and complements in terms of elasticity. Suitable examples are given.

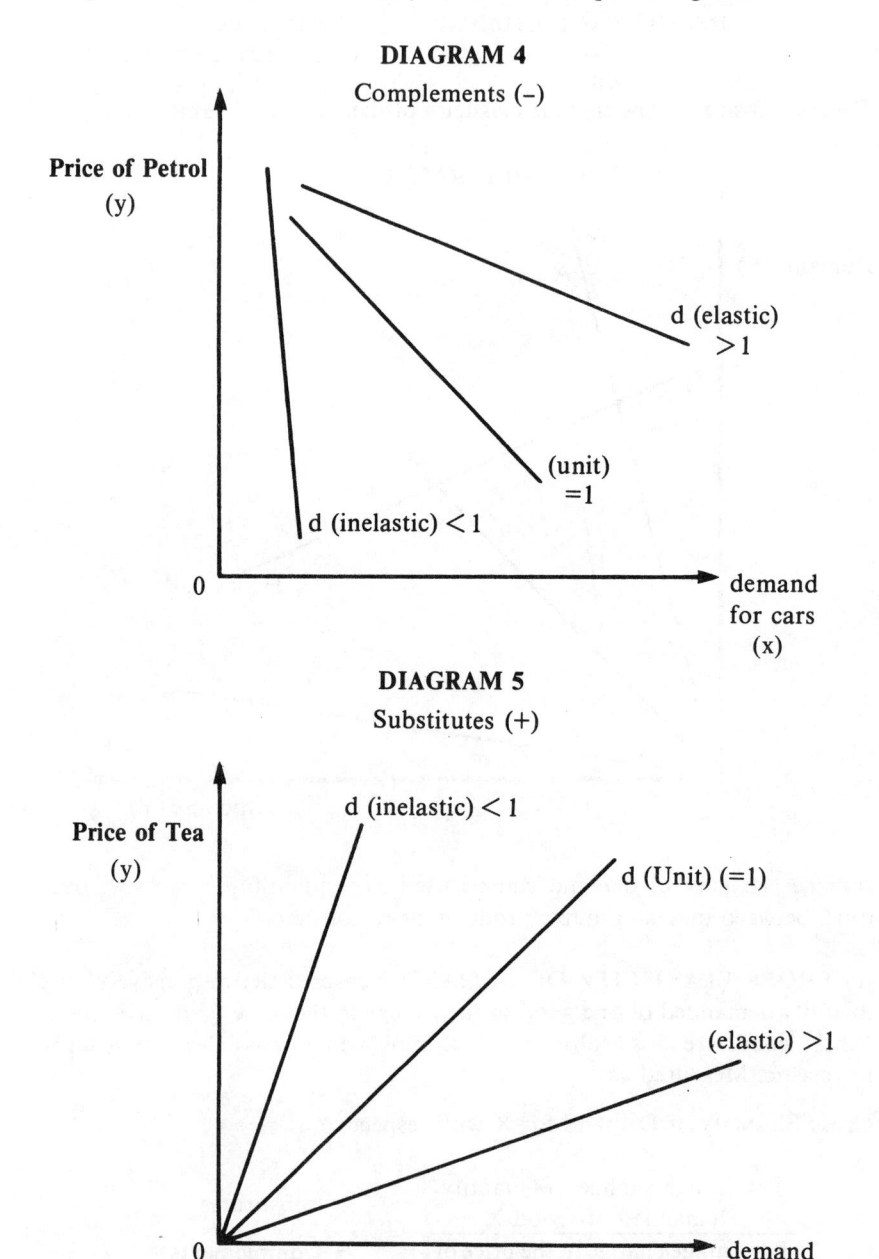

DIAGRAM 4
Complements (−)

Price of Petrol (y)

d (elastic) >1
(unit) =1
d (inelastic) <1

demand for cars (x)

DIAGRAM 5
Substitutes (+)

Price of Tea (y)

d (inelastic) <1
d (Unit) (=1)
(elastic) >1

demand for coffee (x)

Essential Notes on Demand/Supply Elasticity 31

(d) The concept of elasticity also refers to **SUPPLY** and **ELASTICITY OF SUPPLY** can be defined as the **RESPONSIVENESS OF THE QUANTITY SUPPLIED TO CHANGES IN PRICE.**

Diagram 6 illustrates different supply elasticities. It should be noted that any straight line supply curve passing through the origin is unitary. Elasticity of supply = 0 occurs when supply is fixed and cannot be increased, for example Rembrandt paintings.

$$\text{SUPPLY ELASTICITY} = \frac{\text{Percentage change in Quantity supplied}}{\text{Percentage change in Supply Price}} = \begin{cases} = 1 \text{ unit} \\ < 1 \text{ inelastic} \\ > 1 \text{ elastic} \\ = 0 \text{ perfectly inelastic} \end{cases}$$

DIAGRAM 6

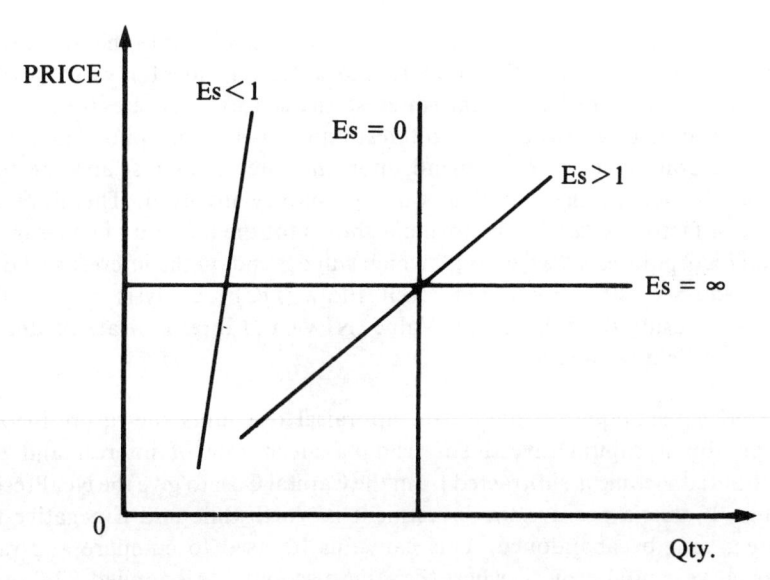

Chapter 8
COMPOUNDING AND DISCOUNTING INVESTMENT ANALYSIS

The economics of investment analysis often require calculations to be made concerning the capitalisation of an income stream over time as well as the yield, interest or discount rate on a capital project. This can apply in the profit motivated private sector and the public sector with, for example, Cost-Benefit Analysis. It is useful to both understand the idea of compounding and discounting and be able to calculate and use appropriate tables to solve quantitative problems. See the Tables and specific examples, below. The idea of compound interest shows how a sum of money invested now and in the future grows over time and therefore it shows the value of savings and how the interest rate affects the principal invested. See specific examples (1) and (3).

The use of discount factors in investment analysis illustrate the idea that a sum of money received in the future foregoes interest and is less valuable than a sum held today which could earn interest. In a sense it illustrates the fact that future income received foregoes interest and thus has an opportunity cost. This foregone income will depend upon the rate of interest and the time period as well as the actual amount of money involved. Therefore the discount factors, given by the formula shown for the Discount factors in the table, incorporates a "weighting" which will depend on the interest and time involved. See (2). Discounted Cash Flow (DCF) analysis applies this reasoning using the Net Present Value (NPV) and Internal Rate of Return (IRR) or yield techniques.

The NPV technique of investment appraisal discounts the future income stream on a capital investment using a given rate of interest and this discounted income is subtracted from the Capital Cost to give the Net Present Value. If this is positive the investment is worthwhile and if negative the project may be abandoned. This can thus be used to compare and rank alternative capital projects where the same discount rate is applied. This often happens in large multinational companies. As higher discount rates are applied the NPV of a project reduces to zero until the discounted income stream equals the capital cost or value. This rate of interest is the yield or the internal rate of return (IRR). When companies seek to maximise the profit yield the IRR technique will be preferred to the NPV. Specific examples (4) below applies both NPV and IRR. Here the constant stream of income is known as an annuity and the principle is the same as above. In this case a property company would see the purchase of the lease as the capital cost and this provides a constant stream of rental income to be discounted; in this case at 20%. If the discount factor had been 25% the NPV would have been negative, as it would if the rental had only been received over say four years, i.e. £300 − 259 = −£41.

SPECIFIC EXAMPLES — see tables over
(1) Compound Interest
Uses 1) Compound Interest. Enables calculations to be made regarding the future value of a present investment. So £100 invested today at 15% interest will be worth £100 × 2.31306 or £231.31 after six years.

(2) Discount Factors
Uses 2) Discount Values. Enables calculations to be made regarding the present value of a sum of money received in the future. So £100 to be paid in 6 years time at an interest rate of 15% over the period is now worth £100 × .432 or £86.40.

(3) Future Value of an Annuity
Uses: Enables calculations to be made regarding the future value of a constant "investment" sum paid annually. So £100 annually invested over six years at 10% interest will be worth £100 p.a. × 7.72 or £772.

(4) Present Value of an Annuity
Uses: Enables calculations to be made regarding the present value of a constant annual income paid in the future. So £100 a year paid as rental income over the next six years at 20% will have a present or current capitalised value of £100 p.a. × 3.32 = £332. If the investment cost £300 to buy the NPV will be £332 − £300 = i.e. £32. i.e. the capital investment is worthwhile. If the investment cost £332 the IRR will be 20%, i.e. £332 − £332 = 0.

COMPOUND AND DISCOUNT TABLES

(1) Compound Interest $P_n = P_o(1+i)^n$

Year	5%	10%	15%	20%
0	1.00000	1.00000	1.00000	1.00000
1	1.05000	1.10000	1.15000	1.20000
2	1.10250	1.21000	1.32250	1.44000
3	1.15763	1.33100	1.52088	1.72800
4	1.21551	1.46410	1.74901	2.07360
5	1.27628	1.61051	2.01136	2.48832
6	1.34010	1.77156	**2.31306**	2.98598

(2) Discount Factors $= P_o \left(\frac{1}{1+i}\right)^n$

Year	5%	10%	15%	20%
0	1.00000	1.00000	1.00000	1.00000
1	0.95238	0.90909	0.86957	0.83333
2	0.90703	0.82645	0.75614	0.69444
3	0.86384	0.75131	0.65752	0.57870
4	0.82270	0.68301	0.57175	0.48225
5	0.78353	0.62092	0.49718	0.40188
6	0.74622	0.56447	**0.43233**	0.33490

(3) $S_{\overline{n}|}$ = Future Value of an Annuity, eg. Insurance Policy, Sinking Fund

Year	5%	10%	15%	20%
1	1.00000	1.00000	1.00000	1.00000
2	2.05000	2.10000	2.15000	2.20000
3	3.15250	3.31000	3.47250	3.64000
4	4.31013	4.46410	4.99338	5.36800
5	5.52563	6.10510	6.74238	7.44160
6	6.80191	**7.71561**	8.75374	9.92992

(4) $a_{\overline{n}|}$ = Present Value of an Annuity, eg. Capitalisation of future rental income

Year	5%	10%	15%	20%
1	0.95238	0.90909	0.86957	0.83333
2	1.85941	1.73554	1.62571	1.52778
3	2.72325	2.48685	2.28323	2.10648
4	3.54595	3.16987	2.85498	2.58873
5	4.32948	3.79079	3.35216	2.99061
6	5.07569	4.35526	3.78448	**3.32551**

Note: 4 is the cumulative summation of 2.

APPENDIX (REFERENCE ONLY)

ARITHMETIC MEAN and STANDARD DEVIATION

$$x = \frac{\Sigma fx}{\Sigma f} \qquad s = \sqrt{\frac{\Sigma fx^2}{\Sigma f} - \frac{(\Sigma fx)^2}{(\Sigma f)^2}}$$

QUARTILE DEVIATION $= \frac{Q_3 - Q_1}{2}$

SKEWNESS

Quartile measure $= \dfrac{Q_3 + Q_1 - 2\,(\text{Median})}{Q_3 - Q_1}$

Pearson measure $= \dfrac{3\,(x - \text{Median})}{s}$

COEFFICIENT OF VARIATION $= \dfrac{100s}{x}$

SPEARMAN RANK CORRELATION COEFFICIENT

$$rs = 1 - \frac{6 \Sigma d^2}{n^2 (n-1)}$$

PRODUCT MOMENT CORRELATION COEFFICIENT

$$r = \frac{n \Sigma xy - \Sigma x \Sigma y}{\sqrt{(n \Sigma x^2 - (\Sigma x)^2)(n \Sigma y^2 - (\Sigma y)^2)}}$$

REGRESSION. Regression line of Y on X: $Y = a + bX$

$$b = \frac{n \Sigma xY - \Sigma x \Sigma Y}{n \Sigma x^2 - (\Sigma x)^2} \qquad a = \frac{\Sigma Y}{n} - \frac{b \Sigma x}{n}$$

STANDARD ERROR OF A SAMPLE MEAN

$$= \frac{\delta}{\sqrt{n}} \quad \text{or} \quad \frac{s}{\sqrt{n}} \quad \text{when is unknown.}$$

STANDARD ERROR OF A SAMPLE PROPORTION

$$= \sqrt{\frac{\pi(1-\pi)}{n}} \quad \text{or} \quad \sqrt{\frac{p(1-p)}{n}} \quad \text{when } \pi \text{ is unknown.}$$

INDEX NUMBERS

$\Sigma w I$ where w = Weight; I = Price relative

	Price	Quantity
Base ; Laspeyres	$\dfrac{\Sigma P_n Q_o}{\Sigma P_o Q_o} \times 100$	$\dfrac{\Sigma P_o Q_n}{\Sigma P_o Q_o} \times 100$
Current : Paasche	$\dfrac{\Sigma P_n Q_n}{\Sigma P_o Q_n} \times 100$	$\dfrac{\Sigma P_n Q_n}{\Sigma P_n Q_o} \times 100$

COMPOUND INTEREST

$P_n = P_o (1 + i)^n$

Present value of an annuity: $a_n = \dfrac{1 - (1+i)^{-n}}{i}$

Sinking fund or future value of an annuity: $S_n = \dfrac{(1+i)^n - 1}{i}$

DISCOUNTED VALUES

$$\frac{A_1}{(1+r)} + \frac{A_2}{(1+r)^2} + \frac{A_3}{(1+r)^3} + \ldots\ldots \frac{A_n}{(1+r)^n}$$

SECTION 3 (QUESTIONS)

Chapter 9
MICRO-ECONOMICS — BASIC CONCEPTS

(1) Diminishing Returns and Marginal Revenue Product.

(2) Working Time to Earn Food 1970, 1980, 1983.

(3) The U.K. Population.

(4) Value Added — Selected U.K. Industrial Output.

(5) Marginal Utility

DIMINISHING RETURNS AND MARGINAL REVENUE PRODUCT

You are given the following information:

Cost per tonne of fertiliser = £140
Fixed cost of land = £3,000
(Assume that no further costs are incurred.)
Selling price of wheat = £2 per unit.

Tonnes of fertiliser applied to a fixed area of land	Total production (units)
0	1,000
1	1,1000
2	1,250
3	1,500
4	1,900
5	2,150
6	2,275
7	2,350
8	2,380
9	2,330

QUESTIONS
(a) With reference to the above data, comment on the relationship between the application of fertiliser and the production of wheat.
(b) What level of fertiliser would a profit-maximising farmer choose to apply? Show the amount of wheat produced and the profit earned. Justify your answer. *(London Economics, June 1983)*

Answer P.132

WORKING TIME TO EARN FOOD 1970, 1980, 1983

The Table shows how much work time the average worker (income) took to earn a selected amount of food between 1970 and 1983.

	WORKING TIME (Minutes)		
	1970	1980	1983
		April of each year	
1lb beef sirloin	47.5	55.8	52.2
1lb fresh cod (fillets)	23.0	27.9	23.9
800g sliced loaf (wrapped)	9.9	8.4	7.2
1 pint fresh milk	5.0	4.3	4.0
1lb pork loin (with bone)	36.1	28.7	23.0
1lb back bacon (smoked)	36.2	31.1	27.4
1lb sugar	4.1	4.0	4.0
1lb butter	18.4	19.5	17.2
1 dozen eggs (size 4)	na[1]	16.8	12.5
14lb potatoes	44.1	25.0	19.8

[1]Eggs were graded in a different manner in 1970.

Source: Social Trends, 1986. C.S.O.

QUESTIONS
1. Identify the general economic principle underlying this table.
2. Which items have become (i) more (ii) less expensive in terms of time worked?
3. Can any general conclusions be deduced from these figures? What changes would have to be made in order to draw a valid conclusion about the cost of food over time?

Answer P.134

THE U.K. POPULATION

Table A shows the age distribution of the United Kingdom's population based on census data for 1931 to 1981.

Table A: Age distribution of the enumerated population in the United Kingdom (figures in thousands)

	1931	1951	1961	1971	1981
Persons (all ages)	46,038	50,225	52,709	55,515	55,039
Under 5	3,531	4,326	4,213	4,505	3,337
Under 18	—	13,248	14,631	15,705	14,241
Under 21	—	15,162	16,667	17,993	16,899
5 — 14	7,643	6,999	8,123	8,882	8,088
15 — 29	11,853	10,328	10,258	11,678	12,402
30 — 44	9,717	11,125	10,526	9,759	10,755
45 — 64	9,877	11,980	13,400	13,384	12,294
65 — 74	2,461	3,689	3,971	4,713	5,045
75 and over	957	1,777	2,218	2,594	3,118

Source: Annual Abstract of Statistics, H.M.S.O., 1984.

QUESTIONS
(a) Outline the main population trends apparent in Table A.
(b) Discuss the economic implications of these trends.

Table B gives data concerning the growth in the population of the United Kingdom between 1931 and 1981, with projected figures until 2021.

Answer P.135

Table B: Population growth in the United Kingdom
(figures in thousands)

	Population at beginning of period	Average annual change			
		Total increase	Births	Deaths	Excess of births over deaths	Net civilian migration and other adjustments
1931-1951	46,038	212	734	603	190	+22
1951-1961	50,290	252	839	593	246	+6
1961-1971	52,807	280	962	638	324	−20
1971-1981	55,610	64	793	666	70	−5
1981-1991	56,252	66	788	679	109	−43
1991-2001	56,912	106	832	691	141	−35
2001-2011	57,968	44	760	681	79	−35
2011-2021	58,403	90	806	681	125	−35

Source: Annual Abstract of Statistics, H.M.S.O., 1984.

QUESTIONS
(c) With reference to Table B:
   (i) Comment on the factors which influenced the growth of the U.K. population between 1931 and 1981.
   (ii) Are these factors expected to maintain their significance during the period 1981-2021?

(d) Table B indicates that the total U.K. population is forecast to be over 58 million in the year 2021. What problems are associated with making such a forecast? *(London, June 1986)*

Micro-Economics – Basic Concepts 41

VALUE ADDED: SELECTED UK INDUSTRIAL OUTPUT

Columns: Main sectors of economic activity	(1) Value added £bn (1984)	(2) Employ- ees '000 (Dec. 1985)	(3) Volume change in output % pa (1975-84)	(4) % share of gdp at current factor cost (1984)
Agriculture, forestry, fishing	6.0	332	3.0	2.1
Energy and water supply	31.5	583	7.7	11.3
Manufacturing	68.4	5,433	−1.1	24.4
Construction	15.8	935	−0.7	5.7
Distribution, hotels and catering	37.0	4,491	0.4	13.2
Transport and communications	19.8	1,266	1.3	7.1
Financial services	37.0	1,881	5.7	13.2

Source: An Economic Profile of Britain 1986.

QUESTIONS

1. What is meant by value added? How is it calculated and why is it used so often?
2. Calculate value added per employee for the sectors and discuss briefly the use of such information. Ignore variation in dates.
3. Briefly outline what columns 3 and 4 indicate about the U.K. Economy 1975-84.

Answer P.136

MARGINAL UTILITY

Given below are the daily utility functions for three cold drinks for a man arriving at a desert oasis with a budget of £28.

Price	Drink A £2	Drink B £4	Drink C £6
Quantity	Total utility	Total utility	Total utility
1	8	8	14
2	14	13¼	27
3	18	18¼	39
4	21	23	49
5	22	27½	55
6	24	31¾	60
7	25	35¾	62

QUESTIONS

Assuming that holding money has no utility for him and that he seeks to maximize his satisfaction, answer the following:
1. On his first visit the only drink for sale is B. How many drinks does he buy and why?
2. In the circumstances of (1); calculate the consumer's surplus.
3. On a return visit, with another £28, all the drinks are available. How will he allocate his budget between the three drinks?
4. What is unlikely about the total utility figures for drink A?

(London, June 1980)

Answer P.138

Chapter 10
MARKET ANALYSIS

(1) U.K. Consumers Expenditure on Alcohol 1971-84.

(2) U.K. Income Elasticity of Demand 1971-81.

(3) Price Elasticity of Demand in Ruritania.

(4) Water Supply in the Community.

(5) The Price of Tea.

(6) Road Pricing in Singapore.

44 Market Analysis

U.K. CONSUMERS EXPENDITURE ON ALCOHOL 1971-84

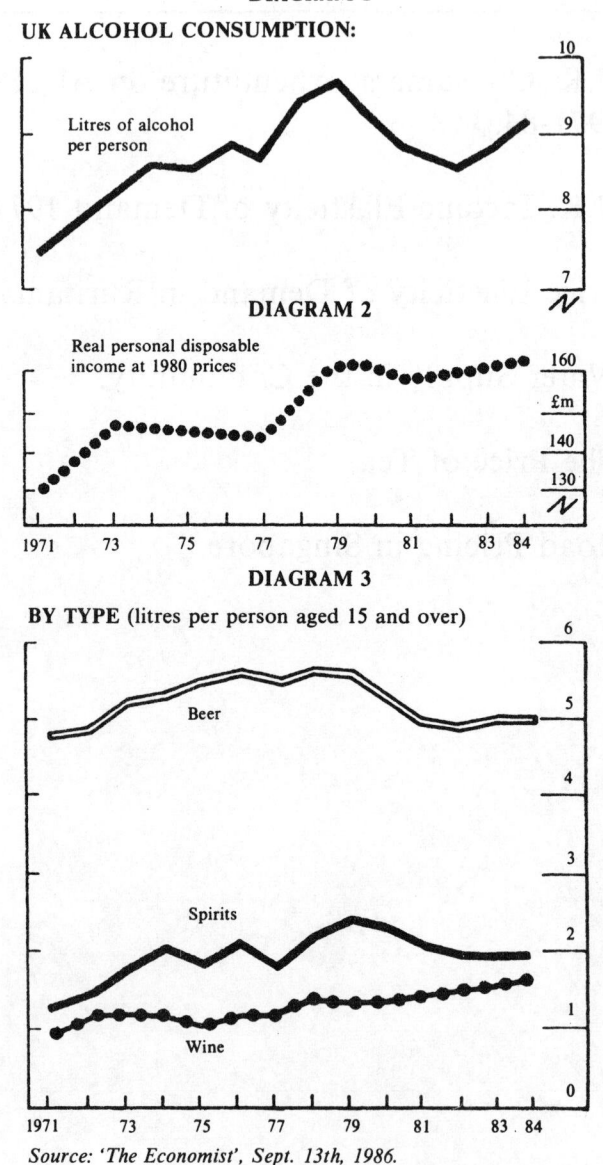

DIAGRAM 1
UK ALCOHOL CONSUMPTION:

Litres of alcohol per person

DIAGRAM 2

Real personal disposable income at 1980 prices (£m)

DIAGRAM 3
BY TYPE (litres per person aged 15 and over)

Beer

Spirits

Wine

Source: 'The Economist', Sept. 13th, 1986.

QUESTIONS
1. Use demand analysis to describe and explain the pattern of consumers' expenditure on alcoholic drink as shown in the diagrams?
2. How could the information in the diagrams be used? *Answer P.139*

U.K. INCOME ELASTICITY OF DEMAND 1971-81

The table below refers to the income and expenditure of United Kingdom households that contain one man, one woman and two children, in 1971 and 1981. Study the table carefully and then, making use of both the data and your knowledge of economics, answer the following questions:

(a) Using the data for 1981:
  (i) assess whether income tax and national insurance contributions were progressive in 1981;
  (ii) using the concept of income elasticity of demand, describe how the expenditure on each of the commodity groups varies with income.

(b) Using the data for the average income group:
  (i) how has the relation between total and disposable income changed between 1971 and 1981?
  (ii) describe the changes in the pattern of expenditure between 1971 and 1981;
  (iii) what factors could account for the changes in (ii)?

(Oxford, June 1985)

	1981 Household Income and Expenditure £ per week					Average income group			
						£ per week		% of Disposable Income	
						1971	1981	1971	1981
INCOME:									
Total Income	119.9	164.0	**194.8**	240.1	327.3	38.3	194.8	114.1	120.9
Income Tax	6.6	16.4	**25.2**	34.4	58.6	3.3	25.2	9.8	15.6
National Insurance Contributions	3.4	6.4	**8.5**	10.5	11.3	1.6	8.5	4.6	5.3
Disposable Income	109.9	141.2	**161.1**	195.2	257.4	33.4	161.1	100.0	100.0
EXPENDITURE ON:									
Fuel, light and power	8.0	7.5	**8.3**	8.6	10.7	1.9	8.3	5.6	5.2
Food	28.3	31.5	**33.6**	37.0	41.5	8.9	33.6	26.6	20.9
Alcoholic drink	4.4	5.0	**5.8**	6.1	8.1	1.1	5.8	3.2	3.6
Tobacco	5.2	4.6	**3.7**	3.4	3.4	1.3	3.7	3.9	2.3
Transport and Vehicles	12.2	16.0	**18.2**	27.1	32.3	3.7	18.2	11.1	11.3
Services	6.7	11.2	**14.6**	18.7	26.8	1.9	14.6	5.8	9.1

Source: *Family Expenditure Surveys for 1971 and 1981; Annual Abstract of Statistics.*

Answer P.140

PRICE ELASTICITY OF DEMAND IN RURITANIA

In Ruritania, a hypothetical country whose currency is the pound sterling (£), the three firms in the car industry together sold in 1985 12 million cars at an average price of £5,000. However, because the economy is in a depressed state the car industry is not working at full capacity and many car workers are not employed for a full working week.

The car workers' union, Vehicle and General Workers, suggest that each producer reduces his price by £200. This action, the Union argues, would result in another 2 million cars being sold while aggregate profits would be maintained at £4,000 million.

(a) Calculate the value of the elasticity of demand (correct to one decimal place) assumed by the Vehicle and General Workers Union. Comment on this value.
(b) Calculate the average cost with an output of (i) 12 million cars and (ii) 14 million cars. Comment on your findings.

A spokesperson for the Ruritanian car industry points out that government economists have estimated that the elasticity of demand for cars is, in fact, −0.5.

(c) Assuming this estimate is accurate, and given the cost conditions assumed in (b) above, what would be the impact on the car industry's profitability of a price reduction of £200?
(d) Other than in the manner suggested by the Union, how might Ruritania's car firms try to increase their sales of cars by acting (i) individually and (ii) as a group?

London, June 1986.

Answer P.142

PRICING WATER SUPPLY IN THE COMMUNITY

FIGURE A

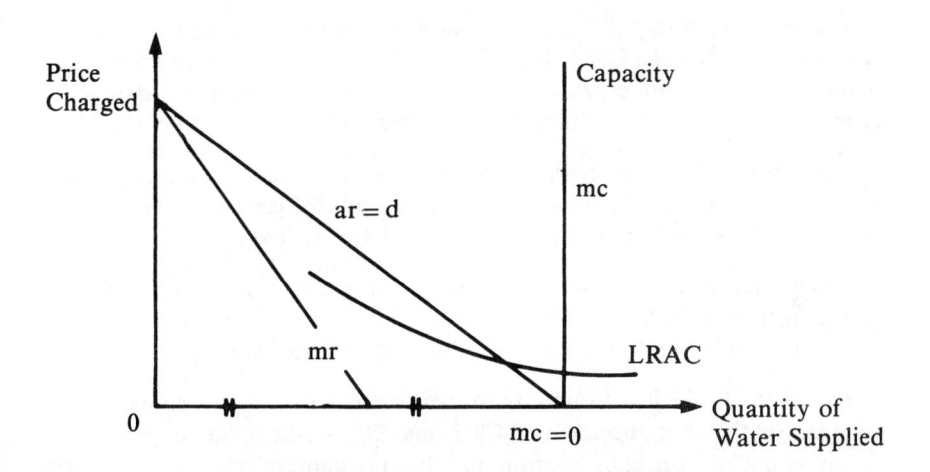

[Figure A: Diagram with axes "Price Charged" (vertical) and "Quantity of Water Supplied" (horizontal). Curves shown: ar = d (demand), mr (marginal revenue), LRAC (long run average cost), mc = 0 along the quantity axis, and a vertical mc line at Capacity.]

A monopolistic water authority can supply water to a community at zero marginal operating costs. The initial cost of building reservoirs and laying pipes is given by the Long Run Average Cost (LRAC). Once capacity is reached, marginal cost rises dramatically. Demand for water is given i.e. (d). A variety of pricing options are available.

QUESTION
On the diagram show the price (p) and output (q) levels when the following objectives are met by the water authority.
(a) Profit Maximising. Use p_1/q_1 and indicate the amount of profit made.
(b) Break-Even in the Long Term. Use p_2/q_2.
(c) Maximise economic efficiency. Use p_3/q_3 and briefly outline the implications of this policy.

Answer P.145

THE PRICE OF TEA

The price of a packet of tea, still Britain's favourite drink, is expected to rise again because the Indian Government has severely restricted tea exports.

Prices soared by about 20% at yesterday's weekly tea auction in London. A spokesman for Brooke Bond Oxo, which with 30% of the British market is the nation's biggest supplier, said, "We are looking at the situation daily and clearly another increase cannot be long deferred".

But both tea traders and retailers could not say yet by how much prices in the shops would rise. Brooke Bond raised its prices by 10% last April and again in December by 8.5% for packet tea and 12.5% for tea bags.

The increases were forced by a continuous rise last year in world tea prices. Consumption in the Middle East, the Soviet Union and developing countries has been growing and in 1983 world demand exceeded supply.

These increases are just beginning to work their way onto the supermarket shelves. But the announcement on Christmas Day by the Indian Government that it would ban, probably for four months, the export of crush, tear and curl (CTC) teas has pushed up prices again.

The CTC process releases the strong flavour and colour from north Indian teas which are the basis of popular blends in Britain. The market leader is Brooke Bond's P.G. Tips. Of the tea drunk in Britain, 80% is CTC, and of that amount India supplies about a quarter.

Source: M. Prest, The Times, 4 January 1984.

QUESTIONS
1. Explain, using a diagram, those factors which increased the price of tea in 1983.
2. How would economic theory explain the decision of the Indian Government to ban the export of CTC teas?
3. What could be the outcome of higher tea prices?
4. Why would Brooke Bond raise the price of tea bags by a greater percentage than the price of packet tea?

Answer P.146

ROAD PRICING IN SINGAPORE

A system of road pricing was introduced in Singapore city centre in 1975. A new licence costing the equivalent of £12 per month was necessary for motorists who entered the city centre between 7.30a.m. and 10.15a.m. Furthermore, the cost of car parking was raised considerably. Cars with at least four occupants (car pools) were exempt from payment of the new licence. The following data shows some comparative figures relating to the new road pricing system.

	March 1975 (before the system was introduced)	August 1975 (after the system was introduced)
Peak hour licence fee (per month)	—	£12.00
Car parking charges in city centre (all day)	£0.70	£2.80
Index of morning peak-hour traffic volume:		
Cars	100	26
Car pools	100	182
Other motor vehicles	100	102
Index of morning bus passenger volume	100	115
Index of time taken for morning peak-hour bus ride	100	70

(Source: P.L. Watson & E.P. Holland, Congestion Pricing: the example of Singapore, Finance and Development, The World Bank, March 1976.)

QUESTIONS
(a) What can you infer about elasticity of demand from the above data?
(b) With reference to the data, assess the road pricing system in terms of resource utilisation.
(c) What additional information would you need in order to make a more comprehensive assessment of the road pricing system?

(London, June 1984)

Answer P.148

Chapter 11
DISTRIBUTION OF INCOME

(1) West End Rents 1985/6.

(2) International Executive Pay Comparisons.

(3) European Living Standards.

(4) U.K. Interest Rates.

(5) Profit Performance of Top Ten UK Motor Car Distributors.

(6) U.K. Private Investment 1975-8.

(7) U.K., U.S.A. Wages and Employment 1979-84.

(8) U.K. Prices, Wages, Earnings and Productivity 1978-83.

(9) Investment in Energy Savings. D.C.F.

(10) Too Equal?

(11) The Changing Structure of Employment

WEST END RENTS 1985/86

West End regains momentum

During the latter part of 1985, rental values in most of the leading thoroughfares in the West End of London were slowly increasing, and retailers and property investors alike looked forward to the anticipated increase in tourists to Central London. The early part of 1986 confirmed the speculation that rents would increase and the slow spiral upwards continued.

However, as a result of the "bombings" in the West End, the tourist trade, particularly from the US, began to slow down significantly. This resulted in a temporary lull in rental values; there was a levelling off period of a few weeks and rents then began to rise.

Over the past two months, however, rental values have begun to accelerate as retailers gain confidence to open shop premises in the major thoroughfares and particularly in Oxford Street.

The demand came from many quarters of the retail industry with Tower Records opening its store in Piccadilly Circus; Dixons opened a large shop for the sale of hi-fi, television and records on two floors at the junction of Oxford Street and Park Street and the new HMV store, which is currently being fitted, located close to the Bournes Development, has an area of about 60,000 sq. ft. At the other end of Oxford Street, close to Marble Arch, the record retailer, Smethers & Leigh, opened its store on three levels with the first floor to ground floor being served by escalators.

Marks & Spencer completed the fitting out of a new furniture satellite opposite its main building adjoining Selfridges. Coloroll acquired the premises in Regent Street, previously occupied by Miss Selfridge, for the sale of fabrics and furnishings. Fashion were also keen to obtain units and Stefanel has recently acquired the Midas store in Brompton Road and In Wear — a European ladies fashion house — leased the property in Kings Road previously occupied by Austin Reed.

With regard to rental values the following 30ft Zone A rates indicate the levels that are currently being achieved. Prime Oxford Street — that is west of Oxford Circus — is in the order of £220/£225, whereas just east of the Circus the prevailing values fall to about £150/£160 per sq. ft. and a similar level is likely to be achieved in the main section of Kings Road, Chelsea. Prevailing values in New Bond Street in the middle stretch of the thoroughfare are about £95/£100 but this figure might increase in a location closer to Oxford Street. There has always been a keen demand for shopping in prime Brompton Road, that is to say between Harrods and Sloane Street, but few units become

52 Distribution of Income

available. If a unit were on the open market, then a figure of £200 per sq. ft., perhaps more, would be achieved.

Current market trends suggest that rental values will continue to increase but it remains to be seen whether they will rise at the same time as they have in earlier months.

Source: Investors Chronicle, 7 November 1986.

QUESTIONS
1. How would economic theory explain (i) specified; (ii) overall levels of shop rentals? Relate your answer to the factors mentioned. Use a diagram to illustrate.

Answer P.150

INTERNATIONAL EXECUTIVE PAY COMPARISONS
(£ Sterling in 1984)

(1)	(2)	(3)	(4)
Country	Gross pay	Net after tax	What that buys
Belgium	33,560	18,190	19,560
Denmark	33,380	17,730	15,830
France	36,670	25,870	25,870
Germany	46,210	27,170	26,380
Greece	26,220	15,240	16,230
Ireland	23,210	12,450	12,210
Italy	35,650	22,050	22,970
Netherlands	36,760	17,900	18,450
Australia	36,930	21,700	19,380
Canada	46,330	30,190	26,250
Japan	58,500	34,920	21,560
Singapore	52,210	37,690	31,940
South Africa	31,810	20,710	22,270
Spain	28,840	19,390	23,360
Sweden	25,130	14,870	13,400
Switzerland	57,570	37,200	28,180
UK	23,650	16,160	16,160
USA	55,290	33,770	28,140

Source: Sunday Times.

QUESTIONS
1. Explain in economic terms the meaning of Columns 3 and 4.
2. Which country provides the lowest spending power for its executives?
3. Account for differences between columns 2 and 3 and between columns 3 and 4.
4. Briefly explain why gross pay levels vary between countries.

Answer P.151

EUROPEAN LIVING STANDARDS

"Living standards per head in 1984 as percentage of European Community average"

	At market exchange rate	At current purchasing power parities
Luxembourg	133	137
Denmark	154	128
West Germany	145	126
France	129	120
Belgium	111	116
The Netherlands	123	111
United Kingdom	108	105
Italy	88	96
Spain	60	79
Ireland	72	74
Greece	49	60
Portugal	27	48

Source: *An Economic Profile of Britain 1986.*

QUESTIONS
1. Explain the difference between the two methods of comparing living standards. Why are there differences between the two methods in terms of respective percentage values?
2. Using your answer to Q1 briefly comment upon the U.K. and Portuguese position in 1984.
3. What are the main drawbacks of using simple indices of living standards as given in the table?

Answer P.152

UK INTEREST RATES

THE PRICE OF MONEY

Savers	% Interest	Tax	Investment Min	£ Max	Withdrawal
BUILDING SOCIETIES					
Ordinary	9.25(a)	Paid	None	15-20,000	On demand
Term	10-11.25(b)	Paid	100	15-20,000	1-5 years
Subscription	10.5(c)	Paid	(1 mth)	100	On demand
CLEARING BANKS					
Deposit	11.5-12	To pay	None	None	7 days
Savings	11.5-12	To pay	10 (mth)	None	7 days
Investment	11.5-12.25	To pay	2-5,000	50,000	3-6 mths
FINANCE HOUSES					
	13.5-14.5	To pay	1,000	15,000	1 mth-1 yr.
FIN FOR INDUSTRY					
	13-13.25	To pay	1,000	50,000	3-5 yrs.
LOCAL AUTHORITIES					
One/Two Years	12.25-12.75	To pay	500	None	1-2 yrs.
Three/Five Yrs.	13.25	To pay	1,000	None	3.5 yrs.
Yearling Bond	12.375	To pay	1,000	None	1 yr.
NAT. GIROBANK					
	11-12	To pay	25p	None	1 dy.-6 mths.
NAT. SAVINGS BANK					
Ordinary	5(d)	£70 free	25p	10,000	£100 on dmd.
Investment	15	To pay	1	200,000	1 mth
N.S. CERTIFICATES					
19th Issue	10.33(e)	Free	10	5,000	5 yrs.
2nd Index-linked	RPI-Linked	Free	10	3,000	1-5 yrs.†
SAYE 3rd Issue†	RPI-Linked	Free	4 (mth)	20	1-5 yrs.*
TRUSTEE S.B.					
Investment	7-13	To pay	5p/£1	None	7 dys-1 mth
Term	10-13.625	To pay	1,000	None	1-5 yrs.

†Retail Price Index for January 277.3, up 13% on year ago index.
*Option of two additional years earns tax free bonus equal to two months contributions.
(a) Gross equiv. 13.21%.   (d) Gross equiv. 7.14% on deposits up to £1,400.
(b) Gross equiv. 14.28-16.07%.   (e) Gross equiv. 14.75%.   (c) Gross equiv. 15%.

Borrowers (INTEREST %)	MINIMUM LENDING RATE 14
BANK BASE RATES 14	PERSONAL BANK LOAN 10 (flat)
MORTGAGE RATE 14	CREDIT CARDS 2-2.25 (mth)

Source: The Sunday Times, 8 March 1981.

QUESTIONS

(a) Discuss the pattern of interest rates shown in the Table.
(b) Explain the significance of the Retail Price Index for both lenders and borrowers, illustrating your answer by reference to the Table.

(A.E.B., Nov. 1982)   *Answer P.154*

PROFIT PERFORMANCE OF TOP TEN PUBLIC COMPANIES (1983/4) — U.K. MOTOR CAR DISTRIBUTORS

Distributor	Franchises held	Turnover 1983/4 £m	Return on capital 1981/2 %	Return on capital 1983/4 %	Profit margin 1981/2 %	Profit margin 1983/4 %
Lex Service	BL, Rolls-Royce, Volvo, CVs - BL, ERF, Seddon Atkinson	887.5	9.6	17.8	3.0	4.3
Kenning Motor Group	BL, Fiat, GM, Mazda, Peugeot/T, Rolls-Royce, VW/Audi	326.3	4.2	12.5	1.4	3.6
Henlys	BL, Datsun, Ford, GM, Renault, Rolls-Royce	237.4	-5.1	-13.7	-1.0	-1.6
Dutton-Forshaw	BL, Ford, GM, Peugeot/T	200.0	-3.3	5.9	-0.6	0.8
Mann-Egerton	BL, GM, Renault	190.4	1.1	16.0	0.2	2.3
Wadham Stringer	BL	165.7	-5.7	8.8	-0.9	1.5
Lookers	BL, GM, Ford, Fiat/Lancia, Nissan, Peugeot/T, Toyota	134.7	9.3	9.1	-1.5	1.0
Appleyard Group	BL, Ford, Rolls-Royce, GM	128.0	-14.3	6.9	-1.5	0.5
Perry Group	Ford	122.5	16.4	13.6	3.8	2.8
T. Cowie	BL, BMW, Colt, Fiat, Ford, GM, Peugeot/T, Saab	104.7	2.0	7.3	0.4	1.1
Average			3.7	10.4	0.8	1.9

Source: Midland Bank Review, Winter 1985.

Continued overleaf

MOTOR CAR DISTRIBUTORS: FINANCIAL PERFORMANCE (1983/4)

QUESTIONS (See table on previous page)
1. (a) Define the terms (i) Return on Capital; (ii) Profit Margin
   (b) Why are they used as a criteria of company performance?
   (c) Calculate **actual** profit and capital figures for LEX Services 1983/4.
2. What could explain (i) the change in the average return on capital for all ten companies between 1981/2 and 1983/4 and (ii) the different returns on capital for individual companies within the sector 1981/2 to 1983/4? Give broad economic and financial reasons.

Answer P.156

U.K. PRIVATE INVESTMENT 1975-81

The table overleaf refers to the United Kingdom over the period 1975-81. Study the table and accompanying notes carefully and then, making use of your knowledge of economics, answer the following questions.

1. Does private sector investment in housing seem to be closely related to:
   (i) personal saving;
   (ii) nominal and real interest rates?
2. What explanations do the data suggest for the behaviour of non-housing investment in the private sector?
3. What additional data would you wish to consult in order to provide a more complete answer to part (2)?

Source: Oxford, June 1984.

Answer P.158

58 Distribution of Income

UK PRIVATE INVESTMENT 1975-81

	PRIVATE INVESTMENT (Annual percentage change)		OTHER VARIABLES (Annual percentage change)					Interest Rates	
	Total (excluding housing)	Housing	GDP at factor cost	Gross trading profits of private companies	Personal saving	Wage rates	Retail price index	Short-term on Treasury Bills	Long-term on dated Securities
1975	-2.6	8.9	-1.1	-16.0	3.5	29.5	24.2	11.1	14.4
1976	2.8	-0.1	2.6	7.6	-7.3	19.3	16.5	12.5	14.4
1977	8.4	-6.5	2.6	16.3	-11.6	6.6	15.9	10.2	12.7
1978	10.7	14.1	3.2	4.6	29.6	14.1	8.3	9.2	12.5
1979	5.9	-13.3	1.8	9.9	19.7	15.0	13.4	14.4	13.0
1980	1.1	-16.1	-2.4	-19.0	7.7	18.0	18.0	15.0	13.8
1981	-2.2	-15.5	-2.4	-12.6	-16.4	10.1	11.9	14.4	14.7

Source: *Economic Trends*, November 1982.

Notes:
1. The figures for the interest rates are averages for the year.
2. All other figures are annual percentage changes, i.e. the percentage change between the figure for a given year and the figure for the previous year.
3. All percentage change figures (except for wage rates and the retail price index) are based on constant price series.

Distribution of Income 59

U.K., U.S.A. WAGES AND EMPLOYMENT 1979-84

Real Wages in manufacturing in the United Kingdom and United States

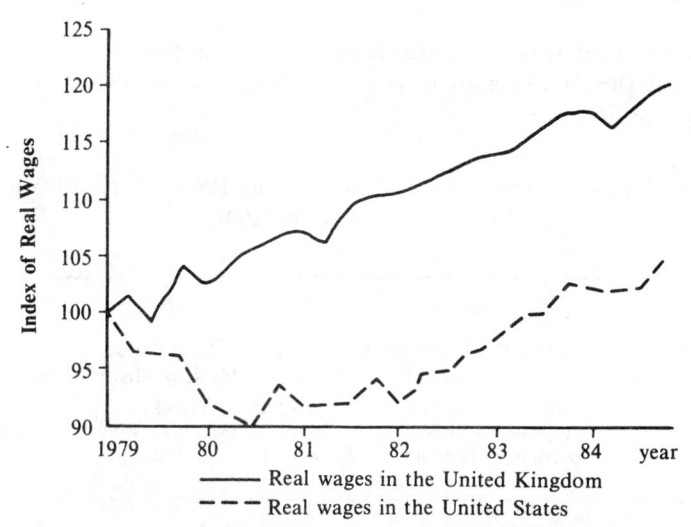

(Graph: Index of Real Wages vs. year 1979–84)
— Real wages in the United Kingdom
--- Real wages in the United States

Employment in manufacturing in the United Kingdom and United States

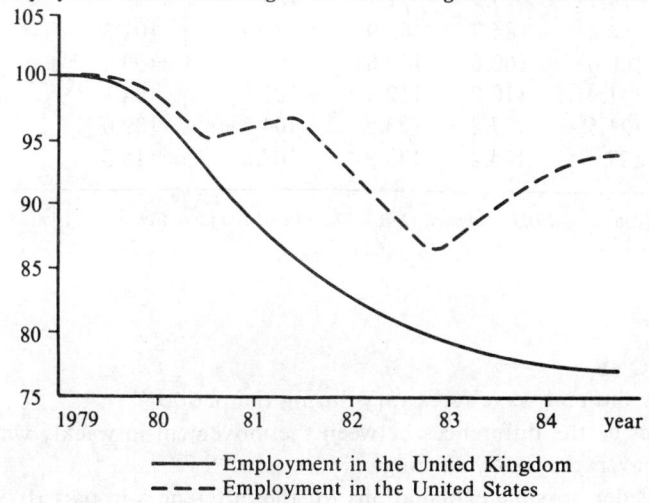

(Graph: Index vs. year 1979–84)
— Employment in the United Kingdom
--- Employment in the United States

Source: *Demand Management and Economic Recovery.*
Sir James Ball. *National Westminster Bank Quarterly Review*, August 1985.

QUESTIONS

(a) Distinguish between real and money wages.
(b) Explain what the diagrams show.
(c) To what extent does the above information support the predictions of the Marginal Revenue Product Theory of Wages? *(S.U.J.B., June 1986)*

Answer P.160

U.K. PRICES, WAGES, EARNINGS AND PRODUCTIVITY 1978-83

The table below refers to the United Kingdom over the period 1978-83. Study the table and then, making use of your knowledge of economics, answer the following questions.

United Kingdom Prices, Wages, Earnings and Productivity, 1978-83
Index Numbers (1980=100)

Columns:

1	2	3	4	5	6	7
Year	Retail Prices (All Items)	Weekly Wage Rates (Whole Economy)	Average Weekly Earnings (Whole Economy)	Output per Person Employed (Whole Economy)	Output per Person-Hour Worked (Manufacturing Industry)	Hourly Earnings (Manufacturing Industry)
1978	74.7	73.7	71.7	100.2	99.7	71.7
1979	84.8	84.7	82.9	102.6	101.3	83.0
1980	100.0	100.0	100.0	100.0	100.0	100.0
1981	111.9	110.2	112.9	101.5	104.3	114.2
1982	121.5	117.8	123.5	104.7	109.0	125.0
1983	127.1	124.4	133.9	107.8	115.3	136.2

Source: A.R. Prest and D.J. Coppock (Eds.), The United Kingdom Economy (10th edition), p.305.

QUESTIONS

(a) How did real wage rates vary during the period?
(b) Describe the differences between the movement in weekly wage rates and average weekly earnings.
(c) Consider possible explanations for the differences in part (b).
(d) To what extent have increases in labour productivity offset increases in earnings in the whole economy and in manufacturing industry?

Oxford, June 1986.

Answer P.161

INVESTMENT IN ENERGY SAVINGS — D.C.F.

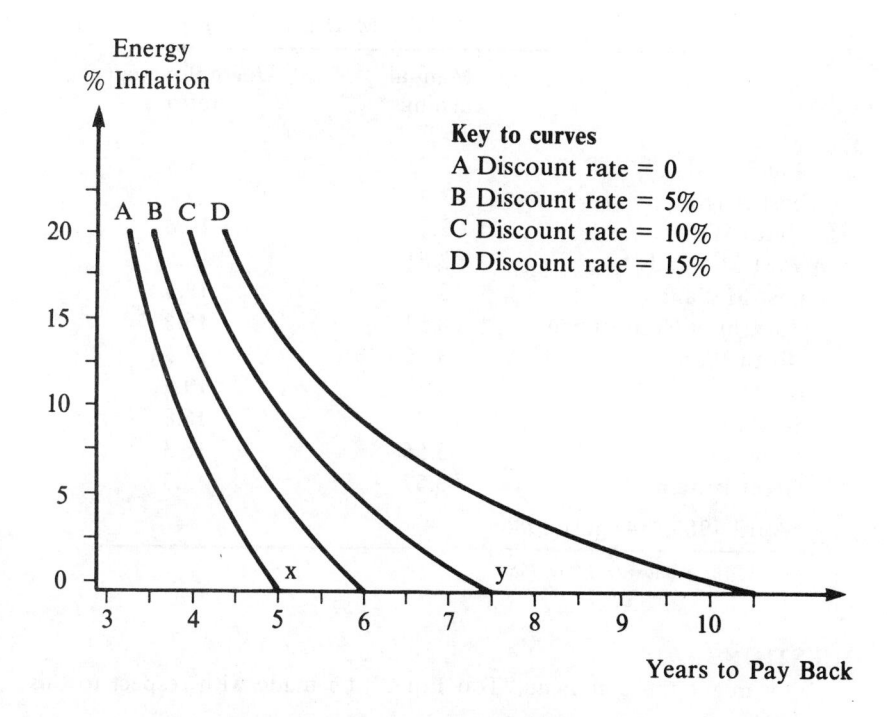

```
Energy
% Inflation
           Key to curves
           A Discount rate = 0
           B Discount rate = 5%
   A B C D C Discount rate = 10%
20         D Discount rate = 15%

15

10

 5

 0       x           y
   3   4   5   6   7   8   9   10
                              Years to Pay Back
```

The chart shows the effects of interest or discount rates and inflation on energy saving payback periods. In the example, if regular yearly energy savings are £200 with an initial investment of £1,000 then after 5 years, with no inflation on energy prices and no capital costs, the investment will be recovered as shown as point X on schedule A. Line C assumes the same conditions but there is now a capital cost of 10% interest p.a. This means the payback period becomes about 7½ years, i.e. point Y.

QUESTIONS

1. Use schedule A and explain what happens to the payback period as energy prices rise.
2. Why does the 10% interest rate shift the original schedule A to C and increase the payback time? Name and describe the economic principle being used.
3. What could the chart illustrate about consumers' buying decisions with regard to energy savings and other home improvements. Relate your answer to actual consumer behaviour.

Answer P.163

Distribution of Income

TOO EQUAL?

MALES (U.K.)

	Manual earnings* £	Unemployment rate† %
South East	3.73	9.8
East Anglia	3.37	9.4
South West	3.37	10.6
West Midlands	3.51	15.5
East Midlands	3.45	12.5
Yorkshire/Humberside	3.52	15.6
North West	3.56	17.3
North	3.62	19.9
Scotland	3.54	16.8
Wales	3.56	16.3
Great Britain	3.57	13.3
*April 1985; †August 1986		

Source: The Economist, 1 Nov. 1986.

QUESTIONS

1. Why might the comment "Too Equal" be made with respect to this Table?
2. How could economics explain the findings in the Table?

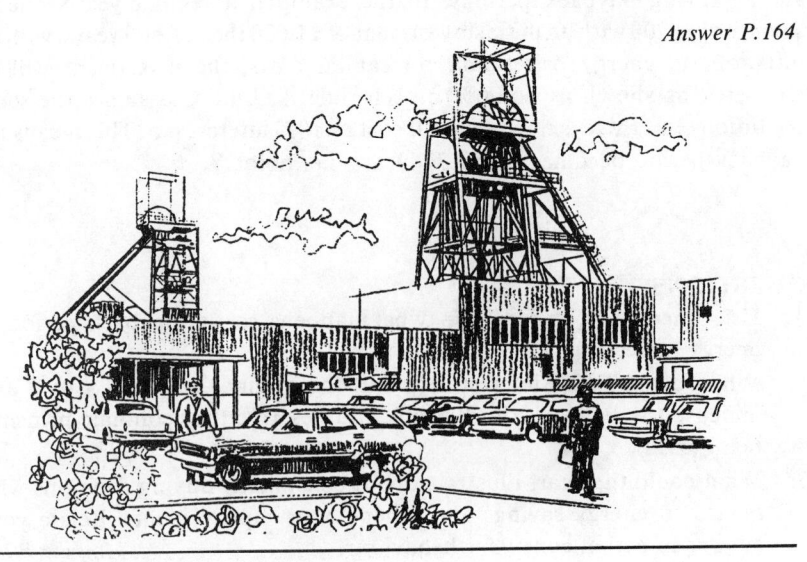

Answer P.164

THE CHANGING STRUCTURE OF EMPLOYMENT

The following table shows the distribution of employment in the United Kingdom in 1973 and 1981.

Employment in the United Kingdom (thousands)

		1973	1981
Total		22,664	21,198
A.	of which:		
	Males	13,773	12,264
	Females	8,891	8,934
		22,664	21,198
B.	of which:		
	Agriculture and mining	795	692
	Manufacturing	7,830	6,038
	Other production industries	1,724	1,472
	Transport and distribution	4,268	4,075
	Service industries	6,462	7,342
	Local and national government	1,585	1,579
		22,664	21,198

(Source: Monthly Digest of Statistics, May 1982, H.M.S.O.)

QUESTIONS
(a) Outline briefly the main changes in the distribution of employment, as shown by the above figures, which occurred between 1973 and 1981.
(b) How might these changes be explained?

London, June 1984.

Answer P.165

Chapter 12
SUPPLY-THEORY OF THE FIRM

---

(1) Price and Costs — A Restaurant Problem.

(2) British Telecom. Telephone Charges.

(3) Full Cost or Marginal Cost Pricing.

(4) Price Discrimination and the Monopolist.

(5) The Monopolist and Competition.

(6) The Publisher as Monopolist.

(7) The Size of the City — "Civis".

(8) Resource Allocation in Oligopolistic Industrial Markets.

(9) Cost Behaviour and Efficiency.

PRICE AND COSTS — A RESTAURANT PROBLEM

A restaurant charges £10 per head for its evening meal. The average number of customers on each night is given below.

Average number of customers

Monday	6	On those nights averaging less than twenty customers, only one waiter is needed. On all other nights two waiters are needed, except Saturday when three are required.
Tuesday	15	
Wednesday	20	
Thursday	20	
Friday	30	
Saturday	45	
Sunday	closed	

The running costs are divided into premises and equipment, food and fuel costs, and waiters' wages. The owner acts as chef and takes as his income all revenue remaining after the costs are paid. Premises and equipment cost £120 a week, which the owner averages out to £20 per working day. Food and fuel costs average £4 a meal. Waiters are normally paid £20 a night each, but on Saturday night the owner needs to pay £30 to attract a third waiter and this is paid to all three on that night.

QUESTIONS
(a) What is the owner's net weekly income?

(b) Explain what part of this would be transfer earnings.

(c) The owner calculates he makes a loss on Monday nights and should thus close. Comment on this.

(d) The owner decides to reduce the price of the meal to £8 on Monday and Tuesday nights, to attract more customers. On both nights the average number of customers rises by five. Compare the elasticities of demand on the two nights.

(e) Comment on the possible effect on profits of charging a different price on different nights.

(f) Explain and demonstrate the relationship between the Average Cost of Labour and the Marginal Cost of Labour on Saturday nights.

S.U.J.B., June 1985.

Answer P.166

BRITISH TELECOM — TELEPHONE CHARGES 1986/7

The following material comes from British Telecom publicity material:

NATIONAL CALLS (UNIT CHARGES)

Did you know that for less than the price of a 2nd class postage stamp, you can make a 3 minute cheap rate call to someone living up to 35 miles* away?

What's more, phone during cheap time and 18p will buy you a 3 minute call to any of your friends or relatives living anywhere in the UK.

Check your Phone Book for details of how these call rates apply to the places you wish to dial. Thus:

*Distance calculated from your local charge point.

Call charge unit fee 4.4p. Prices above one unit are rounded to the nearest penny in these examples.	Cheap Mon-Fri 6pm-8am Sat & Sun all day	
	1st minute	3 minutes
Call Rate a Calls up to 35 miles (56 km) outside local call area	4.4p	9p
Call Rate b1 Calls over 35 miles (56 km) connected over low cost routes	4.4p	13p
Call Rate b Calls over 35 miles (56 km) and calls to the Channel Islands	9p	18p

Standard Mon-Fri 8am-9am 1pm-6pm		Peak Mon-Fri 9am-1pm	
1st minute	3 minutes	1st minute	3 minutes
9p	26p	13p	35p
9p	26p	13p	35p
13p	35p	18p	44p

Supply-Theory of The Firm

Dialling right across the country can cost as little as a local call.
There are 146 low cost (b1) routes throughout the U.K. They are the most heavily-used telephone routes, between major towns and cities (including nearby places in the same telephone charge group).

If you live in an area served by one or more of these low cost routes, you'll find calls to some towns and cities will be much more economical.

LOCAL CALLS

Cheap Rate Mon-Fri 6pm-8am Sat & Sun all day	4.4p buys 6 minutes
Standard Rate Mon-Fri 8am-9am 1pm-6pm	4.4p buys 1½ minutes
Peak Rate Mon-Fri 9am-1pm	4.4p buys 1 minute

(All are **Unit** Call Charges)

EXCHANGE LINES — QUARTERLY RENTAL
Residential
    — Exclusive   £13.95
    — Shared   £12.75
Business
    — Exclusive   £22.55

Source: "Your Guide to Telephone Charges". Effective from November 1986. British Telecom.

QUESTIONS

1. Describe the pricing structure which British Telecom have for Telephone Calls.

2. What could be the economic justification for (i) charging a rental and unit call charge; (ii) charging between areas; (iii) charging between different times of the day?

3. In 1985 British Telecom was "privatised". Explain what this means and outline the supposed benefits of this course of action.

Answer P.167

FULL COST OR MARGINAL COST PRICING

	Products		
Cost Per Unit £	A	B	C
Materials	2.8	5.2	3.4
Labour	3.6	4.0	5.1
Overheads (200% of labour)	7.2	8.0	10.2
Total Cost	13.6	17.2	18.7
Selling Price	15.7	16.1	20.2
Annual Sales	15,000	20,000	18,000

QUESTION
The accountant provides the above information and advises that Product B should be discontinued as it makes a loss of £1.1/unit × 20,000, i.e. £22,000 p.a. Further inspection shows that 40% of overheads are fixed. Should Product B be maintained or discontinued?

Answer P.171

PRICE DISCRIMINATION AND THE MONOPOLIST

A monopolist is faced by the following cost and demand schedules:

	COST		DEMAND	
Q	Fixed (£'s)	Variable (£'s)	Price (£'s)	Demand
1	100	50	70	1
2	100	95	65	2
3	100	130	60	3
4	100	150	55	4
5	100	155	50	5
6	100	160	45	6
7	100	185	40	7
8	100	270	35	8

QUESTIONS

1. What level of output will this firm choose to produce?
2. As a result of a fall in consumers' income the firm's demand schedule becomes as follows:

Price	Demand
60	1
55	2
50	3
45	4
40	5
35	6
30	7
25	8

    How would you expect the firm to respond to this changed situation?
3. What would the firm do if, after the fall in demand, it could engage in perfect price discrimination?
4. What conditions would be necessary for such a policy to succeed?

(SUJB, June 1981)

Answer P.172

70 Supply-Theory of The Firm

THE MONOPOLIST AND COMPETITION

A monopolist, at present producing an unbranded product for the home market only, is faced by the following revenue and cost schedules.

Price	Demand	Fixed Costs	Variable Cost
20	20	200	260
18	30	200	370
16	40	200	400
14	50	200	425
12	60	200	460
10	70	200	500
8	80	200	680

QUESTIONS
(a) Determine the monopolist's equilibrium price and output.
(b) Assuming the same cost conditions, what would the long run equilibrium price and output levels be if the industry were perfectly competitive? (Assume costs include normal profit.)
(c) For what reasons might the cost conditions be different under perfect competition?
(d) The monopolist is faced by imports which enter at the world price of ten. What effect would this have on the firm if
  (i) it maintained its present marketing behaviour;
  (ii) it changed its marketing of the product in response to the different circumstances?
Note: In any calculations, show your working clearly.

(SUJB, June '83, Paper 1)

Use a diagram to illustrate your answer.

Answer P.173

THE PUBLISHER AS MONOPOLIST

A publisher has to decide the price at which to sell a new book. He estimates that the costs incurred before publication amount to £10,000 and that variable costs amount to £1 a copy. In addition, he has agreed to pay the author royalties at a rate of 10 per cent of sales revenue. The publisher's best estimate of the number of books he would sell at different prices is as follows:

Price (£)	Number sold
1.00	60,000
1.25	40,000
1.50	35,000
1.75	20,000
2.00	10,000

QUESTIONS

(a) Which of the above prices would maximise the publisher's profits?
(b) Which of the above prices would maximise the author's royalties?
(c) Publishers often allow authors to suggest the names of people to whom free copies will be sent. In this instance the author has suggested 50 names. Experience suggests that for every such free copy, three further copies are ordered at the normal price. Assuming that the publisher has set his profit maximising price without considering the question of free copies, should he try to persuade the author to increase/decrease his list?
(d) All the above data relate to a book published in black and white. The publisher estimates that publishing in colour would increase his variable costs by 25 per cent and demand by 20 per cent. How would his price be affected if he were to publish in colour instead of in black and white?

(London University, June 1977)

Answer P.175

72 Supply-Theory of The Firm

THE SIZE OF THE CITY — "CIVIS"

"Civis" is a city with marginal transport and production costs, as shown in Fig.1, i.e. MCT, MCP. The Combined Marginal Cost for the city is MC and the present size of the city is at oq_2, with price p_2 the price of the product in the Economy which "Civis" specialises in producing. However, it is envisaged that cheaper imports of this product be allowed into the country at a price of p_1.

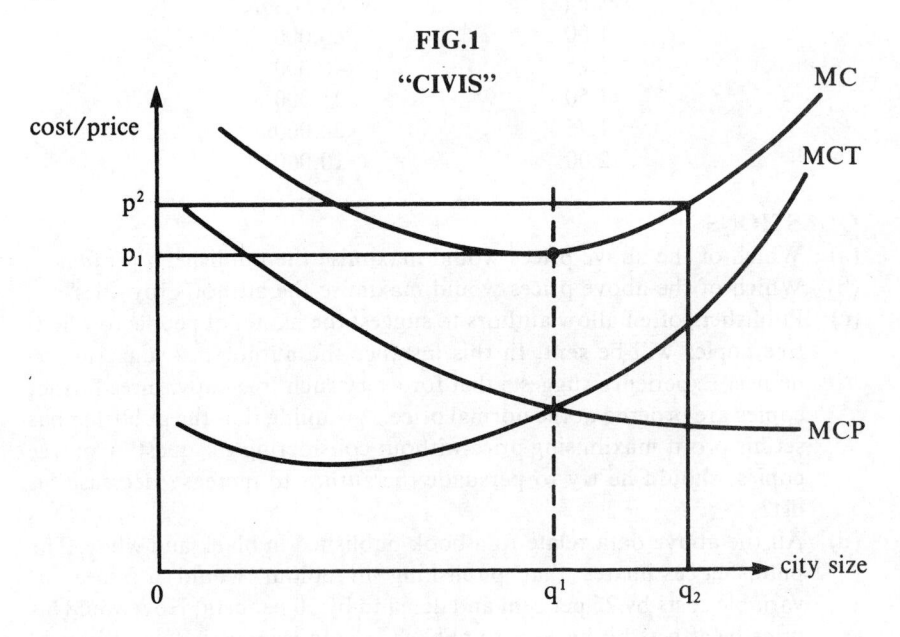

FIG.1

"CIVIS"

QUESTIONS
1. Explain the behaviour of MCT and MCP as shown in the diagram.
2. Why will the city grow in size to oq_2?
3. Discuss the implications of cheap imports on the size of "Civis".

Answer P.176

RESOURCE ALLOCATION IN OLIGOPOLISTIC INDUSTRIAL MARKETS

'Once established, industrial prices tend to remain fixed for considerable periods of time. None supposes that prices of basic steel, aluminium, automobiles, machinery, chemicals, petroleum products, containers or like products of the industrial system will be sensitive to changes in cost or demand which cause constant price readjustment for commodities, such as lesser agricultural products, where producers are still subject to control by the market. This stability of prices, in face of changing costs and demand, is further indication, it may be noted, that in the short run the mature corporation pursues goals other than profit maximisation. Stable prices reflect, in part, the need for security against price competition.'
Source: *The New Industrial State*, J.K. Galbraith; Pelican/Penguin Books.

QUESTIONS
(a) How does Galbraith's description of the operation of industrial markets seem to conflict with the normally suppoed FUNCTIONS of the price system?
(b) Why is it difficult to decide whether the behaviour described in the passage is in the public interest or not?
(c) Does it seem reasonable to assert that 'in the short run the mature corporation pursues goals other than profit maximisation'?

(SUJB, June 1986)

Answer P.177

COST BEHAVIOUR AND EFFICIENCY

The diagram below shows the short-run average total cost functions of three hypothetical companies, A, B and C.

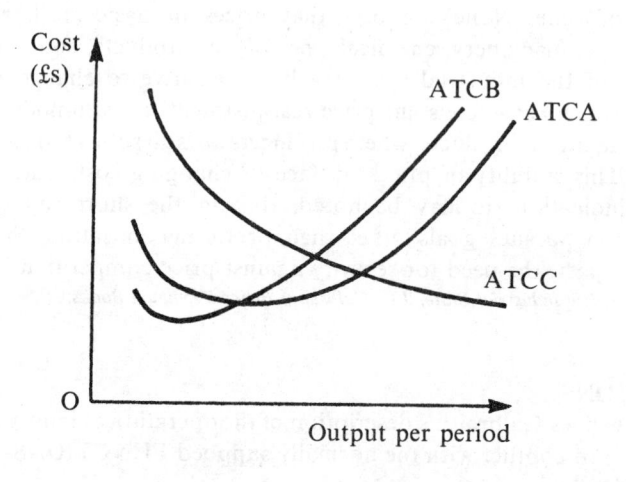

(a) What would you expect to be the characteristics of firms A and C?
(b) Which, of firms A and B, is the more efficient, and why?

(January 1983, London)

Answer P.179

Chapter 13
STRUCTURE OF INDUSTRY, SCALE AND LOCATION

(1) The National Bus Company — A problem of finance.

(2) U.K. Regional Living Standards, 1975, 1985.

(3) The Changing Pattern of Alcohol Sales.

(4) The Book Publishing Industry — Competitive Structures.

(5) Privatisation and Nationalised Industries.

(6) Changing Markets and the Brewing Industry.

(7) The U.K. Woollen & Worsted/Electrical Machinery Industries.

(8) Takeovers: Who Benefits?

(9) British Rail and Transport Resources.

(10) U.K. Cement Industry Restrained by Imports.

(11) U.K. Motor Dealer Outlets and Market Shares, 1984.

(12) U.K. Regional Employment and Output Patterns.

(13) The Structure of the Grocery Trade.

THE NATIONAL BUS COMPANY — A PROBLEM OF FINANCE

The National Bus Company has warned the Government that it must cut services by nearly 60 million route miles this year and reduce staff by 6000. It is being forced to economise to avoid a financial loss which top management blames squarely on the "wholly unreasonable and uncommercial debt burden with which NBC has been saddled."

When the NBC was set up in 1968 it was required to make annual interest payments on its entire commencing capital debt.

"This is an arrangement virtually unknown in the private sector, where a mixture of fixed interest and dividend capital is the norm. It imposes on NBC an annual drain on resources which must be met in even the worst years, including the present general recession, when no private company could afford to pay a dividend and when resources were urgently needed elsewhere," says the National Bus Company's Chief Executive, Mr. Robert Brook.

The interest on this debt cost NBC about £10 million this year. It must pay another £4 million on debts incurred at Government request in 1975 when NBC kept services running while local authorities worked out a new system of subsidising socially important but uneconomic routes. Mr. Brook says this is a "non-commercial millstone". *(Extracted from The Guardian, 5th May, 1981)*

QUESTIONS
(a) Why does the management of the National Bus Company regard the company's debt burden as "wholly unreasonable and uncommercial?"
(b) How do the problems faced by the nationalized bus company in pursuing its aims or objectives differ from those that might be faced by a private bus operator?

(AEB, June 1983)

Answer P.180

U.K. REGIONAL LIVING STANDARDS 1975, 1985

GDP PER HEAD (UK AVGE = 100)		
Region	**1975**	**1985**
North	93.6	92.9
Yorks/Humberside	94.1	91.8
East Midlands	96.1	95.7
East Anglia	92.8	100.7
Greater London	125.9	125.7
Rest of South East	103.6	107.7
South West	90.3	93.9
West Midlands	100.0	92.3
North West	96.2	96.0
Wales	88.7	88.9
Scotland	97.1	97.4
Northern Ireland	80.1	74.1

Source: Economic Trends, Nov. 1986, C.S.O.

QUESTIONS

1. Describe the general feature of Income Distribution in the UK today.
2. Identify the areas with i) lowest GDP per head 1985; (ii) highest GDP per head 1985; (iii) the area with the fastest decline in GDP per head per annum 1975-85; (iv) the fastest annual growth area in GDP per head 1975-85. Show your calculations.
3. How could you explain regional variations in income per head — use general factors to answer.
4. Outline two alternative reactions of government economic policy makers to these statistics?

Answer P.181

THE CHANGING PATTERN OF ALCOHOL SALES

THE CHANGING PATTERN OF ALCOHOL SALES

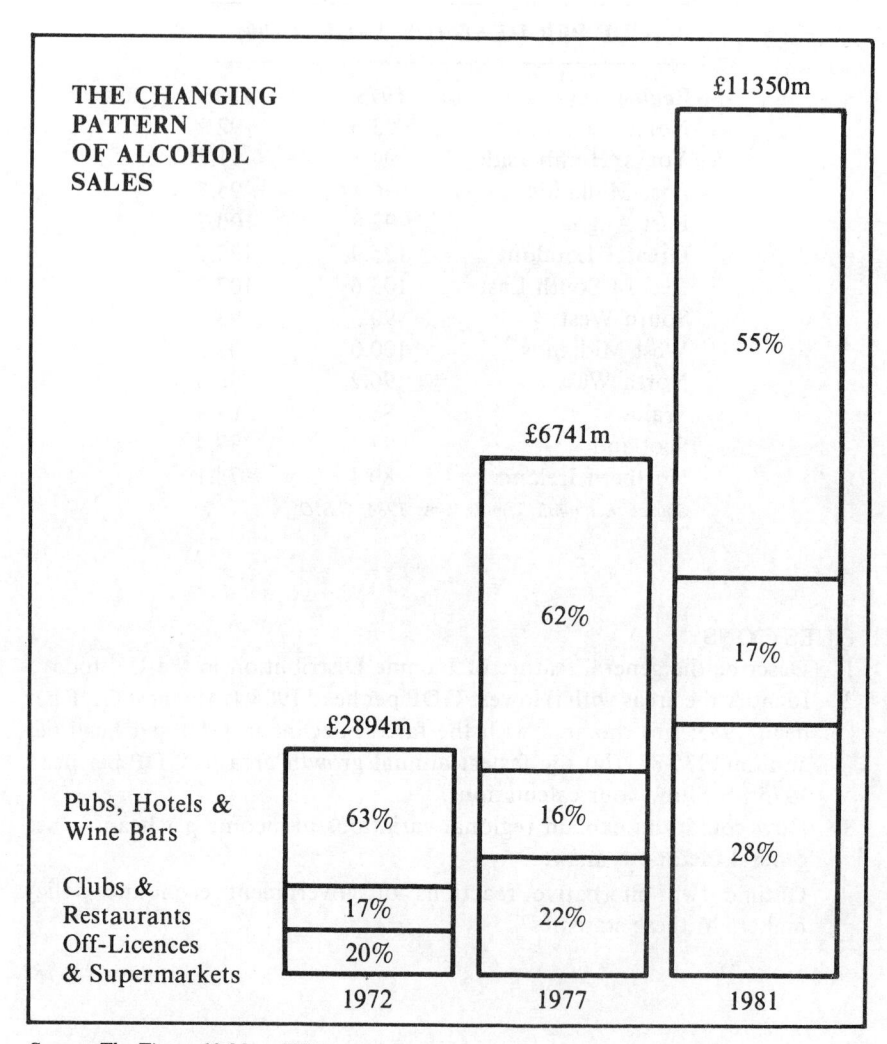

	1972	1977	1981
Total	£2894m	£6741m	£11350m
Pubs, Hotels & Wine Bars	63%	62%	55%
Clubs & Restaurants	17%	16%	17%
Off-Licences & Supermarkets	20%	22%	28%

Source: The Times, 10 May, 1983.

QUESTIONS
What factors might have caused the changes in:
(a) the level of alcohol sales;
(b) the distribution of these sales?

(SUJB, June 1985)

Answer P.183

THE BOOK PUBLISHING INDUSTRY — COMPETITIVE STRUCTURES

The following passage is an extract from an article which appeared in "The Bookseller", 8th October 1983. The Bookseller is a trade magazine and the extract discusses the impact of the rapidly growing book club market in the U.K.; in particular the company Book Club Associates (BCA).

".... Book Club Associates, with its roughly 1.5 million members and 20 or so different clubs (against the 300,000-odd membership of its nearest competitor Leisure Circle) must supply well over 50 per cent of book club editions published in the United Kingdom and must therefore be, both in statutory and in commonsense terms, a monopoly.

It is important to examine what the effect of this particular monopoly has been to date on the book trade, and its members and consumers.

To start at what might seem the logical point, with the originators of the product on which the trade and the clubs depend: the authors. On the vast majority of occasions on which they sell their product in the book club market, they are selling in a market bereft of competition. Occasionally, with a much sought-after book, there is competition at a high level, but the Leisure Circle does not compete for non-fiction books. As non-fiction is well over half the simultaneous publication book club business, this means that over half the purchases made of editions of 10,000 copies or over, up to the high level of around 100,000 copies, are uncompetitive. There is occasionally a flurry of competition at the lowest level of 1,500 to 3,000 copies, but, if a club cannot get the book it wants, there is nearly always another similar title available.

Understatement
To say that this depresses prices is an understatement. The current issue of the *Author* describes an example of an author receiving 0.2 per cent royalty from a club edition: this may be a record, but royalties of between 1.5 and 2.5 per cent are not uncommon. It is very rare for an author to receive a royalty of more than 7.5 per cent of the club price (which is split, usually 50:50, with the publisher). Yet this is the lowest royalty paid as a general rule by the American clubs.

Costs amortised
The effect on publishers of the monopoly is to some extent similar to that on authors. They do not have a competitive market in which to sell book club rights. However, they are not as badly affected as authors because, while the author can look only to royalty as consideration for his licence, a publisher would gain considerable benefit from a book club deal even if there were no royalty paid at all. Up to a print run of approximately 20,000 copies, the

additional copies run off for a book club diminish the unit cost, and about 20,000 copies virtually amortise the basic setting cost, thereby enabling the publisher to show a considerably higher profit per unit. The publisher may use this to lower the list price of the book, thereby selling more copies and benefitting the author, and book club help can also enable a publisher to keep a book in print for longer, which also benefits the author. The author does not, however, receive direct monetary return other than through a royalty.

The effect on booksellers of the BCA monopoly is somewhat different and indeed I think booksellers are more concerned about the effect of book clubs in general than about BCA in particular. They are concerned about a possible impinging on their market and, while on the whole favourably disposed towards book clubs, they are very anxious to ensure that the price-cutting allowed to book clubs is carefully controlled. If book clubs were to grow without restraint, there is no doubt that bookshops, and therefore the consumer, would be drastically affected.
Source: Bookseller, 8th October 1983.

Note: Publishers, protected by the Nett Book Agreement, are able to resell their books, via booksellers, at standard minimum prices. This price is usually much higher than the same book sold through a book club.

QUESTIONS
1. What economic explanation could you offer for the existence of book clubs?
2. Use your knowledge of economics to identify, with examples, the major types of business units and markets outlined in the passage.
3. Discuss the impact of the book club on authors, publishers, booksellers and customers.

Answer P.183

This passage discusses the economic case for privatising certain nationalised industries.

PRIVATISATION AND NATIONALISED INDUSTRIES

A large part of the article of M. Beesley and S. Littlechild* is concerned with an analysis of the prospects for eighteen nationalized industries, which are classified into four groups according to their demand and supply prospects. Demand prospects are described as either good or bad, and supply prospects are viewed in terms of the industry's suitability for competitive or monopoly ownership when transferred to the private sector. Thus, the authors arrive at four categories in a simple two-by-two matrix:
(i) Quadrant A includes industries with good demand prospects, and which are most suitable for single ownership.

(ii) Quadrant B includes industries with bad demand prospects, and which are suitable for single ownership.
(iii) Quadrant C includes industries with good demand prospects, and which are suitable for multiple ownership.
(iv) Quadrant D includes industries with bad demand prospects, and which are suitable for multiple ownership.

The authors place the local distribution of gas, electricity, and telephones and the National Grid in the first category, quadrant A. They all face a reasonably prosperous future, but the high fixed costs (such as underground cables and pipes) make local monopolies the most sensible form of organization after privatization. There would, of course, be dangers of exploitation by local monopolies, although the authors do suggest that private groups could be asked to compete for the franchises for local utility services. In this way the Government would receive the best price from the group most anxious to secure monopoly privileges, and, ultimately, the taxpayer would benefit. However, once the monopoly had been granted, it might be difficult to ensure suitable standards, and the new companies might demand legal guarantees for their monopoly privileges. In turn, this would inhibit the entry of new firms, which represents an important check on monopoly power. Nevertheless, consumers could benefit by the creation of regional organizations which could put pressure on suppliers of electricity, and so prices might be reduced.

Quadrant B would seem to contain the most unlikely candidates for privatization, such as British Rail, the Post Office, and the waterways, since they are facing long-term declines in demand, and are probably best organized as monopolies. Yet the authors are keen to promote, for example, the privatization of BR. Many valuable sites are owned by BR, and privatization might encourage BR to sell some of these. The new rail company, or companies, could then use the proceeds from such sales to maintain a minimum agreed rail network. However, it would seem to remain a very debateable point, since no information is given as to the time-scale. How long could rail companies maintain loss-making lines on the basis of sales of assets, however valuable they might be?

Source: British Economic Survey, Autumn 1983, Oxford U.P., **now** *owned by Longmans.*

Article referred to: Privatisation — *Principles, Problems and Priorities by M. Beesley and S. Littlechild. Lloyds Bank Review, July '83.

QUESTIONS

1. Outline briefly the usual economic arguments advanced for nationalisation. How could the passage be used to argue in favour of certain industries remaining nationalised?
2. How could the best interests of the consumer be safeguarded in those industries privatised in Quadrants A and B?
3. Using the arguments regarding privatisation and quadrants A and B etc., which categories would you place the following industries in: (a) Central Electricity Generating Board (excluding the Grid); (b) the National Coal Board; (c) British Leyland); (d) British Shipbuilders. Give your reasons. What problems could result if these industries were privatised?

Answer P.184

CHANGING MARKETS AND THE BREWING INDUSTRY[1]

Brewing in the UK used to be based on small plants brewing local beers for public houses in the immediate area. This is something like the industry in Bavaria today. Within a century the number of breweries decreased from 2,500 to 100, as large companies bought up the small ones (often for the sake of their outlets), and closed them down. Concentration grew, until by 1975 the biggest nine brewers produced 90 per cent of British beer and controlled a majority of outlets. New plants were built on a larger and larger scale, with the efficient capacity for a modern brewery thought to be around two million barrels per year. Along with this went a 'rationalisation' of the market: the modernising of pubs, changes in beer quality, the replacement of regional and local ales by national ones, and a movement to lager.

Consumer dissatisfaction, spear-headed by the CAMRA movement, led to several brewers realising the market gap that existed. In the mid-1970s the first of the new wave of breweries were established, with capacities as low as 2,000 barrels or less. Against all expectations they prospered, and there are now 110 new small breweries in production. 20 of them are tiny units designed to fit within a public house. The brewers concentrate on cask-conditioned ales, locally distinctive, sold through close outlets.

These small brewers surprisingly have similar production costs to their competitors with plants 1,000 times their size, though they spend much more on brewing materials, and much less on distribution and marketing. The large firms have themselves reacted by bringing back traditional real ales, slimming down their organisations, and re-instituting their old regional structures. In the meantime, only one or two of the new small brewers have failed, and more start-ups are likely.

Source: Lloyds Bank Review, June 1983.

[1] A. Bollard, Pint-Sized Production: Small Firms in the Brewing Industry, ITDG, 1982.

QUESTIONS

1. How would economic theory explain the behaviour of the brewing industry up to 1975?
2. What market conditions have forced the major brewers to adopt new business strategies?
3. How would you describe the overall market structure of the brewing industry today? How far are the characteristics of the market consistent with economic theory?

Answer P.185

THE U.K. WOOLLEN AND WORSTED AND ELECTRICAL MACHINERY INDUSTRIES — A CASE STUDY IN INDUSTRIAL STRUCTURES

size of enterprise by number employed	enter-prises	estab-lish ments	employment total	employment oper-atives	wages and salaries per head oper-atives	wages and salaries per head others	net output total	net output per head	net capital expen-diture
	number	number	thousand	thousand	£	£	£ million	£	£ million
Electrical machinery									
1 — 199	1 046	1 084	21.4	14.4	2 760	3 771	128.2	5 990	7.2
200 — 999	56	88	26.0	17.5	2 919	3 772	174.3	6 686	9.7
1 000 — 1 499	7	25	8.3	5.7	2 937	3 705	50.9	6 094	2.5
1 500 — 3 999	6	24	19.4	12.5	3 088	3 972	98.9	5 105	5.7
4 000 and over	5	68	65.7	38.1	3 303	3 728	483.5	7 355	25.2
total	1 120	1 289	140.9	88.3	3 084	3 771	935.8	6 640	50.3
five largest enterprises percentage of industry			47	43			52		50
Woollen and Worsted									
1 — 199	712	744	23.2	19.3	2 382	3 744	113.2	4 878	11.5
200 — 999	61	97	22.3	19.1	2 509	3 634	119.2	5 349	9.7
1 000 — 1 499	3	9	3.3	2.9	2 537	3 292	13.2	3 959	1.0
1 500 — 1 999	7	40	11.9	10.0	2 559	3 228	69.0	5 790	7.1
2 000 and over	5	58	24.1	20.4	2 511	3 279	113.2	4 695	6.6
total	788	948	84.9	71.7	2 483	3 483	428.0	5 041	35.9
five largest enterprises percentage of industry			28	28			26		18

Source: U.K. Census of Production, C.S.O.

Continued overleaf

QUESTIONS

(a) (i) Describe how the two industries represented in the table compare in overall size of output and employment.

(ii) Outline the major differences in the share of output and employment by size of enterprise in the two industries.

(b) The table shows that wages and salaries are generally higher in one industry than in the other. Provide two possible reasons for this difference.

(c) What data in the table suggests that there may be greater economies of scale in the electrical machinery than in the woollen and worsted industry?

(d) (i) Compare the degree of concentration of market power between the two industries. Justify your answer with information from the table.

(ii) What economic factors would affect the actual market power of the largest enterprise in each of these industries? *Answer P.186*

TAKEOVERS: WHO BENEFITS?

BTR's £1.2 billion bid yesterday for Pilkington Brothers, Britain's biggest glass manufacturer, can only heighten the public belief that the City's principal activity is launching takeovers or fighting them off. This impression is, of course, exaggerated: even financial writers are not immune from the journalist's penchant for personality and conflict. But the truth is not that far removed.

The case for mergers and takeovers as a whole, including — and perhaps especially — unwelcome takeover bids, is that they improve overall management efficiency and hence the productivity of industry and commerce. With a contested takeover some such improvement is to be expected whether the bid is successful or not: a successful bid installs what is presumed to be a superior management, while an unsuccessful bid can have a salutary effect in concentrating wonderfully the minds of the threatened managers. It is further, and plausibly, contended that the mere possibility of a bid keeps the management of possible target companies on their toes.

More generally, those satisfied with the existing situation argue that mergers and takeovers are natural elements in a free market economy which would be distorted and impaired by their restriction.

The consequences of mergers and takeovers have been the subject of growing academic research, though assessment is difficult and the results inconclusive. Certainly it is not true that takeover bids are a necessary condition of a successful economy; the Germans and the Japanese seem to get on well without them. And the objections to contested takeovers are numerous and formidable. For the purpose of this article five main objections will suffice.

First, in many companies long-term planning, particularly decisions on research and development and capital investment, is distorted by the fear of a takeover bid because such expenditure, however desirable for the future, immediately depresses profits and the price of the company's shares. Such inhibition of research and development and of investment cannot be beneficial to the economy.

Secondly, takeover bids exacerbate conflicts of interest between directors and managers on the one hand and shareholders on the other. This applies on both sides.

Taking the predator company first, the interests of its shareholders, like all other shareholders, are in the maximization of earnings per share and a rise in the share price. Such interests, as we have seen, may or may not be advanced by the takeover; in the short term they will almost certainly be depressed by the expenses incurred. To the directors and managers, however, what matters is size: an enlarged company conventionally justifies higher salaries, bigger cars, grander offices, deeper pile carpets and so on.

Source: The Times, 21st Nov., 1986. Author E. Palamountain.

QUESTIONS
1. Explain what is meant by the statement that "mergers and takeovers as a whole . . . improve overall management efficiency and hence the productivity of industry and commerce".
2. B.T.R. is a large, profitable industrial conglomerate, active throughout the world. What economic reasons could explain their bid for Pilkingtons Glass?
3. How is the case argued that mergers and takeovers may not always be successful?
4. Discuss the main arguments against mergers in the light of a) long and short term economic efficiency and b) the divorce of ownership and control.
5. Briefly state the role of the Monopolies Commission in current proposed mergers.

Answer P.188

BRITISH RAIL AND TRANSPORT RESOURCES

Table 1: Financial Results for British Rail's Trading Activities in 1978

INCOME	£ million	EXPENDITURE	£ million
Passengers and freight receipts	1 213	Staff costs	1 113
Support payments from the government	434	Materials, supplies, etc.	615
Shipping	154	Fuel and power	111
Hotels	34	Interest payments on borrowings	49
Catering	50	Depreciation on assets	94
Property rents, etc.	33		
Freightliners	21		
Hovercraft	6		
Rail workshop sales	29		
Other	14		
TOTAL INCOME	1 988	TOTAL OUTGOINGS	1 982

Source: Annual Report of B.R. Board, 1978.

Table 2: Expenditure on Transport and Use of Resources 1976-77

	Expenditure by users (£ million)	Actual resource cost (£ million)
Passenger transport:		
Buses and coaches	1 017	1 471
Private and business motoring	9 060	7 236
Taxis	220	205
British Rail	527	941
London Transport Underground	127	194
Total Passenger	10 951	10 047
Freight:		
Road	9 750	9 787
British Rail	414	446
Total Freight	10 164	10 233

Source: White Paper on Transport, HMSO, CSO.

Study tables 1 and 2 and answer the following:—

QUESTIONS

1. (i) Use Table 1 and calculate the net surplus or deficit on the income account of British Rail's activities in 1978.
   (ii) What other information would be necessary to analyse British Rail's overall level of profitability in 1978?
   (iii) Explain why British Rail's results, as shown in Table 1, would not necessarily be improved by the closure of "unprofitable" branch lines?
2. Suggest an economic explanation for any two of British Rail's activities other than the carriage of passengers and freight by train.
3. (i) In what way does Table 1 indicate that labour productivity is an important issue for British Rail?
   (ii) Why is it difficult for British Rail to raise labour productivity?
4. (i) Explain why expenditure on private and business motoring is greater than resource costs. Use Table 2.
   (ii) Why is the opposite true of buses and coaches?
5. How could you argue in favour of support payments included in British Rail income?

Answer P.190

UK CEMENT INDUSTRY RESTRAINED BY IMPORTS

At first sight the recent fall in sterling could be expected to bring relief to the troubled UK cement industry. But there are still two major problems. First is the destabilising influence of surplus cement capacity throughout Europe. Secondly, the pound's fall has still left UK producers vulnerable to West German and Spanish imports, let alone those from East Germany where the winning of foreign exchange rather than profit is the main objective.

As a result, UK manufacturers are showing signs of anxiety. They are led by Blue Circle Industries (BCI) with 55% of the market. Other large manufacturers include RTZ (formerly Ward and Tunnel) with a 22% share, Rugby Portland with 18% and Aberthaw with 6%.

At present UK cement workers do not compete with each other on price. There is a common pricing agreement and prices are standardised by areas. The arrival of cheap continental cement in large quantities could disrupt this cartel or, at least, force the manufacturers to freeze or even cut their prices in unison. In either event their profitability would be severely affected.

In the last six months or so West German domestic prices have risen significantly, but because of surplus capacity and the need to boost volume, export prices have remained the same. The differential between them and UK prices is still sufficient to encourage importers, despite sterling falling 11% against the Deutschmark in the same period.

Source: Investors Chronicle, 28 January 1983.

QUESTIONS

1. Why might "the recent fall in sterling bring relief to the troubled UK cement industry"?
2. How would economic theory explain the structure of the UK cement market? What might be the economic rationale for its operation?
3. Why might the importation of cement 'disrupt' the cartel?
4. What would explain the pricing policies of West German cement makers?
5. How would UK producers and consumers be affected by the disruption of the UK cement cartel?

Answer P.192

U.K. NEW MOTOR CAR, DEALER OUTLETS AND MARKET SHARES (1984)

Manufacturer	Dealer outlets	Market share %	Outlets per 1% share
GM/Vauxhall	653	16.2	40
Ford	1211	27.8	44
VW/Audi	380	5.5	69
Nissan	425	6.1	70
Volvo	258	3.4	76
BL	1550	17.8	87
PSA Peugeot	530	5.4	98
Renault	400	3.4	118
Fiat	339	2.7	126
Others (small independants)	—	11.7	—

Source: Midland Bank Review, Winter 1985.

QUESTIONS

1. a) Briefly explain each of the column headings.
   b) Calculate overall import penetration of the U.K. market. Ignore Independants.

90 Structure of Industry, Scale and Location

2. How would economic theory explain the structure of the motor car manufacturing market? What would theory indicate about new motor car prices?
3. Which two manufacturers seem to be most economically efficient in their dealer networks? Which economies of scale are at work and give suitable examples.
4. Outline the ways in which the "dealer outlet" network could be improved in terms of future overall efficiency.

Answer P.194

UK REGIONAL EMPLOYMENT AND OUTPUT PATTERNS

Employment (in thousands) and Net Output (in £ million) by standard region UK (1977)

The Census of Production in the UK allows economists to compare regionally output from different industries with numbers employed in those same industries. To make manageable comparisons of output and employment, numbers are often replaced by percentages. As you can see in column 2 in the table overleaf, 4.8% of the 762.3 thousand employed in food, drink and tobacco in the UK work in the North region, or in column 6, 10% of the 6 576.0 £ million output in food, drink and tobacco comes from the Yorkshire and Humberside region. Absolute figures in the tables are italicised.

Structure of Industry, Scale and Location

Employment	1 All manufacturing (in thousands)	% of UK total for each industry		
		2 Food, drink and tobacco	3 Metal Manufacture	4 Instrument Engineering
North	442.5	4.8	10.0	2.6
Yorkshire and Humberside	718.8	11.6	19.1	3.5
East Midlands	583.6	7.1	8.3	3.6
East Anglia	200.8	5.8	0.4	3.8
South East	1 828.3	21.0	6.4	48.1
South West	418.8	7.9	1.4	8.4
West Midlands	986.7	7.4	24.4	5.0
North West	1 027.0	15.0	5.0	10.0
Wales	313.2	2.7	16.8	2.2
Scotland	616.9	13.3	8.1	11.8
Northern Ireland	143.9	3.4	0.1	1.0
UK TOTAL EMPLOYMENT (IN THOUSANDS)	7 280.5	100.0 / 762.3	100.0 / 465.5	100.0 / 156.3

Net Output	5 All manufacturing (£ million)	% of UK total for each industry		
		6 Food, drink and tobacco	7 Metal Manufacture	8 Instrument Engineering
North	3 150.5	4.5	7.6	2.3
Yorkshire and Humberside	4 751.4	10.0	20.7	3.1
East Midlands	3 671.2	7.5	8.4	3.5
East Anglia	1 500.6	6.0	0.5	4.5
South East	14 223.2	23.4	7.5	49.9
South West	2 784.9	7.8	1.4	8.0
West Midlands	6 147.2	6.6	25.5	5.3
North West	7 403.1	14.4	5.3	9.5
Wales	2 158.4	2.2	15.9	2.3
Scotland	4 261.7	14.8	7.1	10.9
Northern Ireland	810.1	2.8	0.1	0.7
UK TOTAL NET OUTPUT (£ MILLION)	50 862.3	100.0 / 6 576.0	100.0 / 2 898.9	100.0 / 934.7

Source: Census of Production 1977, C.S.O.

Continued overleaf

QUESTIONS

(a) (i) Which industry is **least** concentrated geographically and give one economic reason for this.

(ii) Which industry is **most** concentrated geographically and give one economic reason for this.

(b) (i) The table shows measures of net rather than gross output. Why do economists distinguish between the two measures of output?

(ii) Calculate how much labour is required, on average, to produce each thousand pound's worth of net output in food, drink and tobacco in the UK?

(iii) How could you explain why less labour is required to produce each thousand pound's worth of net output in food, drink and tobacco than in instrument engineering?

(c) (i) In manufacturing industry, average wages in the South East region are higher than in Northern Ireland. What information in the tables could imply that this is the case?

(ii) Give reasons for this difference.

(d) Use the table, where possible, and discuss the following problem.

A Japanese manufacturer in instrument engineering wants to build a new plant in the UK. You have been asked to advise on a location. Outline the economic factors that the manufacturer might bear in mind when reaching a decision.

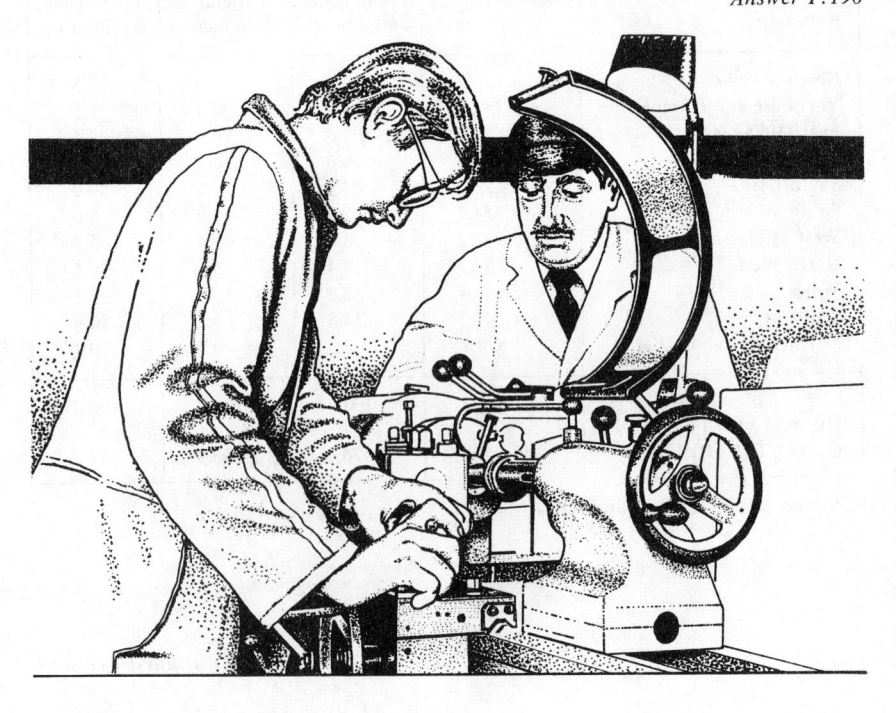

Answer P.196

THE STRUCTURE OF THE GROCERY TRADE

The following figures refer to the grocery retail trade in Britain in 1961 and 1979.

Table 1. Number of grocers' shops

	1961	1979
Multiples	16,522	6,015
All other retail outlets	130,255	62,552
	146,777	68,567

Table 2. % share of grocery sales

	1961	1979
Multiples	26.9	53.6
All other retail outlets	73.1	46.4
	100.0	100.0

Source: Monopolies and Mergers Commission, 'Discounts to Retailers', H.M.S.O., 1981).

QUESTIONS

(a) Describe the main trends in grocery retailing shown by the two tables.

(b) In its report the Monopolies and Mergers Commission commented that 'Multiple retailing offers substantial economies of operation . . . A number of social and economic changes have contributed to the emergence of large retail outlets.'
   (i) What 'economies of operation' are available to multiple retailers?
   (ii) What do you think the 'social and economic changes' referred to in the report have been?

(London, June 1984)

Answer P.198

Chapter 14
INTERNATIONAL TRADE — DEVELOPMENT ECONOMICS

(1) Global Income distribution.

(2) The European Monetary System (EMS).

(3) Selected items from the UK Balance of Payments — The Value of the pound.

(4) Summary of UK Balance of Payments 1974, 1981.

(5) World Trade Patterns.

(6) Free Trade & The Japanese Case.

(7) The problem of floating exchange rates.

(8) Why did the system of fixed parities break down?

(9) The Value of the Pound.

(10) Free trade and the determination of price.

(11) Brazil and international sugar prices.

PRINCIPAL MANUFACTURING STATISTICS IN SINGAPORE (1971-1981)

	Output per worker (dollars at current prices)	Gross domestic capital formation (million dollars at current prices)	Ratio of wages to output (per cent)	Ratio of direct exports to output (per cent)	Gross domestic product deflator (1968 = 100)
1971	36 137	2 744	9.9	44.7	109
1972	34 962	3 354	10.9	47.5	115
1973	42 945	4 000	10.1	54.9	129
1974	67 795	5 592	7.7	59.8	149
1975	67 679	5 035	9.1	57.7	152
1976	76 724	5 492	8.2	62.8	154
1977	82 277	5 339	8.2	62.4	157
1978	83 144	6 344	8.5	63.9	160
1979	96 835	7 850	8.0	64.2	166
1980	113 844	10 015	7.8	60.6	176
1981	131 158	11 553	7.7	60.3	186

Source: *World Development Report, 1981.*

QUESTIONS

(a) (i) How would you establish 'real labour productivity' in Singapore 1971-81?

(ii) How could the table help explain one cause of increase in real labour productivity?

(iii) Give two other causes for increases in real labour productivity.

(b) (i) How does the table reflect the relationship between productivity changes and the improved international competitiveness of firms in Singapore?

(ii) Give three other factors that may have influenced the international competitiveness of firms in Singapore.

(c) Discuss the extent to which productivity gains have been distributed to employees in Singapore 1971-81.

Answer P.199

ECONOMIC PERFORMANCE IN SELECTED ASIAN ECONOMIES

Country	GNP per head				Population 1980 (millions)	No. of years to double population
	1980 (US$)	Average Annual Growth 1960-80 %	Projected Growth 1980-90%			
			High Forecast	Low Forecast		
Malaysia	1620	4.3	6.0	4.3	13.9	36
Singapore	4430	7.5			2.4	59
Brunei	10,640	8.4	4.0	2.9	0.2	29
Sri Lanka	270	2.4			14.7	32
India	240	1.4	2.1	1.0	673.2	28
Indonesia	430	4.0			146.6	34

Source: World Development Report 1982, World Bank and Demographic Yearbook, United Nations, 1981.

QUESTIONS

1. Which country in 1980 had the lowest standard of living? Explain your answer.
2. "Sri-Lanka had a higher standard of living than India in 1960". True or false? Explain your answer.
3. Comparing Malaysia and Singapore, which country is expected to experience the highest growth in GNP between 1980-90 and why?

Answer P.201

GLOBAL INCOME DISTRIBUTION

Region or country	GNP per capita 1976 (US$)	GNP 1976 (US$000 millions)	Population mid-1976 (millions)
North America	7 880	1 877	238
Japan	5 090	574	113
Oceania	5 320	115	22
Europe, excluding USSR	4 280	2 215	518
USSR	2 800	718	257
Middle East	2 250	176	78
South America	1 230	270	219
Central America	1 000	109	109
Africa	420	180	426
Asia, excluding Japan and Middle East	290	586	2 040

QUESTIONS
(a) Comment on the distribution of the world's income and population, as shown in the table.
(b) In 1976 the per capita GNP at market prices of the United Kingdom was £2 090 and that of India was £70. Does this mean that the general standard of living in the United Kingdom was approximately 30 times that of India? *(SUJB 1980)*

Answer P.201

THE EUROPEAN MONETARY SYSTEM (EMS)

The question of whether a region should have its own currency or be part of a larger currency bloc (eg The EMS)* can be decided in principle by comparing the benefits to trade and investment from fixed rates against the extra costs of correcting payments imbalances without flexibility in exchange rates and the cost of administering a separate currency. A number of economic and political considerations will affect this comparison. Perhaps the most important is the requirement that, if a region is to be part of a currency bloc, its inhabitants must have an affinity with those of the rest of the bloc. In particular, there should be a willingness to correct regional payments imbalances by inter-regional transfers of capital and income.

The European Monetary System is an agreement by the member states of the EEC, apart from the UK and Greece, to stabilise the rates of exchange between their currencies. It has been partially successful to date, although its long-run survival probably requires a greater degree of similarity between the economic policies of different member states than has so far been the case.

*Author's brackets.

Source: A Guide to the International Financial System, Banking Information Service, 1984.

QUESTIONS

1. Briefly outline the "(Economic) benefits to trade and investment from fixed rates". Relate your answer to the EMS.
2. What is meant by the statement "the extra costs of correcting payments imbalances without flexibility in exchange rates".
3. Why would it become necessary to correct regional imbalances of capital and income within the EEC? How could this be done?
4. What do you think is meant by 'a greater degree of similarity between the economic policies of different member states'? Why is it necessary for the maintenance of the EMS?

Answer P.203

SELECTED ITEMS FROM THE UK BALANCE OF PAYMENTS — THE VALUE OF THE POUND

	1979 £m	1980 £m	1981 £m	1982 £m	1983 £m
Balance of trade in manufactured goods	+1965	+3872	+2905	+233	−2119
Balance of trade in oil	−731	+273	+3112	+4605	+7001
Balance of visible trade	−3449	+1233	+3008	+2119	−500
Balance of invisible trade	+2796	+2002	+3539	+3309	+2549
Balance of payments on current account	−653	+3235	+6547	+5428	+2049
Investment and other capital transactions	+2307	−1864	−7209	−639	−2044
Balance of Payments *(author's figs.)*	+1654	+1371	−662	+4789	+5

Sterling Exchange Rates

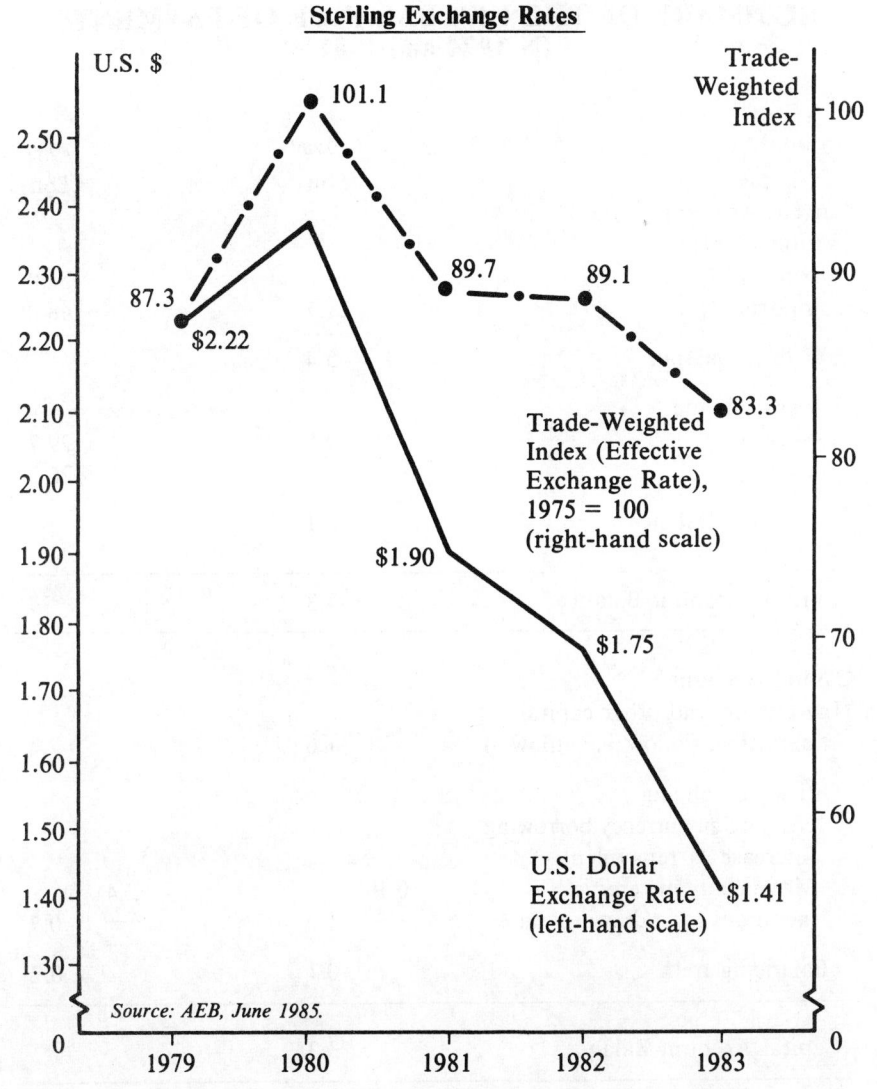

Data points shown on chart:

Trade-Weighted Index (Effective Exchange Rate), 1975 = 100 (right-hand scale):
- 1979: 87.3
- 1980: 101.1
- 1981: 89.7
- 1982: 89.1
- 1983: 83.3

U.S. Dollar Exchange Rate (left-hand scale):
- 1979: $2.22
- 1980: ~$2.38
- 1981: $1.90
- 1982: $1.75
- 1983: $1.41

Source: AEB, June 1985.

Sources: Economic Trends: Balance of Payments 'Pink Book', Department of Trade.

QUESTIONS

(a) Use the table to account for the main changes in the United Kingdom balance of payments on current account over the period 1979 to 1983.

(b) Why may the effective exchange rate of the pound be a better indicator of the United Kingdom's international competitiveness than the dollar exchange rate?

(c) Discuss the nature of any relationships shown by the data between
   (i) the balance of payments on current account and capital flows;
   (ii) the balance of payments and the exchange rate.

(AEB 1985)
Answer P.205

SUMMARY OF THE UK's BALANCE OF PAYMENTS IN 1974 and 1981

	1974 (£bn)	1981 (£bn)
Current Account		
Visible Trade		
Exports		51.0
Imports	21.7	48.0
Visibles Balance	−5.4	
Invisible Trade		
Receipts	10.5	29.7
Payments		26.2
Invisibles Balance	2.1	
Current Account Balance	−3.3	
Capital Account		
Investment and other capital transactions (inflow +; outflow −)	1.6	−7.4
Official Financing		
Net foreign currency borrowing (increase +; repayment −)		
Movements in reserves (additions to −; drawings on +)	−0.1 ── 1.6	2.4 ── 0.7
Balancing Item	0.1	0.2
Capital Account Balance	3.3	

Source: United Kingdom Balance of Payments, 1983 Edition, C.S.O.

QUESTIONS

1. Explain the following terms (i) Capital Account: Investment and other Capital Transactions; (ii) Official Financing: Movements in Reserves.
2. Calculate for 1974 the value of (i) Visible trade exports; (ii) Invisible trade payments; (iii) Official Financing: Net foreign currency borrowing.
3. Calculate for 1981 the value of (i) Invisible Balance; (ii) Visible Balance; (iii) Current Account Balance; (iv) Capital Account Balance.

Answer P.207

WORLD TRADE PATTERNS

In the post-World War II period the volatility of commodity prices in the free-market commodities was greater than before the War, as the calculations of Mr St-Clair Grondona have shown. While between 1950 and 1970 the index of the prices of internationally traded basic materials, as compiled by the UN, remained constant in dollar terms, there were sharp fluctuations up and down with changes in the rate of growth of industrial activity, and of course much sharper fluctuations in *individual* commodities such as sugar. And since 1971, as Professor Sylos Labini has recently shown, the prices of raw materials became far more sensitive to variations in world industrial production than they were before. Whereas in the period 1950-1971 the rise and fall of raw material prices coincided with corresponding changes in the growth rate of world industrial production, but the percentage range of variations in prices was somewhat smaller than that of industrial production, *after* 1971 the extent of price fluctuations in percentage terms was nearly three times as great. Thus the sharp rise in prices in 1972-74 was followed by an almost equally sharp fall in 1974-75, which was again abruptly reversed when world industrial production recovered in late 1975 and in 1976; in fact there can be little doubt that the sharp rise in raw material prices in 1976 (and again, following another sharp fall, in 1978) was the main factor which nipped world industrial recovery in the bud.

Source: Lloyds Bank Review, July 1983. N. Kaldor.

QUESTIONS

1. Why would you expect the price of internationally traded base materials to fluctuate with changes in the rate of growth of industrial activity?
2. Why do post 1971 changes in raw materials prices give cause for concern?
3. What type of institution could you suggest which might be able to solve the problems of unstable raw material prices?
4. Can you suggest any differences between the market structures of primary and industrial products which may explain variations in price movements etc.?

Answer P.208

FREE TRADE & THE JAPANESE CASE

The weakness of the modern argument for the advantages of free trade was ably exposed in a speech delivered in 1970 by Vice-Minister Y. Ojimi of the Japanese Ministry of International Trade and Industry — MITI, the famous ministry to which so much of Japan's successful economic policy is attributed:

After the war (said Ojimi) Japan's first exports consisted of such things as toys or other miscellaneous merchandise and low-quality textile products. Should Japan have entrusted its future, according to the theory of comparative advantage, to these industries characterised by intensive use of labour? That would perhaps be a rational advice for a country with a small population of 5 or 10 million. But Japan has a large population. If the Japanese economy had adopted the simple doctrine of free trade and had chosen to specialise in this kind of industry, it would almost permanently have been unable to break away from the Asian pattern of stagnation and poverty, and would have remained the weakest link in the free world, thereby becoming a problem area in the Far East.

The Ministry of International Trade and Industry decided to establish in Japan industries which require intensive employment of capital and technology, industries that in consideration of comparative cost should be the most inappropriate for Japan, industries such as steel, oil refining, petrochemicals, automobiles, aircraft, industrial machinery of all sorts, and electronics, including electronic computers. From a short-run, static viewpoint, encouragement of such industries would seem to conflict with economic rationalism. But from a long-range viewpoint, these are precisely the industries where income elasticity of demand is high, technological progress is rapid, and labour productivity rises fast. It was clear that without these industries it would be difficult to employ a population of 100 million and raise their standard of living to that of Europe and America . . .

Source: J. Eatwell, "Whatever Happened to Britain", BBC 1983.

QUESTIONS
1. How would the theory of comparative cost advocate Japan concentrating on developing industries characterised by intensive use of labour?
2. How would economic theory explain the Japanese experience of producing and exporting cars, colour T.V.s, videos, etc?

Answer P.208

THE PROBLEM OF FLOATING EXCHANGE RATES

This passage discusses the view of the Deputy Governor of the Bank of England on currency instability.

The implications for the world economy of continuing currency instability would be serious. Mr McMahon, in one of the clearest expositions to date of the economic effects, indicted exchange rate misalignments on three counts.

It reduced investment worldwide by increasing uncertainty and squeezing profits in countries with overvalued currencies. "The result may be a failure of capital formation to respond to the usual extent to the current recovery in consumer demand in the world as a whole."

It pumped up inflation because workers took real wage gains when exchange rates rose, but resisted lower living standards when exchange rate fell.

Most harmful of all, in Mr McMahon's view, it increased pressure for protection in countries at a competitive disadvantage, which was not reversed when circumstances improved.

"I believe that the substantial and enduring exchange rate swings of recent years are likely to have played a significant part in hampering economic performance and impairing the strength of the present recovery."

Source: The Times, 16th November 1983.

QUESTIONS
1. Why might capital formation not respond to the recovery in consumer demand . . . ?
2. How can exchange rate instability pump up inflation?
3. Explain how exchange rate instability could increase the pressure for protection? *Answer P.209*

WHY DID THE SYSTEM OF FIXED PARITIES BREAK DOWN?

The transition to widespread 'floating' among the major currencies in early 1973 was a reaction to the rigidities of the Bretton Woods system of fixed parities. Under this system the fixed but adjustable exchange rate has essentially been viewed as a means of providing a stable basis for external economic and monetary relations. In circumstances of 'fundamental disequilibrium' alterations of the exchange rate could — and should — be used as an instrument for balance-of-payments adjustment. In its first twenty years or so the Bretton Woods system had worked reasonably well. But over time it turned out that countries were not sufficiently prepared to adjust their domestic demand and price level to their exchange rate nor were they, as a rule, willing to adjust their exchange rate speedily enough to their domestic situation or to their fundamental payments position. Thus it was rightly called a system of 'reluctant adjustment' (by the late Professor Harry Johnson). In its final stage of degeneration this sytem had contributed to a distorted pattern of over- and undervalued exchange rates; to a consequent dislocation of productive resources; to an inflation of currency reserves and of the money supply in Europe due to excessive obligatory dollar purchases; and — last but not least — to a never-ending succession of exchange rate crises . . .

. . . In reality, the reasons for the breakdown of the fixed rate system were more complex. The growing external weakness of the dollar — in part due to the Vietnam inflation in the United States, in part to other causes — certainly played an important role. A dollar-based system cannot be stronger than its base. But there were additional reasons: since the beginning of the seventies, *high and widely divergent inflation rates* among a number of major countries made a fixed rate system increasingly vulnerable; they would have necessitated a continuing series of exchange rate adjustments which would have kept the whole system constantly embroiled in speculative expectations and turmoil. Furthermore, *confidence-induced money flows* from one country to another often assumed enormous proportions with the growing internationalization of banking and of money markets, in particular the Eurodollar market. 'The adjustable peg opened the floodgate for disruptive speculation', as Professor Haberler put it.

Source: *Lloyds Bank Review, July 1979.* Author: O. Emminger.

QUESTIONS
1. How and why would countries, under the fixed exchange rate system, fail to adjust their domestic demand and price levels to their exchange rates? Give examples. What was the ultimate impact of these policies?
2. Briefly explain the three main reasons for the eventual breakdown of the fixed exchange rate system?

Answer P.210

THE VALUE OF THE POUND

On a given day the demand for, and supply of, sterling in the foreign exchange market are as follows:—

Price of Sterling (in francs)	11.50	11.80	12.10	13.00
Sterling demanded (£ million)	25	22	20	17
Sterling supplied (£ million)	15	17	20	22

QUESTIONS
(a) What will be the equilibrium exchange rate?
(b) Britain's trade figures show a deficit, and demand for sterling falls by £5 million. What is the new equilibrium exchange rate?
(c) In these new circumstances the British authorities decide to peg the exchange rate at £1 = 12.10 francs. What steps must they take?
(d) If the exchange rate was successfully pegged at £1 = 12.10 francs, would sterling be overvalued or overvalued? *(I.O.B., Part 1, 1975)*

FREE TRADE AND THE DETERMINATION OF PRICE

Commodity x is produced and consumed in two countries A and B. The supply and demand schedules for x in the two countries are as follows:—

Price of x per unit (£)	Country A		Country B	
	Supply	Demand	Supply	Demand
7	70	50	140	40
6	60	60	120	45
5	50	70	100	50
4	45	80	90	55
3	30	90	80	60
2	0	100	70	70

QUESTIONS
(a) What will be the price of x in A and B if no trade occurs between the two countries?
(b) What would be the price if trade occurred and no transport costs were involved?

Continued overleaf

(c) At this price, what would be the imports, exports, consumption and production of x in A and B?
(d) Country A now imposes a tariff of £1 per unit on x. What will be the new price, imports, exports, consumption and production of x in A and B?
(e) Who is likely to benefit from the imposition of this tariff?

(I.O.B., Part 1, 1976)
Answer P.211

BRAZIL AND INTERNATIONAL SUGAR PRICES

'Brazil has also been beset by economic problems during the past four years during which it has become the biggest international debtor owing about $94 billion by the end of 1983. Like Argentina, it too suffered the effects of the international recession which both damaged its trading opportunities and brought, via higher interest rates, a bigger burden of debt servicing. The decline in its economic fortunes is vividly expressed by the dramatic fall in its terms of trade from 114 in 1979 to 84 in 1982 (base year 1980). There are two underlying factors here. First, the rising cost of oil imports which now account for 50 per cent of total imports. Second, the declining value of agricultural exports which fell to 15 per cent during 1980-82. One crop that illustrates Brazil's present difficulties is sugar. Brazil is now the world's biggest producer and third biggest exporter after Cuba and France. It has attained this position by virtue of comparative advantage in that its production costs are about the lowest in the world at approximately US cents 7-9 per pound compared with cents 14-16 per pound in the EEC. Nevertheless, sugar producers in Brazil, as in other developing countries, have suffered from low world prices and increasing competition from the EEC.'

Source: M.J. Roarty in 'National Westminster Bank Quarterly Review', February 1985.

QUESTIONS
(a) Explain the phrases:
   (ii) 'via higher interest rates, a bigger burden of debt servicing';
   (ii) a fall in the terms of trade from 114 in 1979 to 84 in 1982 (base year 1980).
(b) How does the extract appear to support the predictions of the theory of comparative advantage?
(c) Given Brazil's comparative advantage, how is it possible that EEC sugar remains competitively priced on the world market?

(SUJB, June 1986)

Answer P.212

Chapter 15
MONEY AND BANKING

(1) U.K. Monetary Aggregates and GDP.

(2) Monetarism: A Statement.

(3) Why Gold Still Glitters.

(4) Foreign Exchange and Money Markets.

(5) U.K. Financial Balances, 1985.

(6) The Quantity Theory of Money — Cost-Push Inflation.

(7) Unemployment and Inflation.

U.K. MONETARY AGGREGATES AND GDP

TABLE 1

	Amounts (£)		
	1983	1985	all valued at current prices
£M3 (Dec)	64bn	225.6bn	
GDP	125.4bn	306bn	
Retail Price Index	100	110	

Source: "The British Economy in Figures 1986", Lloyds Bank.

QUESTIONS — See Table 1
1. Briefly define (a) £M3 and (b) GDP.
2. Calculate:
   (i) Real GDP in 1985 (1983 = 100);
   (ii) Velocity of circulation in 1983 and 1985.
   Comment on (ii).
3. Why might £M3 suddenly increase?
4. Briefly discuss how a monetarist and a Keynesian might view the findings in 2(ii).

MONETARISM: A STATEMENT

Inflation has come down to levels not experienced in the United Kingdom since the 1960s. There has been a steady recovery in output for almost three years. The aim over the medium term is to continue reducing inflation and to build on recent improvements in the performance of the economy. The Government therefore intends to continue with present policies. The Medium-Term Financial Strategy sets out the framework within which policy operates.

Firm financial policies are the essence of the strategy. This entails control of monetary growth and public sector borrowing. In order to reduce inflation further, the Government intends to continue reducing rates of monetary growth.

Fiscal policy is designed to be consistent with the monetary framework and the Government's objectives for inflation. Falling monetary growth and inflation require a further reduction in the PSBR as a share of g.d.p., to permit interest rates to fall in nominal and real terms.

Source: The Chancellor's Budget Statement, March 1984, C.S.O.

MONETARISM AND THE MEDIUM TERM FINANCIAL STRATEGY: A STATEMENT

QUESTIONS
1. Explain the meaning of the term the 'Medium Term Financial Strategy' (MTFS).
2. Outline the assumed link, in the passage, between inflation and firm financial policies.
3. Outline the relationship between the Public Sector Borrowing Requirement (PSBR) and real and nominal interest rates. *Answer P.214*

WHY GOLD STILL GLITTERS

GOLD is one of those strange subjects which give rise to enormous passions among vociferous minorities. On the one side are the gold-bugs, who are convinced that gold should, must and will come back as the basis of all true money, and that anyone who denies this is an enemy of civilisation. On the other side there is the Anglo-American economic establishment who regard the metal as a barbarous relic and anyone who takes its price movement seriously — as again — an enemy of civilisation.

The difficulty about saying whether gold is losing or regaining its monetary function is that there is ... no hard and fast dividing line between money and non-money. There are at least three main functions of money. It is a means of exchange, a standard of value and a store of value. In an age of rapid, unstable and unpredictable inflation rates, one substance can no longer carry out all three functions — an enforced separation which does more harm than is generally realised.

Gold is least likely to come back as a standard of value ... its real value has fluctuated far too much for the purpose. General price indices are, for all their defects, much more useful for correcting the distortions of shrinking pounds and dollars.

The strongest case for gold is as a store of value. Over long spans of time it has at least maintained and probably increased its buying power over goods and services. It has out-performed not only currency and bonds, but also equities. Unlike investment in property or works of art, the purchase of gold doesn't depend on luck or judgment in picking a particular site or specimen. One gold bar is like another. And it is of course easier to transport, or protect from confiscation, than real estate, pictures or bottles of wine.

But although gold has usually been a good investment to hand on to one's grandchildren, over any shorter period of time it has been highly speculative ... the real value of gold to a U.S. citizen would have more than doubled in the decade from 1929 to 1939 (with many fluctuations in between). On the other hand between 1939 and early 1970, gold lost two-thirds of its real value to the same citizen, before starting on its present erratic climb. Even in the soaring 1970s there have been temporary gold slumps, as in 1975-77, when the real value of an ounce of gold fell heavily.

The greatest intellectual confusion surrounds the relation of gold to money as a means of exchange. We are not on the verge of returning to the use of gold sovereigns as the principal circulating medium.

On the other hand, there is probably some relation between a country's gold stock and its monetary policy. So long as floating is "dirty", and there is some official intervention in the foreign exchange market, the size of a country's reserves will have some influence on the risks it will take with monetary expansion ... gold now accounts for just over 50 per cent of world official reserve holdings ... compared with 32 per cent at the end of 1971. Since 1971, the rise in the gold price has easily overtaken the rise in dollar and other foreign exchange holdings as the main source of the staggering increase in reserve totals, which now stand at well over 500bn SDRs (nearly $700bn), or four times the 1971 level ...

What has finally ended the myth of demonetisation has been the inclusion of gold in the pooling of members' reserves under the European Monetary System.

Central bankers at their monthly meeting this September in Basle expressed concern that the vast expansion in the currency value of gold holdings will weaken the resolve of governments to lower inflation rates and eliminate "balance of payments deficits". But there is a horse-and-cart question here. Is the rise in the gold price weakening ... anti-inflationary resolve; or has a more pessimistic attitude by the market towards the inflationary behaviour of governments, and the security of other assets, triggered off the rise in the gold price?

Source: Financial Times, 20th September 1979. Author S. Brittain.

QUESTIONS
1. Briefly discuss the suitability of gold as a money form in terms of its characteristics and monetary functions.
2. Why do you think gold fluctuates in value so much?
3. Discuss the economic factors behind the concern of "Central Bankers".

Answer P.216

FOREIGN EXCHANGE AND MONEY MARKETS

A. Sterling: Spot and Forward

	Market Rates — day's range	1 month	3 months
New York	$1.5165 — 5285	0.53 — 0.50c premium	1.27 — 0.22c premium
Paris	10.6070 — 6892f	3¼ — 2⅝c premium	7⅜ — 6⅜c premium

Effective exchange rate compared to 1975 was up 0.4 at 75.7.

B. Money Market Rates

Clearing Banks Base Rate   10½%

Discount Market Rate   Overnight: high 11½%   Low 10%

			2 months	3 months
Treasury Bills	Discount % Buying		10¼	9¹³⁄₁₆
	Selling		10⅛	9½

		1 month		
Prime Bank Bills	Discount %	10¹³⁄₃₂ — 10¹¹⁄₃₂	10⁹⁄₃₂ — 10⁷⁄₃₂	10³⁄₃₂ — 10
Trades Bills	Discount %	11¹⁄₃₂	10²⁹⁄₃₂	10²³⁄₃₂

		3 months	6 months
Secondary Market £ C.D. Rates %	10⅞ — 10¾	10¼ — 10⅛	9⅞ — 9¾

	Overnight	1 week	1 month	3 months
Inter Bank Market	11⅞ — 12	11½ — 11¼	10⅞ — 10¹³⁄₁₆	10⅜ — 10¼

Source: The Times, 24th April 1986.

QUESTIONS

1. Explain the meaning of the following:
   a) Sterling: Spot and forward
   b) Treasury Bills
   c) Secondary Market £ CD Rates % (Certificates of Deposit)
   d) Interbank Market
   e) Clearing Banks Base Rate
2. What does Table A indicate about forward sterling rates in New York and Paris?
3. What are the main factors influencing the structure of Table B?

Answer P.218

U.K. FINANCIAL BALANCES, 1985

	Financial balance (saving minus capital expenditure) 1985, £bn	% equiv of gnp at factor cost
Personal	10.5	3.5
Public	−10.3	−3.4
Industrial and commercial companies	6.2	2.0
Financial companies and institutions	1.2	0.4
Overseas	−3.0	−1.0
Residual error	−4.6	−1.5

Each column sums to zero by accounting definition.

Source: *An Economic Profile of Britain 1986.*

QUESTIONS
1. Explain the meaning of "financial balance", illustrating your answer from the Table.
2. Describe the overall flow of funds as shown in the Table.
3. What could explain the behaviour of the Personal sector?
4. Discuss the implications of the Overseas sector figure. Should we act to curtail capital movements overseas?

Answer P.220

THE QUANTITY THEORY OF MONEY — COST-PUSH INFLATION

The table overleaf refers to the United Kingdom over the period 1970-76. Study the table carefully and then, making use of your knowledge of economics, answer the following questions:

QUESTIONS
(a) Describe the association between changes in the money supply and in the velocity of circulation.
(b) Account for the association found in (a).
(c) Is there any relationship between GDP and the unemployment rate during this period?
(d) What contributions do cost-push factors make to inflation over this period?

Oxford, June 1983.

Answer P.221

	Money Supply (M_3)	Velocity of Circulation	Retail Price Index	GDP at Constant Prices		Wage & Salary Earnings	Import Prices
	Annual % change	Annual % change	Annual % change	Annual % change	Unemployment % rate	Annual % change	Annual % change
1970	9.4	2.6	7.7	2.0	2.6	13.6	2.1
1971	12.1	0.3	9.2	1.4	3.8	9.5	5.1
1972	25.4	-11.9	7.7	4.3	3.4	15.5	9.5
1973	28.8	-11.4	10.4	3.9	2.3	12.5	38.9
1974	12.7	3.0	18.1	-1.3	2.8	25.4	35.9
1975	7.8	14.6	25.3	-0.4	4.8	21.6	13.3
1976	10.8	6.0	15.0	4.2	5.5	12.4	27.2

Source: Economic Trends Annual Supplement, 1981.

Note: 'Annual percentage change' refers to the percentage change between the end of a given year and the end of the previous year. The unemployment rate refers to the last quarter of each given year.

UNEMPLOYMENT AND INFLATION

QUESTIONS
(a) Explain the interpret the diagram below.

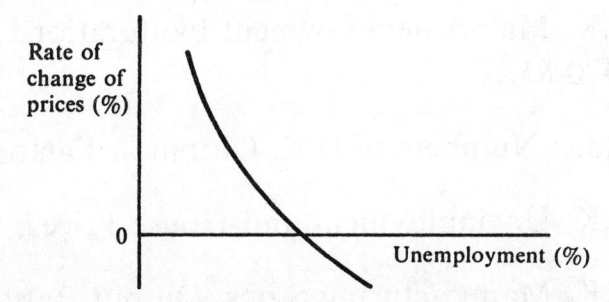

[Diagram: downward-sloping curve with "Rate of change of prices (%)" on the vertical axis and "Unemployment (%)" on the horizontal axis, origin at 0.]

(b) In the light of the following figures, comment on the Phillips curve and the British experience during the period 1971-76.

Year	Rate of change of Retail Price Index (%)	Unemployment (%)
1971	9.5	3.4
1972	6.8	3.7
1973	8.3	2.6
1974	15.9	2.6
1975	24.2	4.0
1976	15.7	5.4

(June 1983, London)
Answer P.223

Chapter 16
MACRO-ECONOMICS, NATIONAL INCOME ACCOUNTS

(1) Freewhorn — National Income Accounts.

(2) GDP Expenditure Based 1981-85.

(3) A Macro-Economic problem.

(4) U.K. Output and Expenditure, 1984-7.

(5) Macro-Economic Indicators — Living Standards.

(6) Macro-Economic Forecasts of the U.K. 1986/7.

(7) National Income Calculations.

(8) U.K. Male Unemployment by duration, 1970-85.

(9) Index Numbers of U.K. Output at Factor Cost.

(10) U.K. Unemployment and House Prices, 1985.

(11) U.K. Manufacturing Stock/Output Ratios.

(12) "Will U.K. Manufacturing Recover?"

(13) The Costs of Unemployment.

(14) The Economy in Equilibrium.

(15) Interpretations of the PSBR.

FREEWHORN — NATIONAL INCOME ACCOUNTS

Freewhorn is an island economy with no international trade, no government sector and no subsistence farming. In this economy there are 300 cattle of which 200 are killed for beef every year and the remaining 100 bred to keep the stock of cattle at 300. The only other product is 5000 tonnes of grain per annum, half of which is eaten by the inhabitants of the island and the other half by the cattle.

QUESTIONS
(a) Calculate a measure of the island's National Income. Show all your workings.
(b) The island hires a team of economists to do an economic survey. They decide to remain and become residents. The economists' fees are recorded in the National Income account as services, which increases the recorded National Income. Discuss this in the light of the island's living standards. *Answer P.225*

GROSS DOMESTIC PRODUCT EXPENDITURE BASED (U.K.) 1981-85

£ million

	1980	1981	1982	1983	1984	1985	Percentage Average 1960-1975
AT CURRENT MARKET PRICES:							
Consumers' expenditure		152 544	167 362	182 877	195 711	213 208	52.4
General government final consumption	48 936	55 358	60 478	65 932	69 886	74 012	14.5
of which: Central government	29 993	33 873	37 126	40 770	43 350	45 975	
Local authorities	18 943	21 485	23 352	25 162	26 536	28 037	
Gross domestic fixed capital formation	41 774	41 612	44 683	48 775	55 567	60 118	15.2
Value of physical increase in stocks and work in progress	-2 844		-1 306	651	-356	528	0.7
Total domestic expenditure	225 100	246 704	271 217		320 808	347 866	82.8
Exports of goods and services	63 097	67 861	73 060	80 399	91 750	102 304	17.2
of which: Goods	47 422	50 977	55 565	60 776	70 367	78 051	
Services	15 675	16 884	17 495	19 623	21 383	24 253	
Total final expenditure	288 197	314 565	344 277	378 634	412 558	450 170	100.0
less Imports of goods and services	-57 868	-60 675	-68 122	-77 582	-92 390		
of which: Goods	46 061	47 617	53 234	61 611	74 751	80 162	
Services	11 807	13 058	14 888	15 971	17 639	18 441	
Gross domestic product at market prices	230 329	253 890	276 155	301 052		351 567	
FACTOR COST ADJUSTMENT:							
Taxes on expenditure	36 441	42 492	46 641	49 113	52 496	56 812	
Subsidies	5 718	6 416	5 862	6 333	7 723	7 710	
Taxes less subsidies	30 723	36 076	40 779	42 780	44 773	49 102	

Source: U.K. National Accounts 1986, C.S.O. *Continued overleaf*

CALCULATE

(i)   GDP at factor cost for 1983.
(ii) Value of stocks and work in progress for 1981.
(iii) Value of imports of goods and services for 1985.
(iv) Consumers' Expenditure for 1980.
(v)   Total Domestic Expenditure for 1983.
(vi) Gross Domestic Product for 1984 at market prices.
(vii) The percentage of (a) consumers' expenditure and (b) general government final expenditure represented of total final expenditure for 1985. Compare to the percentage average for 1960-75 and comment.
(viii) The Index Number Value of GDP at market prices for 1982 with 1980 = 100.
(ix) Calculate the Marginal Propensity to (a) consume (b) import, between 1984-5. (Take GDP at market prices as Income).

Answer P.226

A MACRO-ECONOMIC PROBLEM

In an economy the following values occur:

Consumption	$= 0.8\ Y$ Disposable
Net Investment	$= 260$
Government Spending	$= 400$
Exports	$= 300$
Imports	$= 0.2\ Y$
Income Tax	$= 0.5\ Y$ (there are no indirect taxes)

Y = National Income.

QUESTIONS

(a) At what level of National Income will equilibrium occur?
(b) Because of unemployment the government wishes to increase total spending by 600. By how much must it increase its own spending to achieve this?
(c) What will this do
   (i) to the budgetary position;
   (ii) to the Balance of Payments?
(d) Explain, with aid of a diagram, the meaning of the term *deflationary gap*.

(SUJB, June 1981)

Answer P.227

UK OUTPUT AND EXPENDITURE, 1984-87

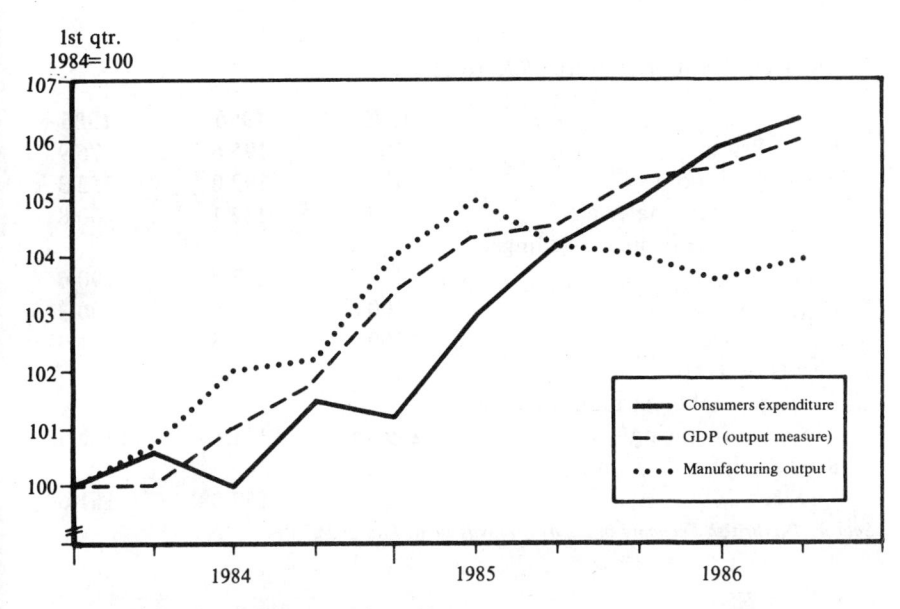

1st qtr. 1984=100

— Consumers expenditure
— — GDP (output measure)
• • • • Manufacturing output

Source: Midland Bank Review, Autumn 1986.

QUESTIONS
1. Explain why there can be variations in the trends of each variable shown on the chart?
2. Discuss the possible implications of the overall trends shown with respect to UK performance in 1986/87.

Answer P.228

MACRO-ECONOMIC INDICATORS: LIVING STANDARDS

Below are price indices from 1975 to 1985.

	1975	1980	1985
1. Retail Prices	100	195.6	276.9
2. of which: Food	100	192.0	252.3
3. Basic materials	100	182.1	250.8
4. Average price of new dwellings (on mortgage)	100	213.7	290.6
5. Import prices	100	172.4	250.3
6. Export prices	100	196.5	281.9
7. Terms of Trade	100	114.0	
8. Average weekly earnings of men in manufacturing	£59.74	£111.64	£170.58
9. Row 8 adjusted for inflation 1975 = 100	£59.74	£57.08	£61.60

Source: The British Economy in Figures, Lloyds Bank Ltd. 1986.

QUESTIONS
1. Explain fully rows 8 and 9 and show how the adjusted figures are calculated for row 9.
2. Calculate the terms of trade for 1985 and briefly explain how changes occurred in the terms of trade 1975-85.
3. In the light of the above figures, discuss the relationship between living standards and inflation.
4. How useful are such indices when discussing living standards?

Answer P.230

MACRO-ECONOMIC FORECASTS OF THE UK, 1986/87

"Clearly if the oil price stabilises at about the Government's Budget forecast figure of $15 a barrel the **PSBR target** can be achieved without too much trouble. If, as we assume, such stability were to gain credence gradually there would be a consequent strengthening of sterling, and we would expect interest rates to fall more or less in line with our past forecasts, with base rates down to 9% by the end of the year. In spite of the electoral uncertainties, we expect that further downward movement in interest rates will occur in 1987 to bring base rates down to $7\frac{1}{2}$% by the fourth quarter, still a **real rate of interest** of over 5%.

As regards growth in the economy, industrial production has been less than expected this year so far and although some pick-up is likely over the rest of the year, it may not be enough to achieve the overall rise built into our earlier forecast. An exception to this expected recovery is of the oil and gas extraction industry, output of which was slightly lower in the first half of 1986 than in the same period last year. The expected medium-term decline in North Sea production could well be accelerated by the reduction seen in the oil price which makes it unprofitable to continue extraction when wells are close to exhaustion. However, total output has been holding up better than industrial production and this year's growth figure is likely to be only a little less than the 2½% figure predicted in our last *Review*, with growth around 3% in both 1987 and 1988. Much of the impetus for this is likely to come from consumers' expenditure, which in the first half of this year is preliminarily estimated to have been about 4% more in real terms than in the same period of last year. With buoyancy set to continue, as **real personal disposable incomes** are boosted by tax cuts and high wage settlements, we have increased somewhat our estimate for growth in spending this year, while for 1986 as a whole predicting a small decline in the **savings ratio** to accompany the lower level of inflation. Growth in consumer spending in real terms is expected to continue at around 3½% a year over the rest of the forecast period.

The net trade balance, though, is expected to provide a **negative contribution to growth** this year following the positive part played last year; this is in large part due to a reversal in net trade in oil. We expect growth in non-oil imports to remain moderate, but toward the end of the decade a falling rate of export growth will become more significant as a result of an expected cyclical slowdown in world trade.

The balance of payments is one area where our forecast is particularly subject to error over timing. We continue to expect a decline in the current account balance into substantial deficit by the end of the forecast period, but the risk that the decline could be faster has increased, particularly in the event of another oil price collapse. Thus, although we still expect a positive current account this year our earlier forecast has been revised down somewhat, to £2bn, with the move into deficit now expected during 1988 instead of 1989."

Source: Midland Bank Review, Autumn 1986.

QUESTIONS
1. Explain the following:— (bold in the text)
    (a) real rate of interest
    (b) the savings ratio
    (c) the P.S.B.R. Target
    (d) real personal disposable incomes
    (e) negative contribution to growth.
2. Explain how the writer argues that interest rates may fall to 9% by the end of the year. What are the main assumptions of the passage re interest rates?

3. Distinguish between industrial production and total output and briefly outline the economic factors likely to influence each.

NATIONAL INCOME CALCULATIONS

QUESTION

From the data below calculate the gross national product at factor cost.

	£M
Imports	42,000
Exports	43,000
Value of physical increase in stocks	1,300
Capital formation	25,000
Government expenditure	29,000
Consumer expenditure	84,000
Taxes on expenditure	20,000
Subsidies	3,000
Net property income from abroad	400

(Certified Accountants, Level 1, June 1984)

Answer P.232

U.K. MALE UNEMPLOYMENT BY DURATION, 1970-85

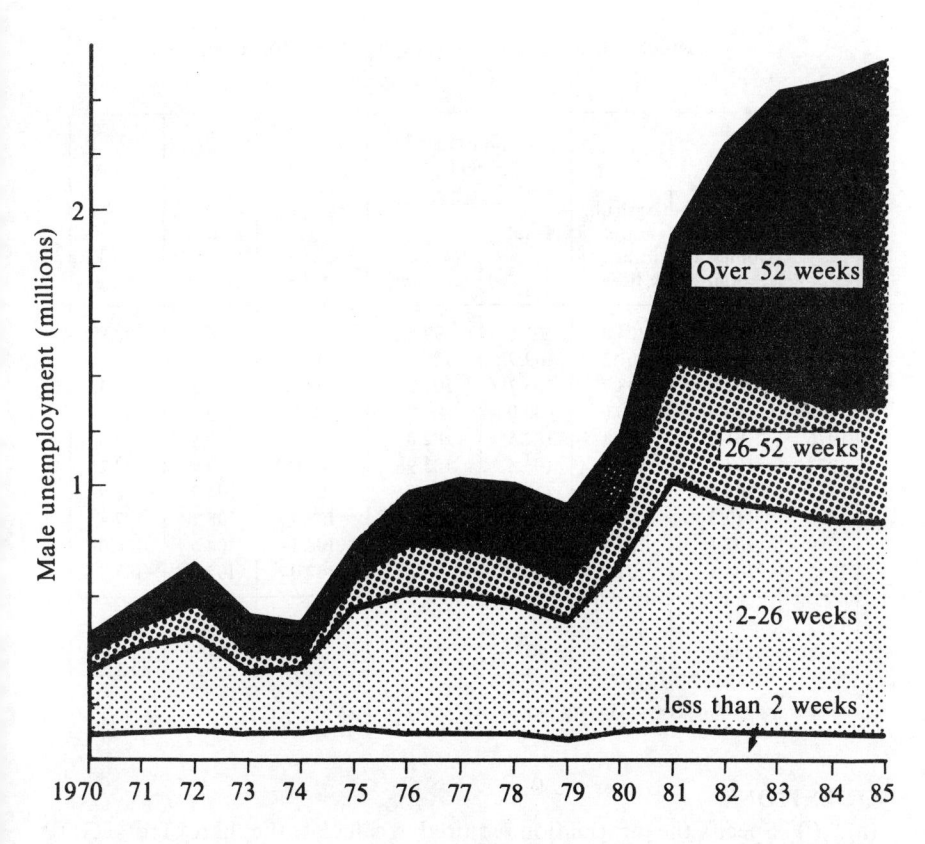

Source: "Economics", Winter 1986; and "How to Beat Unemployment" by R. Layard, Oxford 1986.

QUESTIONS
1. Describe the main trends shown in the diagram.
2. What could explain the overall change which took place after 1981?
3. What do the types of unemployment shown indicate about economic policies aimed at reducing unemployment. Give examples of suitable schemes.

Answer P.234

INDEX NUMBERS OF UK OUTPUT AT FACTOR COST

Index Numbers of UK Output at Factor Cost
(1975 = 100)

	Gross Domestic Product	Agriculture, forestry & fishing	Industrial Production		Transport and Communication	Distributive Trades	Other Services
			Total	Manufacturing			
1972	97.9	104.0	101.6	99.6	93.5	100.9	93.8
1973	103.6	107.3	109.7	108.6	100.5	106.8	96.6
1974	102.0	108.7	105.7	107.5	100.7	103.3	97.3
1975	100.0	100.0	100.0	100.0	100.0	100.0	100.0
1976	101.8	92.1	102.5	102.0	99.1	100.8	102.8
1977	104.6	103.9	106.8	103.9	102.0	99.5	104.2
1978	108.1	112.0	110.6	104.5	104.6	104.3	106.9
1979	110.3	111.9	113.3	104.7	109.8	108.1	107.8
1980	107.1	122.6	105.7	95.2	108.3	104.6	108.0
1981	104.5	121.7	100.3	89.2	107.0	104.1	107.3
1975 weights	1 000	28	407	283	88	101	376

Source: Economic Trends Annual Supplement 1983, C.S.O.

QUESTIONS

(a) (i) Specify the information required to calculate the share of total GDP produced by any one sector of the economy.

(ii) Estimate the share of GDP produced by the "Service" sector in 1975.

(b) Consider 1975 to 1981 data only and identify which area of the economy grew (i) at the fastest rate and (ii) contributed most to the growth of real GDP. Explain your answer.

(c) If labour productivity grew by 1.8% between 1975 and 1976 in all sectors, (i) estimate from the data the likely change in aggregate employment in that year and (ii) identify a sector of the economy where unemployment is likely to have increased in that period. Carefully explain your answer.

(d) Use the Table to compare the (i) extent to which 'Industrial Production' and other services are affected by changes in the level of economic activity and (ii) provide a suitable explanation for any difference you find.

Answer P.236

FIG.1

U.K. UNEMPLOYMENT AND HOUSE PRICES, 1985

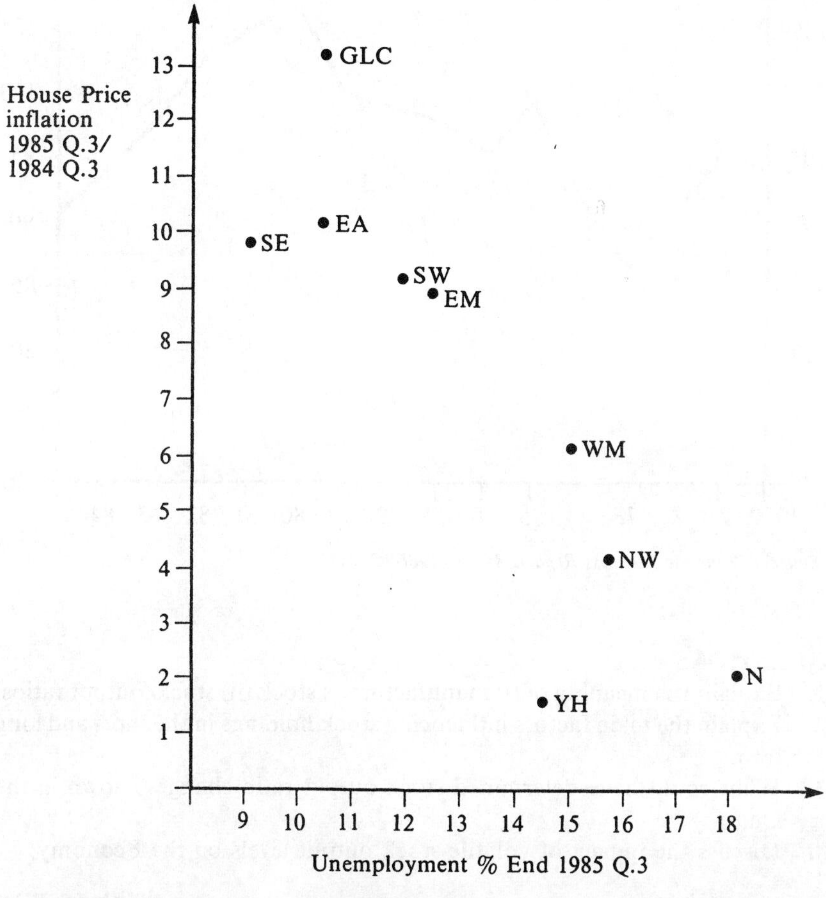

Note: The regions are keyed as follows:
SE, South East; GLC, Greater London; EA, East Anglia; SW, South West; EM, East Midlands; WM, West Midlands; YH, Yorkshire and Humberside; NW, North West.

Source: Building Society Association Bulletin, January 1986.

QUESTIONS

1. Describe the association between the two variables in Fig.1.
2. Explain the relationship in Q.1.
3. Discuss the possible implications of your findings.

Answer P.238

U.K. MANUFACTURING STOCK/OUTPUT RATIOS

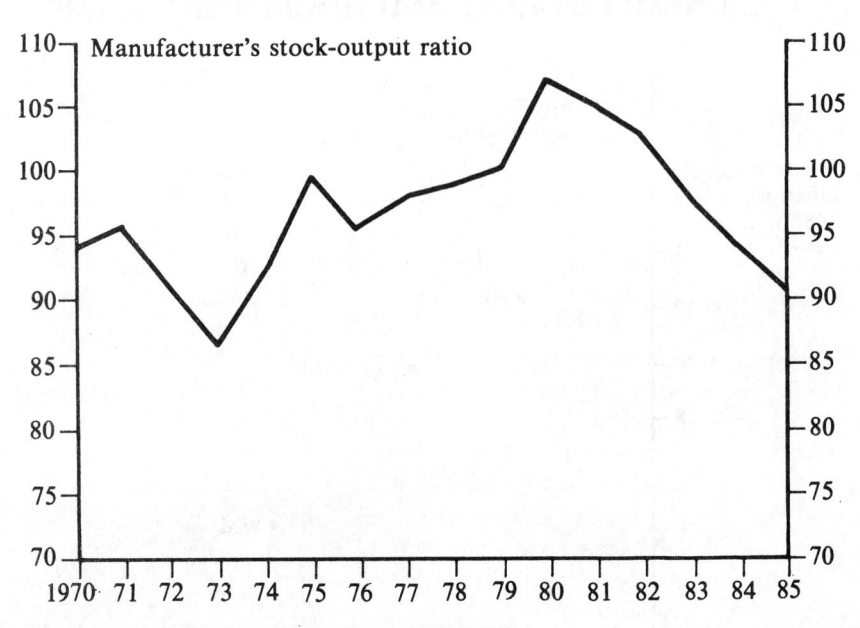

Manufacturer's stock-output ratio

Source: Economic Progress Report, August 1986, C.S.O.

QUESTIONS
1. Explain the meaning of (i) manufacturer's stock (ii) stock/output ratios.
2. Explain the main factors influencing stock holdings in the short and long term.
3. What could have determined stock output ratio changes shown in the Chart.
4. Discuss the impact of volatile stock output levels on the Economy.

Answer P.240

"WILL U.K. MANUFACTURING RECOVER?"

"The claim that, as the value of North Sea Oil production declines and the oil account surplus reduces, manufacturing will automatically recover, depends largely on the assumption that a fall in the exchange rate will automatically produce a new competitiveness for manufacturers. But have we then to assume that sterling will of its own accord obligingly find its appropriate level, in an orderly manner? Recent history suggests otherwise. The exchange rate does not respond in some automatic manner to oil price movements, or to movements in the current account of the British balance of payments, or to calculations of British industrial competitiveness. It is, for example, heavily influenced (sometimes perversely) by international capital flows, which are dictated by a range of complex considerations. And there are many other elements in our competitive position that have to be put right. Moreover, the Treasury assumption of 'automatic' recovery in manufacturing output seemed to us to take little account of the time and effort needed to put new products into the market, particularly when capacity has vanished. It is right to argue that world markets will want new products, different from those that were produced five years ago; but one proven way to produce new products is from established businesses and factories.

It has also been argued against us that the balance of trade will automatically balance. It does not balance in USA nor in Japan, but over time it will have to balance with us. We can close the gap by importing less; and this can be done by producing more manufactured goods for the home market or by squeezing demand down. We can also close the gap by exporting more manufactured goods. Either way, we must increase the output of manufactured goods which we can sell competitively against all-comers."

Source: Royal Bank of Scotland Review, September 1986.

QUESTIONS
1. Explain the mechanism by which falling North Sea Oil values leads to an automatic recovery of the U.K. manufacturing sector. Why might this not happen?
2. How is it argued that the Balance of Trade may not automatically balance? What assumption is made about U.K. home demand?

Answer P.241

THE COSTS OF UNEMPLOYMENT

Budgetary Cost of 2.88 million unemployed, in £ million

Foregone taxes		Benefit costs	
Income Tax	3 137	Unemployment benefit	1 646
National insurance		Supplementary benefit	2 618
contributions	2 613	Other	368
Indirect Tax	2 563		
Total	8 313	Total	4 632

Source: Dilnot and Morris 1981, 'The Exchequer Costs of Unemployment' taken from National Westminster Bank Quarterly Review, February 1983.

QUESTIONS
(a) Calculate the approximate cost to the Government of each unemployed person.
(b) To what extent do the above figures represent the full cost to the economy of unemployment? *Answer P.242*

THE ECONOMY IN EQUILIBRIUM

Recorded below are some figures for a hypothetical economy.

	Weeks 1	2	3	4 .....n
1 Output (=income)	100	90	82	75.6 ..50
2 Investment	10	10	10	10 10
3 Consumption goods produced (=consumption goods demanded in previous week)	90	80	72	65.6 ..40
4 Planned (ex-ante) savings (=20% of row 1)	20	18	16.4	15.1 ..10
5 Consumption goods demanded (=80% of row 1)	80	72	65.6	60.5 ..40
6 Excess supply (=row 3 minus row 5)	10	8	6.4	5.1 ...0
7 Planned savings minus planned investment (=row 4 minus row 2)	10	8	6.4	5.1 0

(Source: W. Beckerman, 'An Introduction to National Income Analysis', Weidenfeld & Nicolson, 1968).

Continued overleaf

QUESTIONS
(a) Specify and briefly explain the process which is at work over time in the case of the above economy.
(b) The last column on the right shows the values of the variables for a national income equilibrium.
   (i) What assumptions are necessary for this equilibrium to be reached?
   (ii) When will the equilibrium be reached?   *(June 1981, London)*

Answer P.243

INTERPRETATIONS OF THE PSBR

'The Treasury is proposing further cuts in expenditure when output and employment are falling fast. It is the recession itself which is responsible for the increase in expenditure through increased unemployment benefit which, by automatic stabilization, counteracts the fall in private sector income. This form of public spending, together with the related falls in tax revenue, must mean that the public sector borrowing requirement should be allowed to fluctuate with the trade cycle. The PSBR should never have a fixed target value.'   *(Source: Times Newspapers Ltd.)*

QUESTION
Explain why you agree or disagree with this statement.
(London, June 1982)

Answer P.244

Chapter 17
PUBLIC FINANCE

(1)   The Composition of the U.K. National debt.

(2)   The impact of taxation on the poor.

(3)   The structure of U.K. taxation, 1974-81.

THE COMPOSITION OF THE U.K. NATIONAL DEBT

COMPOSITION OF THE UNITED KINGDOM NATIONAL DEBT
(£m at 31 March, percentages of totals in brackets)

	1970	1974	1978	1982
Treasury bills and other floating debt	4,989 (15.1%)	6,339 (15.8%)	12,703 (16.1%)	5,778 (4.9%)
Gilt-edged securities and other marketable securities	19,720 (59.6%)	26,747 (66.7%)	51,300 (64.9%)	91,025 (77.2%)
National Savings securities	3,558 (10.8%)	4,075 (10.1%)	5,828 (7.4%)	14,990 (12.7%)
Externally held debt	4,115 (12.4%)	2,735 (6.8%)	7,777 (9.8%)	4,198 (3.5%)
Other debt	697 (2.1%)	229 (0.6%)	1,475 (1.8%)	1,968 (1.7%)
Total National Debt	33,079	40,125	79,083	117,959
Gross National Product at market prices	51,661	84,529	165,493	270,657
	1969/70	1973/74	1977/78	1981/82
Cost of servicing the National Debt, including management and interest costs	1,458	2,341	5,929	11,205

Source: *Financial Statistics. C.S.O.*

QUESTIONS
(a) Explain briefly what is meant by the National Debt.
(b) (i) What have been the main changes in the composition of the National Debt over the period shown by the data?
　　(ii) Explain why the changes have occurred.
(c) Discuss whether the data support the view that the National Debt is a burden to the nation.

(AEB, June 1984)
Answer P.245

THE IMPACT OF TAXATION ON THE POOR

The following passage is adapted from an article by Michael Meacher, M.P., in *The Guardian,* 4 August 1982.

"Three years after the present Government reduced the highest rate of income tax to 60 per cent, there are still 120,000 families today who are subject to a marginal tax rate of more than 80 per cent. However, they are not the rich, but the poor.

They are families with children where the working head earns between £47 and £87 a week, that is as little as only a quarter to a half of the current national average wage. Yet liability to income tax at 30 per cent and national insurance contributions at $8\frac{3}{4}$ per cent, plus the loss of 50p of family income supplement for each extra £1 earned, cripple such families with poverty surtax.

Their position is even worse if rent and rate rebates are added in. As a result, the Department of Health and Social Security estimates from the evidence of its Family Expenditure Survey, that there are more than 250,000 poor families subject to a marginal rate in excess of 50 per cent (not reached at the top end of the income scale till the £19,000 - £23,500 bracket). Within these 250,000 there are even 50,000 poor families subject to a marginal rate in excess of 100 per cent, i.e. each extra pound they earn makes them actually worse off than before. These extraordinary consequences flow from a tax structure which has become distorted out of all recognition as a result of decades of incremental adjustment at successive annual budgets."

QUESTIONS
(a) What does the author mean by the marginal rate of taxation?
(b) Explain how the tax structure may have caused the consequences outlined in the passage.
(c) Discuss the likely economic effects of the situation described in the passage.
(d) Explain how the government could reduce or eliminate the problem outlined in the passage. *(AEB, June 1985)*

Answer P.247

THE STRUCTURE OF U.K. TAXATION, 1974-81

Study the table below and then answer questions (a) to (c).

Taxes as a percentage of total taxation in the United Kingdom

	Year							
	1974	1975	1976	1977	1978	1979	1980	1981
Taxes on:								
Personal income	33.4	38.2	38.2	35.1	32.9	31.4	30.0	29.3
Corporate income	9.6	6.2	5.1	6.5	7.5	7.6	7.7	8.4
Property (rates, etc.)	12.6	12.6	12.1	12.0	12.0	12.1	11.9	13.4
Goods and services	27.1	25.4	25.8	26.2	26.6	27.0	29.5	28.3
National Insurance	17.1	17.4	18.6	20.1	20.9	21.8	21.1	19.8
Total (rounded)	100	100	100	100	100	100	100	100

Source: Lloyds Bank Economic Bulletin, October 1983.

QUESTIONS
(a) Define (i) direct taxation and (ii) indirect taxation. Give *one* example of each tax from the above table.
(b) Examine the progressiveness of the tax system during the period 1974 to 1981.
(c) What might be the economic implications of the major tax changes shown in the table?

(London, June 1985)

Answer P.249

/ Micro-Economics – Basic Concepts

SECTION 4 (ANSWERS)

Chapter 18
MICRO-ECONOMICS — BASIC CONCEPTS

DIMINISHING RETURNS AND MARGINAL REVENUE PRODUCT

ANSWERS
(a) When the data is plotted, as in Fig. 1, the relationship between the two variables indicates that at low levels of fertiliser input there are increasing returns of wheat output. Thus increasing fertiliser from 1 to 2 tonnes increases production by 150 units and from 2 to 3 tonnes output of wheat rises by 250 units. However, after 4 tonnes decreasing returns set in so by 8 tonnes of fertiliser input total wheat output falls. See Table 1.

FIG. 1   DIMINISHING RETURNS

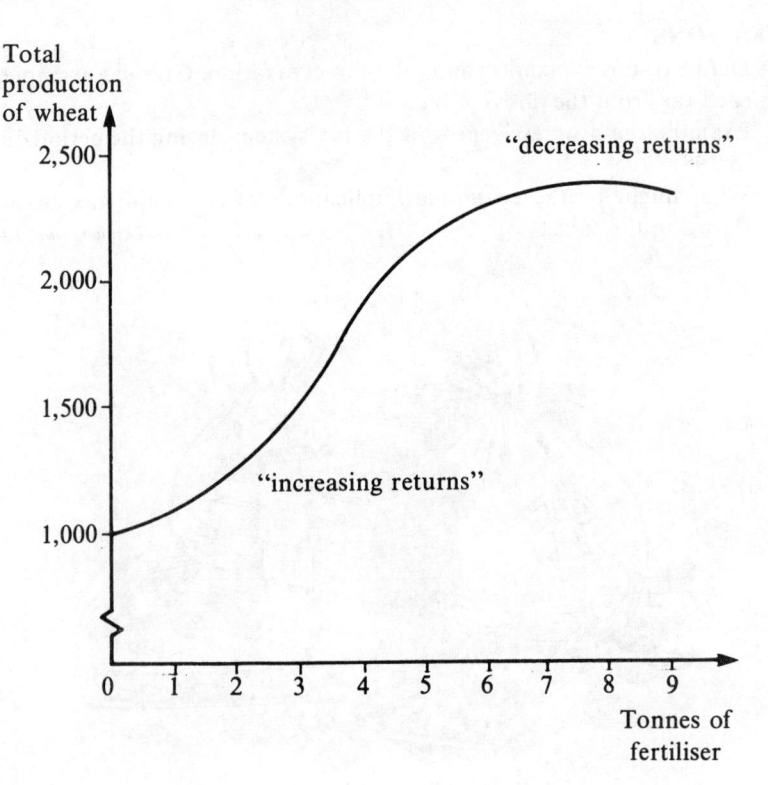

TABLE 1

Tonnes of fertiliser	Total production	Change in total production (MPPf)	Marginal revenue product (MPPf × Price)
0	1,000		
1	1,100	(1,100 − 1,000) 100	200
2	1,250	150	300
3	1,500	250	500
4	1,900	400	800
5	2,150	250	500
6	2,275	125	250
7	2,350	75	150
8	2,380	30	60
9	2,330	−50	−100

MARGINAL REVENUE PRODUCT AND THE OPTIMUM USE OF FERTILISER

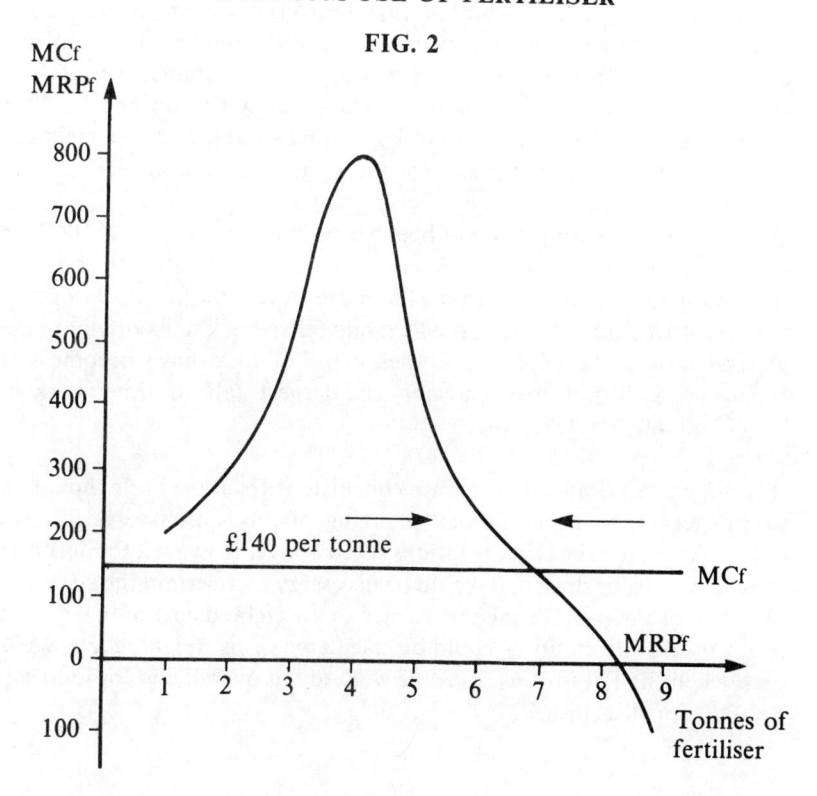

FIG. 2

134 Micro-Economics – Basic Concepts

(b) The profit maximising farmer will employ fertiliser up to the point where marginal cost equals marginal revenue product. As can be seen, marginal cost is always £140 per tonne and marginal revenue product is obtained by multiplying marginal product (see Table 1) by the constant price of £2 per unit. It can thus be calculated that MC = MRP at just over 7 tonnes of fertiliser input. Thus with 7 tonnes the Total Revenue is £2,350 (see Table 1) × £2 = £4,700 and Total Costs are land costs of £3,000 plus fertiliser at £7 × 140 = £3,980 so profit is £4,700 – £3,980 = £720. One way of seeing this relationship is by Fig. 2. At low levels of production, i.e. less than 7, marginal revenue is higher than marginal cost so profit can be further exploited by producing more but at higher levels marginal cost exceeds marginal revenue so profits fall and production would be reduced. Profits are therefore maximised at 7 where marginal costs and revenue are equal.

WORKING TIME TO EARN FOOD 1970, 1980, 1983

ANSWERS

1. The comparison of the amount of time the average income earner had to give up, in order to buy a variety of foodstuffs, implies the use of the economic principle of 'opportunity cost'. For example, 1lb of beef sirloin in 1970 cost $47\frac{1}{2}$ minutes in work time given up and by 1983 52.2 minutes of work time had to be worked so beef had become more expensive by around 5 minutes for the average income earner.

2. Using the above example, 1lb of beef has become $\frac{52.2}{47.5}$ minutes × 100% or 9.9% more expensive since 1970. A comparison of 1lb of fresh cod over the time shows that it became 21% more expensive (in time worked) between 1970 and 1980 but by 1983 it had fallen back to its original time worked cost. Otherwise most other items of food have become less expensive with potatoes showing the largest fall in time worked, i.e. $\frac{19.8}{44.1} \times 100\% = 45\%$ less.

3. It is difficult to draw any accurate conclusions from the table though in overall terms the general 'cost' of living of foodstuffs seems to have fallen, except for the two exceptions listed above. However, for accurate conclusions to be drawn, it would be necessary to ascertain the spending 'weights' of the average income earner so a weighted cost of living — in terms of time given up — could be calculated. This weighted average is used when the Retail Price Index is worked out overall and for food etc. See Statistical section.

THE U.K. POPULATION

ANSWERS

(a) Between 1931 and 1981 the U.K. population grew from 46 million to 55 million, an increase of about 19.6%. The population grew most rapidly between 1931 and 1951 and thereafter remained relatively static at around 55 million. The age structure of the country has also experienced changing trends over this period. The number of elderly, those over 64, has gradually increased, roughly trebling over the whole period, due mainly to a fall in the death rate, and the number of those over 75 has increased at a faster rate than those between 65-74. At the same time the trend for the younger age groups show an increase to 1961 when during the 1960's there was an increase in the birth rate, which works its way through the 1970's etc., in the form of an increase in those under 21. Thus the young and old together increased as a percentage of the working population so the "dependancy ratio" would have increased over this period.

(b) Overall population increase could well have stimulated more economic growth and efficiency as resources were worked more extensively and intensively, at least until the early '80's. The population size could be thought of as increasing to an economically optimum level. On the other hand, the increase in the dependency ratio meant that demand patterns would require, for example, more education, health and care services to look after young and old. As these are labour intensive in nature, with productivity less likely to increase, it implies extra tax revenues to finance pensions and other social services. This could put a greater strain on the economy and would require the working population to increase productivity so that economic growth could generate tax revenue for social services and also employment for the working population.

(c) (i) The main factors affecting population changes are the birth and death rates together with the net migration rate. In the case of Table B it can be seen that the rapid increase in the population 1931-71 was due to a stable death rate and a rising birth rate. The net migration rate over the whole period balances out, though of course the positive rate in the period 1931-51 could have been of people of child bearing age, so the significance of the migration rate does depend upon the ages of those entering the U.K. The gradual stabilisation of the population after 1971 can be seen to be due to a decline in the birth rate and a negative net migration rate. The slight rise in the death rate is because the overall life expectancy has risen so there are more old people likely to die.

(ii) During the period 1981-2021 overall birth rates are expected to exceed death rates as in the past. Birth rates are expected to be more stable than 1931-81 and in line with 1971-81 levels. Death rates are expected to be stable and slightly up on 1931-81 due to the fact that the population is expected to age. Net migration rates are expected to be negative and relatively constant and follow the pattern for 1971-81. In all, the increase in the population 1981-2001 is expected to follow the same factors as for 1971-81 but not show the same excess of birth over death rates as for 1931-71, due to the stabilisation of the death and birth rates.

(d) Population forecasts, as with other economic forecasts, are often inaccurate when compared to actual figures. This is due to the problems of forecasting in the social services which are:—

(1) Forecasts of human behaviour patterns often depend on previous experience repeating itself. This cannot be relied upon because unforeseen circumstances arise and human behaviour changes. Whilst the death rate may be predictable because of the state of medicine etc., birth rates can change due to human inclination and economic circumstances. Again, net migration figures can be different to those predicted because of the economic state of other countries which is beyond our control. These latter influences could dramatically change the predicted population sizes.

(2) Forecasts depend upon accurate information being available in the first place. This may not be the case. The statistics themselves may be incomplete, dated and inaccurate and they may not include, for example, true statistics of immigration figures. If base figures are inaccurate, then forecasts will also be inaccurate.

(3) Population trends, as such, often ignore other important factors which could have a significant impact or influence and which may not be included in the analysis. Thus the projection is based upon a rather narrow outlook and can ignore trends which could be important in predicting future population growth. For example, economic growth rates have been analysed in the U.S.A. and findings indicate that it has uncertain effects on birth rates often related to socio-economic factors.

VALUE ADDED — SELECTED U.K. INDUSTRIAL OUTPUT

ANSWERS
1. "Value added" shows the value of output net of inputs. In order to calculate value added at the unit or industry level, the cost of materials is

deducted from sales and the residue is the value added by labour, capital and land. It is used in National Income accounting so as to avoid double counting when the sales of different units are added together. Calculations and comparisons of value added can indicate relative levels of worker or capital efficiency in terms of units or industries over time, between industries or between countries, i.e. it is the prime indicator of efficiency and productivity. It serves as a basis for estimating value added tax (VAT) and can show up tax paid at each stage of production.

2. Calculations of value added per employee or worker are done by dividing Total Value Added (1984) £m by employees '000 1985. In this case dates vary but nevertheless each figure provides a rough indicator. Value added per employee for the sectors are as follows:—

   1) Agriculture, etc.   = £18,072
   2) Energy etc.   = £54,031
   3) Manufacturing   = £12,589
   4) Construction   = £16,898
   5) Distribution etc.   = £ 8,239
   6) Transport, etc.   = £15,639
   7) Financial services   = £19,670

   Relative sectoral value added figures indicate overall output per head figures but this does not say anything about employee productivity because often capital usage varies between industries. Thus capital intensive sectors, e.g. Energy, employs fewer people than Distribution which is a labour intensive sector, so one would expect value per head to be higher, etc. Furthermore, overall value added and employee figures fail to show up different occupational output rates within each sector. Distribution, etc. covers a range of industries and occupations and efficiency and labour usage rates will vary. Nevertheless, such figures, when compared to other countries or other periods, do serve as useful indicators of relative efficiency levels and possibly overall earnings figures. Furthermore when aggregated in the economy, sectoral value added figures are the basis for National Income calculations. They also help to explain the different returns to labour and capital in terms of wages, interest and profit variations between sectors and specific industries and firms.

3. Column 3 provides an overall indication of the changing structure of the U.K. economy between 1975-84. Column 4 indicates the overall significance or weighting of each sector. Thus the annual decline of the manufacturing sector at 1.1% cumulates to 11.1% which, when compared to 1984 figures shows that it has fallen from around 34% to around 26% of gdp. This is an economically significant decline and the implications of

these changes are enormous. Investment and employment losses in manufacturing have been considerable, between 1971-79, about 208th jobs per annum. Furthermore the construction industry has declined by about 7%. On the other hand, energy (oil production), transport and financial services have all grown. Indeed "Financial Services" has almost doubled in size and now accounts for 13.2% of total output. In conclusion, we can see that the U.K. has experienced a decline in its manufacturing sector which has been partly balanced by a growth in service sector activities such as transport and finance. Thus employment and investment has fallen in manufacturing but has increased in financial services, which has had an impact on relative living standards and regional levels of income, growth, house prices and overall opportunities, etc.

MARGINAL UTILITY

ANSWER
(1) The objective of the rational consumer will be to maximise total utility when spending his £28 budget. As the consumption of B increases so does total utility and by spending all his income on 7 units of B (£4 × 7 = £28) total utility will be $35\frac{3}{4}$ units. The assumption is that holding money has no utility and he seeks to maximise satisfaction.

(2) (a) Consumer's Surplus (C.S.) is the excess value a consumer gains when he purchases at a lower price than he would have been prepared to pay, i.e. the price is £4. Thereafter the C.S. increases from £4 to £6 and equates to the extra utility gained. From the 4th to the 6th drink total utility or the C.S. gained is $31\frac{3}{4} - (6 \times 4) = 7\frac{3}{4}$. Note: There is no extra utility from the last unit because it costs £4 and this equates with the extra 4 units of utility gained or $35\frac{3}{4} - 31\frac{3}{4}$.

(b) If holding money has no utility any price above a zero yields a consumer's surplus so $35\frac{3}{4}$ limits represents consumer's surplus.

(3) The consumer aims to allocate expenditure to maximise total utility over all three drinks. To do this he sets the prices to the marginal utility at the margin. This requires a calculation of the marginal utility of each drink (A, B, C) over the price range £1-£7. Then each marginal utility is divided by the prices £2, £4, £6. The consumer maximises total utility, with the limited budget of £28, when 3A, 1B, 3C are drunk at a MU/price ratio of 2.

(4) The law of diminishing returns implies that more consumption of the same good leads to continuous diminishing marginal utility. However, the marginal utility of A is 6, 4, 3, 1, 2, 1 which does not behave in a diminishing manner, i.e. the marginal utility of the 6th drink yields more than the MU of the 5th! This increasing marginal utility is most unlikely in the case of the consumption of a cold drink.

Chapter 19
MARKET ANALYSIS

U.K. CONSUMERS' EXPENDITURE ON ALCOHOL 1971-84

ANSWERS

1. Demand factors which influence consumption are:— real income, real prices, the distribution of income, taxation, relative prices, advertising, taste, population, availability, etc., and all of these can be used to explain the behaviour shown in the diagrams. Real personal disposable income, i.e. income after inflation and taxation, has a major influence on the consumption of alcohol per person and the general trends are closely related, except for the period 1982-4 when other factors outweighed income alone, see Diagram 1. However, consumption of specific types of alcohol does not always follow income changes, see Diagram 3. Beer consumption between 1973-77 rose though incomes fell and as disposable incomes rose between 1979-84 beer sales per person fell. The consumption of spirits generally follows personal disposable incomes, though, for example, sales fell after 1979 in the face of rising incomes. Comparing consumption by types it can be seen that wine sales have grown whilst beer and spirits have fluctuated. It could be that wine has a higher and more stable income demand elasticity. In the case of beer it might be argued that for some income groups it has a "negative" income elasticity so that as incomes rise people switch to more 'up market' drinks, e.g. wine or spirits. Other reasons might be that tastes have changed in favour of wine due to increased foreign holidays introducing people to wine drinking or because of increased advertising by wine importers. At the same time real and relative alcohol prices will influence demand. All prices may have risen between 1979-82 which could account for the overall fall in alcohol consumption. Between 1971-79 the real price of alcohol fell but after 1979 deliberately increased taxation meant that prices kept pace with inflation, which reduced consumption. The relative price of wine may be less than that of beer and spirits due to lower relative indirect taxation and this could encourage wine sales at the expense of beer and spirits. In fact over this period beer and spirits prices rose due to tax increases and oligopolistic brewery price increases for beer. Again the availability of wine has increased as more supermarkets now hold comprehensive wine stocks because of the U.K. joining the EEC. Over the period 1971-84, the population structure changed and the young seem to prefer wine and lager products, whilst the traditional beer drinkers are now perhaps those on lower incomes and the more elderly population groups who drink less. However, it should be noted that the diagrams only show overall income and sales behaviour so it is difficult to be conclusive in terms of actual income or age groups.

2. The information displayed in the diagrams indicates trend relationships between disposable incomes and the consumption of alcohol in the U.K. 1971-84. It is therefore of use to the economist in building up reliable and predictable models of economic behaviour which can test economic hypotheses regarding demand theory. The producer and retailer of alcohol would be able to see past demand changes and hence extrapolate likely future patterns of demand. This could help in determining output, employment and investment levels in both the company and the industry, which would also change in structure as specific sectors grow or decline in importance. The decline of the "Distillers" Company from 1982-6 is evidence of the changing fortune of the "spirits" sector in the U.K. Perhaps companies could plan to increase exports if U.K. sales growth potential appeared limited! Lastly, substantial tax revenues are forthcoming from all alcohol sales and so the government (Chancellor) could plan its future income and expenditure strategy based on future disposable income and price changes.

U.K. INCOME ELASTICITY OF DEMAND 1971-81

ANSWERS
(a) (i)   A progressive system of taxation is one where the percentage of income going to taxation, etc. increases as incomes rise. In order to assess whether Income Tax and National Insurance contributions were progressive in 1981, both have to be added together for each income group and then calculated as a percentage of the income groups. This is done in the Table.

		GROUPS			
1. Total Income	£119.9	£164.0	£194.8	£240.1	£327.3
2. NI + Tax as a % of (1)	8.3	13.9	17.2	18.7	21.3

It can be seen that as incomes increase from £119.9 to £327.3 the percentage that N.I. and tax represent increases from 8.3 to 21.3 and so the deductions of Tax and National Insurance were progressive in their impact. A closer inspection reveals that National Insurance contributions rose faster than Income Tax.

(ii)   Income elasticity of demand measures the responsiveness of demand to change in real income (disposable) or

$$\frac{\% \text{ change in demand}}{\% \text{ change in real income}} = \frac{(+) > 1}{(-) < 1} = 1$$

For the most part income elasticity will be positive, except for inferior goods (−), and will be usually elastic (> 1) or inelastic (< 1) with respect to Income.

In the case of measuring income elasticity with respect to each commodity over the income range in 1981, the calculations are as follows: The disposable income range is £109.9 to £257.4, i.e. a percentage change of 134.2%. The percentage change in spending for each commodity group is calculated over the income range so:

Fuel, Light & Power 8.0 to $10.7 = \dfrac{2.7}{8} = 33.75\%$

so income elasticity for fuel, etc. $= \dfrac{+\ 33.75\%}{+\ 134\%} = +.252$

which shows a positive but inelastic income elasticity. Completing the same calculations for the other commodity groups, the findings are as follows:

	Food	Alcoholic Drink	Tobacco	Transport	Services
Income elasticity =	.348	+ .626	− .253	+ 1.20	+ 2.24

In other words, food and drink consumption is little influenced by income levels but for transport and services, income increases bring forth disproportionate increases in spending levels. Tobacco appears as an "inferior" good in the sense that as income levels fall, spending, as a percentage of income, increases, and vice versa.

(b) (i)   For the average (median) income group, disposable income in 1971 of £334 represented 87.2% of weekly income earned whilst in 1981 the comparable figure was 82.7%, i.e. £161.1 as a percentage of £194.8. This was due to the rise over time, in the average rate of tax and national insurance. This was caused by inflation pushing up wages, and hence marginal tax rates, faster than inflation corrected tax bands allowed so that the average tax and national insurance paid weekly by the average income group rose from 9.8% to 15.6% and 4.6% to 5.3% respectively. This is confirmed by the fact that between 1971-81 total income rose by 408% but disposable income by only 382%.

(ii)   The pattern of expenditure between the two dates is reflected in the percentage of disposable income each commodity group represented. For example, the average income earner spent 5.6% of disposable income (weekly) on fuel, light and power in 1971 and 5.2% in 1981. In other words, there was a slight decline in the householder's spending budget between the two dates on this commodity. A comparison of similar figures shows budget spending falls on food and tobacco but alcoholic drink, transport and services all show average householder spending percentages increasing over time, e.g. food fell from 26.6 to 20.9% and services rose from 5.8 to 9.1% etc.

(iii)   Demand analysis can help explain the spending patterns illustrated in (b) (ii). For example, relative prices inclusive of indirect taxes, taste, advertising, real income, population changes, taste changes, government policies, etc. can be applied in the analysis. Conservation policies, increasing real costs and improved housing designs could all help explain static spending levels with respect to fuel and light, etc. Spending on food reflects a low, inelastic demand with respect to income, a static or declining population and the growth of healthy eating habits which have reduced food intake and hence spending levels. The rise in spending on alcoholic drink could reflect lower real prices, as taxation has failed to keep pace with inflation, social patterns and the increase in the number of outlets selling alcoholic drink coupled with extensive advertising. Tobacco sales have suffered due to the health risks and changing social habits, e.g. "No Smoking" areas. Also cigarette prices have moved ahead of inflation so "real" prices have risen. The increase in the growth of motoring, the family car, the decline in rail provision and extension of the motorway system helped increase spending levels on transport, etc. At the same time this commodity exhibits a high income elasticity as transport provision is considered a necessary social and business function. Lastly, as income levels rise, most economies display a shift in spending towards the service sectors and the statistics in (b) (ii) confirm these changing social patterns. The growth of leisure and spare time have all contributed towards rising service sector provision which is again highly income elastic; even though these services have shown relative price increases above the average. Improved local authority provision of sports facilities etc., have also contributed and changing population structures have increased the demand for social, health and education services. Commercial services such as insurance and banking are also necessary to the average income earner as they are purchased, for example, with all forms of house tenure and consumer durables. Thus as private house purchase has increased, the services of the solicitor, surveyor, insurance man and banker etc. have risen to facilitate these transactions.

PRICE ELASTICITY OF DEMAND IN RURITANIA

ANSWERS

(a)   Price Elasticity of Demand = $\dfrac{\text{\% Change in Demand for cars}}{\text{\% Change in the Price of cars}}$

Change in demand for cars = $\dfrac{+2m}{12m} = +.167$

Change in price of cars $\dfrac{£-200}{£5,000} = -.04$

therefore overall price elasticity = $\dfrac{+.167}{-.04} = -4.175$
of demand for cars   = -4.2 to one decimal place which is highly elastic. It suggests revenue and sales will dramatically increase with car price reductions.

(b) (i) Average cost of 12 million cars equals the selling price times number sold less profit constant at £4,000m
so £5,000 × 12m − Total Cost = Total Profit
(Total Revenue) £60th m − Total Cost = £4th m.

$$\frac{£56\text{th m}}{12\text{m}} = \text{unit cost per car}$$

£4,667 = per car at 12 million

(ii) Average cost of 14 million cars again equals the selling price times number sold less profit constant at £4,000m
so £4,800 × 14m − Total Cost = Total Profit
(Total Revenue) £67.2th m − Total Cost = £4th m.

$$\frac{£63.2\text{th m}}{14\text{m}} = \text{unit cost}$$

£4,514 = per car at 14 million

In other words, the average total cost of the extra 2 million cars falls from £4,667 to £4,514 per car, i.e. £153 per car whilst the selling price falls by £200 overall so each car produces a lower profit margin, i.e. £5000 less £4667 or £337 per car at 12 million to £4800 less £4514 or £286 per car at 14m. In effect the increase in total revenue is at a lower rate than the change in total cost so resources are more efficiently used at 12 million since profit levels are higher on each pound of sales.

(c) If price elasticity were − 0.5 then sales and hence profitability would be:-
Given change in price of cars £5,000 to £4,800 = − .04 (4%)
substituting into price elasticity of demand formula gives
$$\frac{+ x}{-.04} = -.5 \text{ where x equals the change in demand (unit)}$$
so x = −.5 x − .04
i.e. x = .02 or 2%
so demand changes by 12m × 2% = 240 thousand extra cars.
therefore the total cost and revenue and hence profit with £200 price reduction will be:
Total Revenue = 12,240,000 × 4,800 = 58,752,000,000
Total Cost   = 12,240,000 × 4,514 = 55,251,136,000

Profit   £3,500,864,000

In other words, even if it is assumed average costs fall to £4514 per car because of the higher output levels (unrealistic) profits fall from £4,000m to £3,500m. (Assumes average costs as per 14m cars).
or if average costs fall at a constant rate between 12 to 14m cars the average cost of 12–24m cars is:—
$$£4,667 - \frac{.24}{2} \times (£4,667 - £4,514) = £4,648.$$

Thus Total Cost = £4,648 × 12.24 = £5.6,896m giving profits of £58,752m less £56,896.4m = £1,855.6, i.e. less than the £35,008.64 above.

(d) (i) Each car firm may attempt to boost sales by exporting overseas, by engaging in retail competition, e.g. by increasing dealer discounts or by extending free warranty periods, etc. Note price cuts are excluded. Overall advertising levels could also increase and the firm could improve the performance or value for money of each car, e.g. stereo systems could be included as a standard item. However, since the industry is only composed of three firms it is effectively an oligopoly so the above retail price cutting actions will be followed by the other firms and overall individual firms sales may not increase, i.e. "kinked demand curve" behaviour pattern may apply. If they individually raised the price of their cars, the other two may not and so individual sales and profit would fall. If they individually cut prices, all will follow so overall sales will fall.

(ii) If the firms acted as a group, e.g. a cartel, they could attempt to raise revenue by increasing the general price level of cars. Since price demand elasticity is presumed to be low, e.g. −.5, this may raise revenue and profits in the whole industry. Otherwise they could research the whole industry and discover the demand elasticities in each segment. In high elasticity segments they could reduce the prices and in low elasticity markets they could act in concert to raise price. Otherwise they could act together to encourage the government to boost demand in the economy, perhaps lower tax on cars or petrol and again they could act together to restrict foreign car import competition and generally encourage overall export sales. They could also encourage the government to encourage motoring by cutting petrol tax and/or protect home markets by imposing import tariffs etc.

WATER SUPPLY IN THE COMMUNITY

ANSWERS
See Fig.

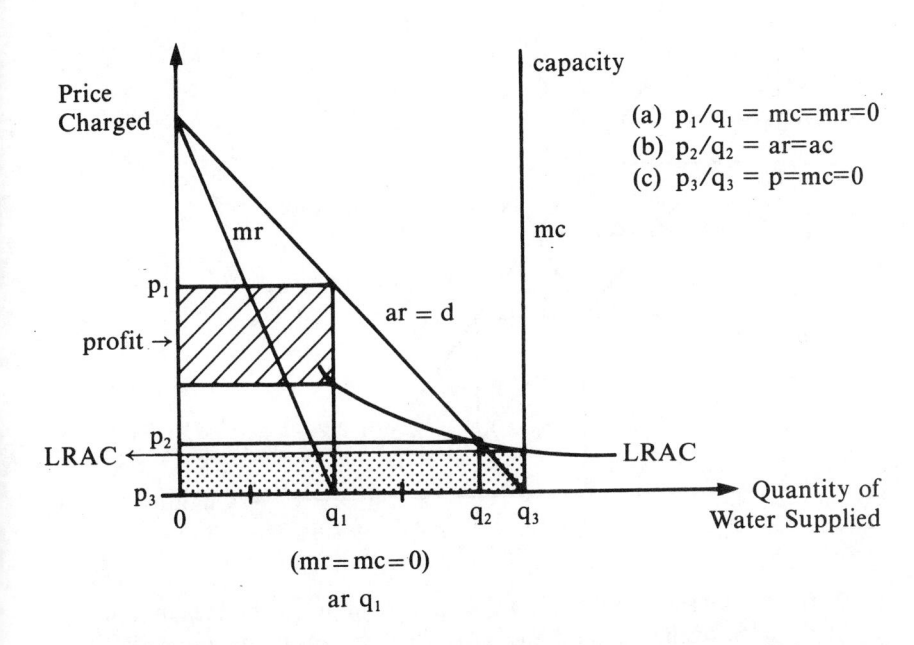

(a) $p_1/q_1 = mc = mr = 0$
(b) $p_2/q_2 = ar = ac$
(c) $p_3/q_3 = p = mc = 0$

(c) When maximum economic efficiency is the objective, price will be set to marginal cost which is zero and output will be expanded to q_3, which is the full extent of demand with a zero price. At this price/output level economic benefits are maximised and all consumers will use water freely; since it has no opportunity cost, i.e. zero marginal cost. Indeed because a zero price increases water use, and possibly overall standards of hygiene, overall social benefits are maximised and economic welfare and efficiency are optimised. However, at p_3 the Long Run Average Cost is positive and to maintain commercial solvency and future investment in water resources a payment, equivalent to the dotted area, will have to be met. This will be done by either the government, who pay a subsidy, or by users in the form of a fixed rental payment. The different pricing policies reflect how water is seen by the community. If it is a private good then p_1/q_1, if a public good then p_2/q_2 and if a merit good p_3/q_3.

146 Market Analysis

THE PRICE OF TEA

ANSWERS

FIG. 1

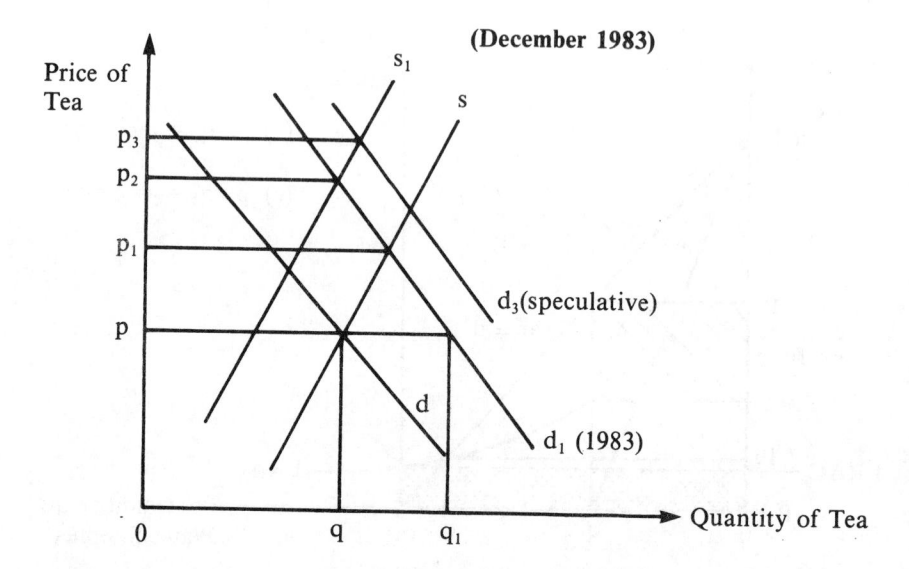

(December 1983)

[Diagram: Price of Tea vs Quantity of Tea, showing supply curves s and s_1, demand curves d, d_1 (1983), and d_3 (speculative); price levels p, p_1, p_2, p_3 on vertical axis; quantities q, q_1 on horizontal axis.]

1. Market analysis would explain the increase in the price of tea in terms of shifts of both the demand and supply of tea. Assuming an equilibrium (see Fig.1) price and output of op/oq, the increase in demand for tea in the Middle East etc. in 1983 would shift demand to d_1 so at op demand would exceed supply by $oq_1 - oq$. This would, as the diagram shows, increase price to op_1 — this occurred with the 10% and $8\frac{1}{2}$% increase by Brooke Bond. The reduction in supply from s to s_1, due to the Indian Government's ban, pushed the price even further from op_1 to op_2 as supply reduced. Lastly, short term speculative demand, d_3, could push the price even further up to op_3 in anticipation of the price increase due to future demand increasing in developing countries, etc.

An alternative but similar analysis could explain the market behaviour as follows: Assume the price and quantity equilibrium of op/oq (see Fig.2) and world demand increases to d_1, thus pushing up price and output to op_1/oq_1. In the short term supply could be cut back to s_1, ie. become inelastic, if the Indian Government impose a short term ban on exports. This will push up price to p_2 and output back to oq_2. S now becomes the long term world supply which increases as more land comes into tea cultivation and the long term equilibrium now moves to op_1/oq_1.

FIG. 2

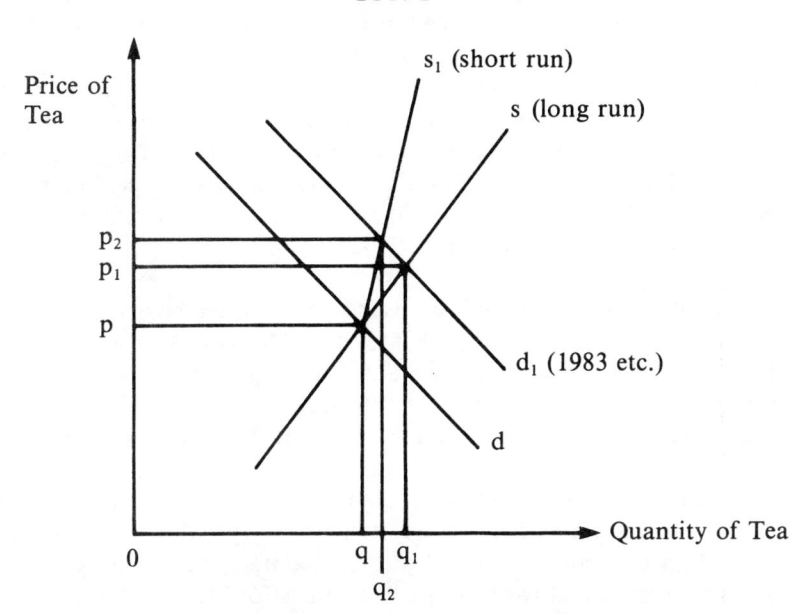

Figure: Price of Tea vs Quantity of Tea showing s_1 (short run), s (long run), d_1 (1983 etc.), and d curves, with prices p_2, p_1, p and quantities q, q_1, q_2 marked.

2. Tea is Britain's favourite drink and Brooke Bond Oxo is a monopoly supplier with 30% of the market and the market brand leader. 80% of all tea drunk is CTC and India supplies 20% of that; in effect India supplies 20% of all the tea drunk in Britain through a monopoly supplier, Brooke Bond. Under these circumstances India is therefore a monopoly supplier and if U.K. demand is inelastic then a reduction in output (due to a ban) will increase revenue faster than the fall in output, i.e. demand is inelastic. In view of the fact that Brooke Bond had raised tea prices by large amounts in 1983, the Indian Government could perhaps note monopoly price rises by Brooke Bond and they may feel justified in banning exports of CTC in order to re-negotiate their own prices and profit margins with Brooke Bond, and generate more export revenue. Overall they may not fear a loss of U.K. markets because of price rises since long term world demand is increasing to fill the overall gap which could result.

3. The outcome of higher tea prices may be analysed in terms of demand factors. Thus as tea prices rise and substitute products become cheaper, e.g. coffee, tea consumption may in the long term fall as more people switch to coffee and other suitable beverages. Furthermore it may attract new tea investment in those regions suitable for tea production and overall may stimulate more intensive tea production methods in existing areas such as India, Sri Lanka and China, etc. Thus overall investment in new and existing tea areas will help to improve the incomes and wellbeing

148 Market Analysis

of people in less developed countries. It is also possible that competitive food producers could pursue tea tasting substitute products or they may boost the appeal, by advertising, of other substitutes. If demand for tea does fall due to price increases, existing suppliers could aim to be more efficient in tea production in order to cut costs and hence prices. Finally, excessive tea prices supplied by a market monopoly, e.g. Brooke Bond, could lead to high profits, public alarm and possible investigations by the Monopolies Commission. It could boost India's export earnings and increase the U.K.'s import bill for tea.

4. The ability of Brooke Bond to raise the price of tea bags by a greater percentage than the price of packet tea would be based on the belief that demand conditions vary. If demand for tea bags is more inelastic than packet tea, then the supplier could differentiate price to maximise profits due to more inelastic demand for tea bags. At the same time if different income groups purchased tea bags and packet tea and if tea bags exhibited higher income elasticity than packet tea then, assuming high income earners purchased tea bags, it might be profitable to increase the price of tea bags more than packet tea to maintain overall sales levels. It could be argued that tea bags are substitutes for "tea" and as incomes rise, people switch to tea bags because of the convenience factor. As incomes rise, people switch to tea bags and away from packet tea (inferior good?) so along with the increased price of tea there is a high income elasticity for tea bags working in favour of the tea bag price increase. Lastly, higher tea bag prices could be the result of increased costs of production, packaging or processing, etc.

ROAD PRICING IN SINGAPORE

ANSWERS
(a) The new system of road pricing in Singapore consists of two elements, namely a new conditional charge to enter the city (£12) and a quadrupled price for city car parking of £2.80, though for car pool commuters the charge will be as before, i.e. $0.70 \times 4 = £2.80$. "Other motor vehicles" presumably refers to commercial vehicles, vans and lorries etc., who have to make essential journeys for selling, distributing, etc. In all cases the new system refers to peak hour travel when, it may be speculated, those entering the city did so for essential work purposes.

The index numbers indicating the volume of "cars" travelling in show a fall in non-pooled users from 100 to 26, i.e. 74, possibly because these users will be paying more than four times as much to park, i.e. 70p to £2.80 plus the £12.00 licence to enter. From this we may infer that non-pooled car use is highly elastic with respect to price. On the other hand, "car pools" or shared travel, increases from 100 to 182 because in relative terms the price has become less than non-pooled travel, though the same as before for each traveller. In a sense there is a high cross-elasticity of demand between "cars" and "car pool" travel if they can be viewed as substitutes. In money terms the price of car pool travel is the same as before, though in real terms it may have fallen if inflation has risen so it is difficult to infer too much about "car pool" price elasticity. Overall demand for car and car pool travel has increased very slightly, $26 + 182 = 208$ over 200, even though the price overall has gone up indicating a highly inelastic demand for car travel generally. Possibly an overall increase in real income has caused this increase so demand for "car" travel is elastic with respect to income! With regard to other motor vehicles the volume index changes from 100 to 102, a marginal change, reflecting the inelastic demand for this form of motor travel in the face of substantial price increases. It is difficult to infer anything about the demand for bus travel elasticity because, although volume has increased from 100 to 115, no information is given about bus prices.

(b) The resources being utilised refers to:— car and road use, car parking both on and off street, buses, petrol, etc. From the volume indices etc., it would appear that slightly more people are entering the city to work but fewer cars are being used and so less car parking will be needed. Therefore cars are being used more efficiently so there will be fewer cars on the roads, journey times will improve, less petrol will be consumed etc. (In all, the private and social marginal cost of travel for each worker entering the city will fall.) At the same time more workers use buses and the speed of bus travel improves by 30% (100 to 70) because of fewer cars, less traffic jams etc., i.e. social bads or externalities reduce. As the workers use fewer vehicles, journey times improve and car parking needs reduce, so overall travel efficiency should increase leading to lower resource costs. In effect the new price system releases previously used resources, such as land for parking, cars, petrol, police, etc., which could be used elsewhere, and so a more efficient use of resources could result from this road pricing system. On the other hand, it could be argued that in order to collect the £12 per month fee more people will be needed and motorists may have to wait to pay their fees, etc., representing a waste of resources. However, since fewer cars will be entering the city, fewer traffic wardens, etc. will be needed to collect the £2.80 and hopefully fewer parking fines will be incurred which will reduce the need for law enforcement and the administration of parking fines, etc.

(c) Demand for car travel and parking responds not only to price changes but to other factors namely, income, taste, population, the price and availability of substitutes and complements, seasonal influences, etc. In order to make a comprehensive assessment of the new road pricing system, information as to whether any of these variables have changed would be required. For example, the increase in bus travel may have been due to lower bus fares, improved bus comfort or a more regular service. The price of individual car travel may have increased because of lower petrol costs, tyre prices, servicing charges etc., and this may have led to fewer cars entering Singapore. Over the period March to August the number and structure of the workforce may have changed, so the pattern of travel demand is represented by a new workforce and/or seasonal influences. Similarly, long-term information on disposable income, income tax, traffic management, road works, the population structure, would all be required. The government could have introduced an intensive advertising campaign designed to educate the public towards public transport and away from single car use.

Chapter 20
DISTRIBUTION OF INCOME

WEST END RENTS 1985/6.

FIG. 1
Demand for Central London Shop Locations

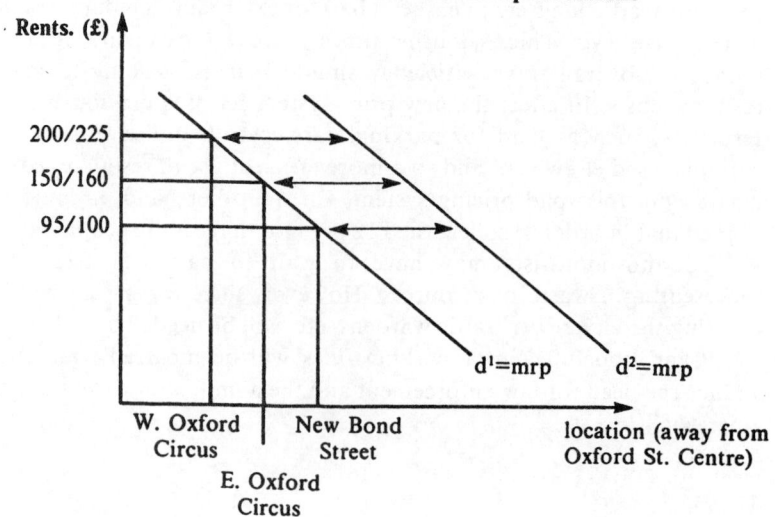

Rents. (£)

200/225
150/160
95/100

d^1=mrp d^2=mrp

W. Oxford Circus | New Bond Street | location (away from Oxford St. Centre)
E. Oxford Circus

ANSWERS

1. (i) Economic theory predicts that with a limited supply (scarcity) of available land in a central location, as in the West End of London, demand will be the main determinant of overall levels. Demand for shopping space is a derived demand and is based upon the marginal revenue product available from each square foot used; in this case for retail purposes. Retailers will bid up rents until marginal revenue product (sales) is just equal to the rents payable inclusive of profit. This means with reference to Fig.1 that the rentals or price charged will reflect relative marginal revenue and hence "who will go where" viz shopping thoroughfares. This means high turnover shops will be able to afford up to £200/£225 per sq. ft. per annum in the highest trade areas West of Oxford Circus and slightly lower marginal revenue product (Sales) shops will have to locate East of Oxford Circus and so on. This gives the general shape of the demand schedule as indicated in d^1. In a sense, there are individual demand schedules along d^1 for different locations from the centre of the West End and the analysis is similar to the productivity of labour and the different wage levels afforded by the employer.

(ii) Once the locations are valued and traders have decided what they can afford there will be dynamic influences at work within the market. Thus as specific demand for clothes, Hi-Fi or records booms, then those retailers involved may find the value of their marginal revenue (per sq. ft.) rises so they may be able to move towards the more expensive zones and less profitable retailers may have to move to the cheaper areas etc. At the same time, the overall demand for shopping within the West End can be subject to factors such as bomb scares or a tourist boom or slump etc., which will shift the whole curve d^1 to d_2 if there is a boom or from d^2 to d^1 if there is a slump. This means with respect to paragraph 1, demand was moving to the right but this was halted by those factors detailed in paragraph 2. If overall trade picks up though and demand shifts to d^2, each zone or area specified will find its rents rising (in real terms). In general terms then supply and demand or market forces generally determine the level of rents in an area though financial considerations such as acceptable yields on interest rates in the stock market also have an influence.

INTERNATIONAL EXECUTIVE PAY COMPARISONS

SHORT ANSWERS

1. Column 3 is disposable money income.
   Column 4 is real disposable income.
2. Sweden with £13,400 p.a. real disposable income. This is the same as spending power.

3. Column 2 less taxation and national insurance gives Col.3 and after deflating for inflation rates we have Col. 4.
4. International pay variations for executives exist because of different market forces, i.e. supply and demand, plus government factors. Supply reflects the relative scarcity of executives whilst demand for executives, possibly most important in the short term, reflects the profitability of each economy and industrial section together with the productivity or profitability of those employed. At the same time, individual government pay policies, historical and social factors and overall comparability factors will all have a role to play.

EUROPEAN LIVING STANDARDS

ANSWERS
1. In order to make meaningful comparisons of international living standards, some simple numerical measure has to be used. In this case per capita levels are compared to an EEC average and expressed in terms of relative exchange rates or in terms of purchasing power. Living standards are then expressed as a percentage of the EEC average = 100. The exchange rate technique translates the per capita income into an acceptable yardstick, e.g. the U.S. dollar, whilst the purchasing power parity method compares income with relative price levels in each country. The problem with the exchange rate method is that exchange rates are not always reliable because they can be distorted and hence over or under valued in terms of other currencies, e.g. the U.S. dollar. In other words, high internal interest rates can overvalue a currency and hence living standards, even when real earnings within the country are falling. The exchange rate could thus indicate "unreal" high living standards. The purchasing power parity method relates respective earnings and price levels so the "real" value of incomes is compared in each country. However, in order for this to be reliable, income receivers in each country must buy the same basket of goods and indirect taxation levels must be comparable. These two factors may not apply so even the purchasing power parity method has its drawbacks. In theory, as inflation increases in one country and purchasing power falls, the value of its exchange rate should fall so both measuring techniques should give the same answer in the long term. The fact that they do not in the short term is because exchange rates can be distorted as mentioned above, and as illustrated in the table. Nevertheless because of the volatility of current international exchange rates, it is widely accepted that the purchasing power parity method may be the best, albeit limited, measure of living standards.

2. In 1984 U.K. living standards appeared higher according to the exchange rate than the purchasing power method, whilst in Portugal the opposite was true with the exchange rate indicating living standards were almost fifty percent below those indicated by the purchasing power method. In terms of answer 1, the U.K. has an exchange rate overvalued in terms of internal prices, whilst Portugal has effectively a lower exchange rate than would be indicated according to internal prices. The equality of both measures would only arise if those prices selected for the purchasing parity method were the only goods traded internationally and if capital account movements and influences were ignored. In the case of the U.K. the current account within the Balance of Payments includes oil exports which may strengthen the pound but would not necessarily be included in the basket of goods used in calculating the purchasing power method. Again capital movements, excluded in purchasing power in the U.K., would be attracted by higher U.K. interest rates and would thus boost the exchange rate; though this would be excluded in the purchasing method. Applying this to the Portuguese case the opposite experience applies so the exchange rate is lower than that implied by the price of internal goods. This can be due to two factors. The current account may be in deficit because Portugal is unable to export goods, or goods selected within the purchasing power method are not included (traded) in the Balance of Payments. On the other hand, they may not be able to find export markets for their internally produced goods and they may have an inelastic demand for imports. At the same time, the Portuguese Balance of Payments may be pushed further into deficit by an adverse capital account which weakens the currency internationally but would not immediately affect or reflect the real earning power of consumers and earners in Portugal.

3. The main drawbacks of both measures are:—
a) They are both narrow measures of living standards as they both relate a hypothetical income level to a sample of goods and fail to include other influences on living standards such as the existing stock of passenger cars, telephones, T.V.'s, doctors and social services such as schools and provision for the elderly, etc.

b) Both measures concentrate on current incomes and prices and exclude the overall standards maintained by the existing stock of houses or other forms of the capital stock, e.g. roads, hospitals, bridges, etc.

c) Both measures ignore actual earnings and employment prospects within a country or region, e.g. unemployment rates and benefits should also be included.

d) Living standards cover a range of factors other than merely earnings, etc. Overall weather conditions, environmental and health conditions, freedom, etc., are all part of social living standards.

e) Many argue that the "Black Economy" or the hidden economy is large and therefore many earnings will be unrecorded. This means that official figures could underestimate true figures in all countries.

f) As outlined in Q1 both indicators have weaknesses and drawbacks so are unreliable as complete measures of living standards.

U.K. INTEREST RATES

ANSWERS

(a) The pattern of interest rates refers to the variety of actual rates paid to lenders and charged to borrowers. The Table itself identifies different savings institutions and the circumstances under which savers lend their money are given by the column headings along the top. The range of interest rates paid is from 5% to $14\frac{1}{2}$% and between 14 and 25% for borrowers, so obviously the pattern reflects significant savings and borrowing factors. These can be identified and discussed as follows:—

1) The ease with which savers can withdraw their money is an important factor since it reflects liquidity. Those accounts where money can be easily and quickly withdrawn pay a lower rate than those where money is tied up for a period. Examples are Building Societies, Clearing Banks and Local Authorities, where a three tier structure reflects withdrawal conditions such as 'on demand', '7 days notice', '1-2 years notice', etc., and where higher rates are paid when savings are left for longer time periods. This reflects compensation for giving up liquidity.

2) The tax liability of the lender will also influence interest rates in two ways. Some rates are quoted tax paid (the grossed up interest paid equivalents are given in notes (a) (b) and (c) and these are lower than the rates where depositors have to declare and possibly pay tax on interest earned, e.g. the Clearing Banks. Otherwise for National Savings Certificates. The low rate is because no tax is payable so bringing the effective rate paid in line with tax payable rates.

3) Traditionally low National Savings rates, e.g. 5%, and T.S.B. rates have reflected the origins of the institutions and the saver. The T.S.B. was set up in the nineteenth century for small savers and their savings and interest rates were to some extent guaranteed by the government, so offsetting higher rates. Furthermore, with small unit savers, the administrative costs were higher on each account and low interest rates reflected this fact. As can also be seen, high interest rates are normally paid in those institutions where investment minimums are large, so both

Finance Houses and Finance for Industry rates are well above average.

4) Variations in borrowers rates reflect both the security of the borrower and the nature of the loan. Thus mortgage rates are lower than loan and overdraft rates since the security of a house is greater than other speculative and less certain bank loan ventures. In fact, banks and overdrafts would normally be at a rate well in excess of Banks Base Rate so making them 4 or 5% more than mortgage rates. Whilst the personal bank loan of 10% flat appears even lower than mortgage rate, it should be realised that repayments on these loans start immediately so that the amount of the loan is reducing from the very beginning. In other words, the grossed up effective rate of a 10% (flat) bank loan would usually be around 20% p.a. This reflects the cost and risk of the loan. Again Credit Cards charge a monthly interest rate compounded up so 2% per month would be at 24% (2x12) per annum. This reflects the cost of maintaining the credit card service and a large provision for risk and bad debts. However, if outstanding debts are cleared monthly, it is possible to view credit cards as providing an interest free service.

5) A comparison of rates paid to savers and those charged to borrowers indicates the profit and cost margins the institutions charge. The Minimum Lending Rate has now been discontinued (since 1983) but the Clearing Banks still set a Bank Base Rate which serves as the benchmark for other interest rates, both long and short term. The Bank's Base Rate reflects the cost of money in the wholesale or discount markets and from this rate savings rates are determined, taking into account the costs of operations, etc. The differences between savings and borrowing rates will vary between the institutions and will reflect normally the market power of the institution and the costs of operation. Thus institutions providing for the small saver, e.g. TSB, on a national basis will find costs high and therefore the difference between the two rates will be higher than for an institution taking in large unit savings on a centralised and limited scale, e.g. Finance Houses.

(b) The Retail Price Index measures the inflation rate and in this case was 13% higher than the previous year. The rates of interest quoted in the Table are nominal rates and after taking off the inflation rate, "real interest" rates can be calculated. Thus real interest rates can be positive, greater than zero or negative, less than zero. After correcting for inflation, for example, the real interest rate received by Ordinary Share Account holders in Building Societies was minus .21% (tax payable) or minus 3.75% (tax paid) both negative. This means that lenders lose but borrowers gain since the real interest rate paid can be less than zero (negative). Of course, if inflation falls faster than interest rates, lender gains. In 1986 interest rates to lenders of around 7% were about 4%

above inflation, so lenders gained. From the Table two observations can be made:—

1) Most savers were paid a negative real rate as most rates were less than 13%. However, the position of Building Society term and subscription account holders depended upon whether the calculations are made before or after tax is paid. The tax situation now (1987) is that tax is payable on all accounts and is non-recoverable even for those now paying tax at the standard rate. Thus it is best to view all Building Society Accounts for 1981 as receiving negative real rates on savings. National Savings Certificate holders of index linked accounts would have received at least rates equivalent to inflation and SAYE 3rd issue holders would effectively receive positive interest rates because interest rates were linked to the RPI and hence inflation.

2) Lastly, it can be seen that all borrowers pay positive rates to the institutions in 1981. For example, mortgage holders pay +1% and personal bank loans could cost up to (20%–13%) 7% above inflation, at a positive borrowing rate.

PROFIT PERFORMANCE OF TOP TEN U.K. MOTOR CAR DISTRIBUTORS

ANSWERS

1. (a) (i) Return on Capital = $\dfrac{\text{Earnings Before Interest \& Tax}}{\text{Net Assets} = \text{Capital employed}}$ %

   (ii) Profit Margin = $\dfrac{\text{Earnings Before Interest \& Tax}}{\text{Sales Turnover}}$ %

(b) Return on capital and profit margin are two widely used measures of corporate financial performance. They relate comparative "profitability" between industries, firms and are used as a basis for investment comparison over time, and between industry sectors. Essentially "return on capital" indicates the efficiency of the capital resource in terms of it generating a reward (profit) and the "profit margin" indicates how much of each pound of sales is profit. These ratios are then used by "investors" and the "stock market" to determine relative equity or share prices and likely future investment levels.

(c) Using the Lex Service figures the profit margin on £887.5m sales was 4.3% so profits or Earnings Before Interest and Tax (EBIT) was £887.5 × 4.3% = £38.16m. This represented a 17.8% return on capital so if £38.16m = 17.8% return on capital then capital invested was **£214.39m** $\dfrac{(£38.16m)}{(17.8\%)}$. Similar analysis can indicate actual capital and profit for other distributors. The same calculations for average turnover, capital and profit figures for the ten companies in 1983/4 were £249.7m, £45.6m and £4.74m respectively.

2) (i) The increase to the industry's return on capital between 1981/2 to 1983/4 was from 3.7% to 10.4% and this could have been due to:

(1) Improved dealer margins given by manufacturers anxious to sell cars and reduce their stocks, in the face of high interest rates and depressed consumer demand during 1981/2.

(2) Rationalisation in the industry resulting in fewer, more efficient retailer distribution networks.

(3) Economies of scale in buying and selling cars, e.g. "fleet" distribution to company buyers and Car Hire Companies. See The Perry Group.

(4) Reduction in the holding of spare part stocks and general running down of other car stocks after 1981/2.

(5) Improved national sales due to rises in consumer earnings and company profit levels.
Note: Corporate buyers account for around 65% of all new cars sold.

(6) Improved profit margins on second-hand car sales which many distributors maintain.

2) (ii) Differences in profitability between dealers in the same industry or sector are explained by:—

(1) Management efficiency greatly varies between companies. See Lex Service and Henly's figures. For example, Dutton-Forshaw and Mann-Egerton both capitalised at around £27m with sales of around £200m each in 1983/4, experienced different profit rates. Mann-Egerton generated £4.38m profit in 1983/4 and Dutton-Forshaw only managed £1.6m. Obviously management efficiency varied since the product range seems similar.

(2) Marketing "set-ups" differ. Some dealers sell slow moving models with high profit margins, e.g. Rolls Royce. Others sell fast moving, low profit margin models, e.g. Mini Metro.

(3) Regional variations. Some dealers are based in high income growth regions, e.g. the South East (Lex), others are more widely dispersed over some depressed areas such as the North, e.g. Cowie.

(4) Some dealers are "fleet" orientated, e.g. Perry Group, selling only Fords and so marketing costs are relatively low, and by standardising and reducing the number and range of the models held, savings can be made on spares, etc. Profits then rise.

158 Distribution of Income

(5) Small general dealers are often unprofitable because they are unable to concentrate their sales effort and exploit marketing economies of scale.

U.K. PRIVATE INVESTMENT 1975-81
ANSWERS
CALCULATIONS FROM THE TABLE (Selected)

Date	Personal Saving	Private Investment		Nominal Interest/Real Interest			
		Non-housing	Housing	Short	Long	Short	Long
1975	3.5	-2.6	8.9	11.1	4.4	-13.1	-9.8
1976	-7.3	2.8	-0.1	12.5	14.4	-4.0	-3.1
1977	-11.6	8.4	-6.5	10.2	12.7	-5.7	-2.2
1978	29.6	10.7	14.1	9.2	12.5	+1	-4.2
1979	19.7	5.9	-13.3	14.4	13.0	+1	-.4
1980	7.7	1.1	-16.1	15.0	13.8	-3.0	-4.2
1981	-16.4	-2.2	-15.5	14.4	14.7	+2.5	+2.8
		(Annual percentage change)				(Averages for year)	

(1) (i) Although initially the direction of the two variables coincides, at least for 1975-81 thereafter there does not seem to be any close relationship between personal saving and investment in housing.

(ii) Nominal short and long term interest rates are corrected for inflation by the Retail Price Index, to show 'real' rates, but again there does not seem to be a close relationship. The closest relationship is between investment in housing and real long term rates in terms of the signs, though not for magnitude. However, by 1981 this is no longer true.

(2) Comparisons of non-housing investment with other variables in the table reveal a broad relationship with changing levels of output (GDP) and a closer relationship with the trading profits of companies and with some real interest rates. Non-housing private investment is specifically in plant, machinery, factories, computers and stock, etc. and according to Keynesian theory it will be influenced by a variety of factors including levels of consumption, saving and profit income as well as real interest rates. The data seems to broadly confirm these predictions with respect to all though there are exceptions for particular years. For example, there seems to be a relationship between Gross Trading Profits and investment for most of the years except 1980. Again theory suggests that borrowers, (investors) are better off when real interest rates are negative

Distribution of Income 159

and between 1975-78 real interest rates are broadly negative and non-housing investment rises. The positive real interest rates in 1981, together with a downturn in the economy, would explain the negative investment, though overall business psychology and attitudes could also play a major role. In fact the downturn in investment in 1981 was mainly due to destocking caused by the expensive cost of borrowing, e.g. high real interest rates. It would have been interesting to analyse the data in terms of monthly changes in GDP investment and interest rates, etc. Note: Interest rates are averages for the year.

(3) In order to provide a complete answer to (2), economic theory suggests that other important determinants of private non-housing investment may be relevant. In particular government policy regarding future capital and current expenditure plans for the economy would be important. If, for example, the government indicated its intention to inject extra spending into the economy in order to stimulate growth, then businessmen could respond by themselves adopting a more optimistic attitude and increasing private non-housing investment in plant and machinery, etc., as Keynes indicated. Again taxation and capital expenditure policies affect the real cost of investment and businessmen will be influenced by this and corporate tax rates on profits, etc. This would affect the gross trading profit figures and provide more accurate net trading profit figures which could be more indicative viz investment. Much private non-housing investment is provided for export markets so data on the value of the pound, U.K. trade competitiveness and overall world trade data would be useful. If the exchange rate were high and exports uncompetitive, investment in export manufacturing sectors would be affected. Overall total investment will be a composite of investment over many sectors and so to obtain a better idea each sector could be analysed in terms of its investment levels, e.g. oil, mechanical and electrical engineering data could give a more precise picture of non-housing investment and therefore the factors which may influence it.

Many explanations of private non-housing investment behaviour incorporate a lagged relationship between changing levels of output and investment, a variant on the Accelerator Theory of Investment, so perhaps data covering a wider time span would be useful in order to obtain a more accurate picture. Since much investment in the U.K. is undertaken by large multinationals, perhaps it would be relevant to consider multinational investment patterns and how economic growth and profit/profitability levels vary throughout the world. World wide interest rates would be relevant, in comparison to the U.K. ones given in the table.

160 Distribution of Income

Lastly, in order to obtain a more complete picture to part (2), perhaps the specific forms of private investment undertaken could be given along with amounts, e.g. plant, machinery, stocks, etc. Without specific data on actual industrial performance and investment undertaken, it is very difficult to gauge a complete understanding of determinants of non-housing investment from the data provided.

U.K., U.S.A. WAGES AND EMPLOYMENT 1979-84

ANSWERS

(a) Money wages are actual wages earned by labour and would be based on current prices, etc. Money wages when corrected for inflation will indicate the buying power or real wages earned. It is usual to deflate money wages by a Price Index, e.g. 1979=100, in order to obtain accurate real wage levels.

(b) In the case of the U.K. manufacturing worker, since 1979 real wages earned have shown an upward trend and employment a downward trend. In the former case the trend is a straight line or generally constant, whilst employment fell fastest between 1980 and 1981 and thereafter the rate of employment has fallen at a slower rate. In the U.S.A. manufacturing sectors real wages and employment have shown a different pattern. Between 1979 and 1982 real wages show a downward, though fluctuating trend. It is not until 1982 that real wages rise roughly in line with U.K. rates. Initially U.S.A. employment in manufacturing falls but then increases in 1981 before falling once again in 1982. Employment recovers in 1983 showing the U.S.A. employment is subject to fluctuations and seems to be less related to real wage behaviour than the U.K. experience.

(c) The Marginal Revenue Product Theory of Wages is a micro-economic theory which relates the marginal cost of employment (real wages) to the marginal value of the output produced. Diagrammatically the marginal revenue product schedule is downward sloping, reflecting diminishing returns and means, in the competitive case, that as the real wage falls, to equate with a lower marginal revenue product, more workers are employed and vice versa. An increase in the overall output of the workforce or a rise in the price of the final product can shift the whole mrp schedule to the right so that higher real wages (mrp) can be associated with the same or an increasing workforce. In the case of the U.K. overall, the rise in real wages between 1979 to 1984/5 is about 20% whilst employment fell by about 22%, which may confirm the predictions of the theory. However, the relationship is not clear cut as there are varying rates of employment falls but a roughly constant real wage increase. Again, mrp theory is concerned with employment and wages at the unit or firm level and tends to ignore macro-economic considerations. The diagrams refer to overall manufacturing behaviour and do not provide specific experience of real wages and employment in specific manufacturing sectors or firms. During this period the U.K. manufacturing sector was subject to high interest and exchange rates and overall a generally depressed home demand, all of which may have shifted the mrp to the left because of lower product prices rather than falling labour productivity. This, together with rising real wages, would certainly reduce employment levels.

In the case of the U.S.A. the initial fall in real wages was still accompanied by employment falls, which can be explained in terms of a shift of the mrp schedule to the left at a faster rate than the real wage wall, which should generate employment along the mrp schedule. The second phase shows reasonably stable real wages and slightly increasing employment, which could be due to overall demand for output and labour increasing. The last two phases show conflicting behaviour with real wages rising but employment falling, then rising. Initially the rise in real wages led to a cutback in labour demand and employment, i.e. leftwards along the schedule, but then employment also rose. This can only be explained in terms of an overall increase in demand for output and labour — reflation* — which shifted the overall demand for labour to the right faster than real wage costs. However, the overall inconsistency in the case of the U.S.A. throws some doubt on the validity of mrp, and U.K. evidence seems too general to confirm the theory which may be better explained in terms of macro-economic considerations.

*President Reagan maintained an increasing overall Budget Deficit during the early and mid 1980's.

U.K. PRICES, WAGES, EARNINGS AND PRODUCTIVITY 1978-83

ANSWERS
(a) Calculate Real Wage Rates:
Actual weekly wage rates are compared to Retail Prices in order that real wages can be assessed. Comparing the first two columns it can be seen that in 1978, 1979 adjusted weekly wage rate indices would have been slightly below retail prices so real wage rates would have been negative. For 1980 real and actual wage rates were the same since this is the base year. Thereafter the index of retail prices from 1981-3 is always above actual weekly wage rates, so in effect real wages would have been falling,

162 Distribution of Income

indeed for 1982 the difference is 121.5 to 117.8, a fall in real wages of $(117.8 \div 121.5) \times 100 = 97\%$.

(b) Weekly wage rates specify the hourly or weekly rate for the job whilst weekly earnings covers actual earnings received before deductions. In the Table it can be seen that initially weekly wage rates exceed earnings until 1980 but thereafter earnings increase faster than the wage rate. In fact the difference rises from 2.7 to 5.7 and by 1983 earnings exceed wage rates by 9.5 points.

(c) Earnings include wages, overtime and bonuses etc., and the excess difference of this over the wage rate is known as the 'wages drift'. After 1980 this wage drift steadily increases as overtime working and bonuses increased in industry. This may be because with a reduced workforce, after the reduction in manufacturing industry from 1980, longer hours were worked by the remaining workforce. If this workforce was in expanding firms then rather than employ extra labour, management prefer to pay overtime to those already employed. If wage rates fail to increase with output and earnings, this may reflect overall the weakness of Trade Unions to effect improved basic wage rates and after 1980 the power of Trade Union negotiators certainly fell in the face of unemployment and reduced union membership. On the other hand, weekly wage rates were ahead of earnings between 1978-9 and this may be because workers were not able to work to make up earnings. In other words, because of short time working, strikes or other industrial disturbances, actual earnings failed to keep up with wage rates. At the same time, if management closed down and laid off manpower, perhaps due to excessive Trade Union wage rate claims, then clearly actual earnings will be below these published negotiated wage rates. Lastly, it could be argued that whilst weekly wage rates are negotiated for industrial operatives, overall average earnings include all workers, that is to say salaried and non-salaried. This being so, if industrial wage rates are ahead of salaried earnings, then the differential will be in favour of those paid a weekly rate.

(d) Marginal Revenue Product Theory attempts to relate increases in earnings to increases in the value of output produced, i.e. output per person. For the whole economy between 1978-9 increases in labour productivity (column 5) more than offset increases in wages (4). However, from 1981 onwards, productivity failed to increase as fast as earnings so that by 1983 earnings had increased by around 40 points on 1980 compared to an output rise of only 7.8 points since 1980, i.e. earnings far outstripped output. In manufacturing, this trend was copied. From 1978-9 output (6) far outstripped earnings until 1980.

Thereafter the opposite occurred so that by 1983 earnings had increased by 36.2 points on 1980 but output per person had only increased by 15.3 points. The differences between output and earnings from 1980 was far less marked for manufacturing than for the whole economy.

INVESTMENT IN ENERGY SAVINGS. D.C.F.

ANSWERS

1. Schedule A shows that with a zero interest or discount rate but increasing energy prices, the payback period shortens. This is because the annual savings will increase as energy prices rise and so the £1,000 investment will be recovered much earlier. For example, with $7\frac{1}{2}\%$ inflation the initial investment will be recovered after 4 years. ie. Clearly, as inflation rises the compound savings increase disproportionately so sloping the schedule upwards to the left.

2. If capital costs 10% then this represents the opportunity cost of borrowing and will reduce the annual savings accordingly. Discounted Cash Flow Analysis uses this idea — see Statistical Section — and future annual savings are discounted by the cost of interest foregone in order to calculate the present value of this future stream of money saved. Deducting this discounted income stream from the initial investment gives the Net Present Value. This can be worked out using the discount factor formula $\left(\frac{1}{1+i}\right)^n$ where i is the cost of capital and n the number of years. This formula gives the discount factor weights in decimal form for years 1 to 7 as shown.

    After Yr   1   2   3   4   5   6   7

    $$£200 \times \frac{1}{.909} + \frac{£200}{.826} + \frac{£200}{.751} + \frac{£200}{.683} + \frac{£200}{.621} + \frac{£200}{.565} + \frac{£200}{.513} = £973.6$$

    which represents the present value, after seven years, of £200 annual savings. This approximates to £1,000 invested. If similar calculations were carried out when capital cost 5% and 15% then break-even payback time would be around 6 and $10\frac{1}{2}$ years, as shown with schedules B and D.

3. Home improvements such as double glazing or attic insulation are made for a variety of reasons. These may be to make financial savings, to increase the value of the property and to improve the comfort of the home. If strict economic considerations were applied then investment in home improvements will be dependent upon annual savings discounted by the cost of capital or the current interest rate. Therefore as inflation increases the value of savings or as interest rates fall, then payback time

164 Distribution of Income

shortens and home improvements will become more economic. If the opposite occurs, and when householders change home every seven years or so, then the likelihood of home improvements becomes less worthwhile. However, there are other considerations. Consumers may be more interested in comfort and such improvements may lead to less maintenance and upkeep, e.g. Aluminium double glazing. Finally, the improvement may increase the capital value of the property in excess of the actual investment cost. In other words, a variety of influences affect the consumer when such investment decisions are made.

TOO EQUAL?

ANSWERS
1. The free market theory of wages maintains both supply and demand of labour (marginal revenue product) are important in determining wage levels. If unemployment rates vary between regions, the implication is that labour supply is in surplus in high unemployment areas such as the North (19.9%) and this will act to force down wages and earnings. Similarly in the South relative unemployment rates are lower, surpluses are less and vacancies occur, so wage levels should be relatively more. In the Table, male hourly earnings are generally the same but unemployment rates are not so the inference is that either the statistics are unrepresentative, unreliable, invalid, incorrect or that the labour market is somehow being distorted and thus not subject to free market forces, i.e. wages and earnings are 'too equal' given the apparent unemployment rates.

2. Free market labour economists believe that current UK labour markets and wages are not free and are therefore unresponsive to changing market conditions. They contend that too many wages are determined by national agreements, providing for similar overall rates, which do not take into account local variations in unemployment or the cost of housing etc. Because of this insistence on national wage levels, negotiated by Trade Unions and employer representatives, employers adjust their local labour needs to match the value of the output produced. As income, spending and the value of output varies between areas, so does employment levels. In terms of the demand (mrp) for labour schedule, the South, at a given wage level, will employ more than the North. Furthermore, others allege because of distortions to the labour market, the inconsistency illustrated in the Table can prevail. That is to say, there is immobility of labour otherwise unemployment rates would become less divergent, i.e. workers would move to fill vacancies from high unemployment regions. They argue that immobility of labour

occurs because of varying housing costs and supplementary benefits which do not provide enough incentive to look for work. At the same time, market imperfections exist such as insufficient information about job opportunities and Trade Unions and Professional Associations refuse to allow local wages to reflect market conditions. This leads to wage inflexibility and voluntary unemployment. On the other hand, if the variation in unemployment primarily reflects differences in long term unemployed, e.g. in the North, the Table could be explained. Most economists contend the long term unemployed exert little or no influence on the labour market as they have no skills in demand and so they are not actively competing for work. ie. It is those **in** work that bargain for wages not those **out** of work. If this is the case and the number of short term unemployed is similar throughout the regions, then it would be reasonable to expect similar regional wage levels as displayed in the Table.

THE CHANGING STRUCTURE OF EMPLOYMENT

ANSWERS
(a) The main changes to the distribution of employment:
  (1) **Overall** decline in employment though women's employment rose whilst male employment fell.
  (2) The **structure** of employment changed considerably with employment declining in Agriculture etc., Manufacturing and Production, Distribution and gains in employment in service industries. Local and national government employment remained stable.

(b) Brief explanations of (a): (1) Downturn in the economy due to world recession; (2) Decline in manufacturing because of high interest rates, poor export performance, larger less labour intensive manufacturing units, increased import penetration by foreign firms in UK manufacturing markets; (3) Growth of leisure and service industries because of shorter working week, rise in incomes in SE, unemployment, changing social habits and leisure pursuits (often women employment); (4) Other production industries downturn due to knock-on effect from decline in manufacturing and labour saving capital innovations; (5) The transport and distribution jobs losses were due to larger container units requiring fewer lorries etc., the growth of larger multiple distribution networks replacing traditional wholesale/retail networks, high energy costs led to rationalisation and more efficient systems.

Chapter 21
SUPPLY-THEORY OF THE FIRM
PRICE AND COSTS — A RESTAURANT PROBLEM

ANSWERS

(a) Owner's net weekly income is the difference between total revenue (TR) and total costs (TC).

		£
Total Revenue = 136 meals @ £10 =		1,360
less Total Cost: comprises premises	120	
food	544	
waiters	250	
	914	
So Net Weekly Income =		**£446**

(b) Transfer earnings are the minimum wage necessary to keep the owner as the chef, i.e. what the chef (owner) could obtain elsewhere as a chef. Thus £446 less owner's acceptable **profits** equals that part which is the transfer earnings.

(c) The loss on Monday, in full cost terms, equals TR − TC=£60−£64=loss of £4. However, the premises cost of £120 or £20 per night still has to be paid and on Monday there is at least a positive contribution of £16 towards the fixed costs of the premises. This gives Total Revenue of £60 less **Total Variable Cost only** of £44, i.e. net contribution of £16. So the owner should open on Monday night.

(d) **Price Elasticities of Demand:—**

Before Price Reduction		*After Price Reduction*	
Monday	6 @ £10	11	@ £8
Tuesday	15 @ £10	21	@ £8
Monday Price Elasticity =		$\frac{.83}{.20}$	= 4.15 elasticity
Tuesday Price Elasticity =		$\frac{.33}{.20}$	= 1.65

Demand is far more price elastic on Monday than Tuesday night; though on both nights elasticities are greater than 1 (one) when the price falls from £10 to £8 a meal.

(e) **Profit Before/After Price Change** = (Variable Cost only)
Before TR — TC = £210 — £124 = +86
After TR — TC = £248 — £184 = +64
Change of £22 or less profit after price cuts.

$$\left(\begin{array}{c}\text{ignore Premises Costs of £20}\\ \text{a night, i.e. same}\\ \text{costs regardless of price.}\end{array}\right)$$

(f) **Average Cost of Labour** (waiter) on Saturday is £30 per person, as opposed to an average cost of labour £20 for the other nights.
Note: ignore chef as a labour cost.

Marginal Cost of Labour (waiter) on Saturday equals the cost of the extra waiter (3rd).

e.g. 2 @ 20 = 40   Total Cost of 2
      3 @ 30 = 90   Total Cost of 3
      ─────
      £50   M.C. of the 3rd.

So between Friday and Saturday night, the average cost of labour increases from £20 to £30 a waiter. The average cost has risen because the marginal cost of the 3rd waiter on Saturday increases from £20 to £50 or £20 plus 3 × £10 (30–20) = **£50**

BRITISH TELECOM — TELEPHONE CHARGES 1986/7

ANSWERS
1. British Telecom have a pricing tariff which seems to incorporate three factors. In the first place there is a fixed quarterly rental which depends on whether the subscriber use is domestic or business and also whether the domestic line is shared or exclusive. Secondly, there is a variable cost factor, the Unit Charge, which depends upon the time of the day, the duration of the call and the destination of the call. With regard to the time of the day, there are three times: cheap, standard and peak. The "cheap" rate is the lowest, the standard is roughly twice as expensive as the cheap rate, whilst the peak rate is around three times as expensive as the cheap rate. In most cases, though not all, it is also proportionately cheaper to phone for three minutes than for one; though in the case of the Standard time costs this does not seem to be the case. Lastly, cost increases as the destination of the call distance increases from local (up to 10 to 20 miles) to call rate "a", "b" and "b1" (around thirty five miles and over). Call rate "a" is for short distances outside "local" rates and calls

"b1" and "b" are both over thirty five miles. Rates "b1" are charges connected over low cost (well used) routes, whilst "b" rates are for the more isolated and less used routes. Note: there are **other** National tariff charges dependent upon whether calls are made by the user (STD) or connected by the operator etc., but these lie outside the scope of the data.

2. (i) In order to appreciate why rentals and unit calls are used, it is necessary to understand the Overall Cost Structure of British Telecom. British Telecom has a great deal of capital invested in exchanges, cables and other communication systems. These go to make up the fixed costs it must cover and for which the subscriber pays a rental. This could be seen as an average fixed cost. At the same time there will be variable power and labour costs etc. (marginal costs) which will vary and depend upon the time of the day and the distance the call covers and so on, i.e. unit charges.

(ii) As mentioned above, the unit call charges can be seen as variable (marginal) costs and in a sense these will vary the greater the distance covered. This is why overall local costs are low and calls over 35 miles generally high. Of course, this is not true in all cases and indeed between large towns where extensive exchange systems have been installed, increased use is encouraged by lowering variable costs in order to exploit capital economies of scale. Furthermore, more intensive use ("long" phone calls) is also encouraged over the destination tariff so as to exploit capital economies of scale.

(iii) Over the whole system, charges vary according to the time of the day the call is made and economics can explain this in two ways. As above, one could argue that "peak" rates are high because the system incurs high variable labour and power costs, possibly because the system operates above its most efficient level. A more usual explanation is that rates vary because price discrimination is practiced in order to generate a demand for the overall system which maximises profit. Price discrimination is possible when users can be identified and separated and also when demand elasticities vary. Therefore the high peak rates can be seen as a relatively high charge to businessmen who have an inelastic demand for communications and who, therefore, will be willing to pay. This would also include domestic users who have to make essential calls. The cheap off peak rates can be seen as attempts to encourage the domestic user, who has a generally more elastic demand schedule for the most part, to use the phone rather than the postal service to communicate. The first and second class internal letter post rate illustrates "differential" pricing since the two services are being offered, based upon speed of delivery. Thus discriminatory pricing can be seen as a way by which British Telecom maintains an even flow of demand on the service. If for example peak rates were not used, demand may be so excessive between 9.00am and 1.00pm that other expensive capital equipment would have to be installed which might then lie idle for the rest of the day. This problem of expensive over capacity which other Nationalised Industries have to cope with has to some extent been solved by using differential pricing. Naturally, though price discrimination is exercised by the monopolistic British Telecom, it could also be argued that even in the case of time call rate variations, some operating variable costs will differ at different times of the day so price discrimination may not be the complete answer.

3. Prior to 1985 British Telecom (BT) had been a Nationalised monopolistic supplier of telephone/communication systems in the UK. In 1985 the government "privatised" BT by selling its assets, in the form of ordinary shares, to the British public, and this allowed BT to operate as a fully fledged equity owned Public Company rather than a public corporation. It was argued that by transferring ownership from the taxpayer to the shareholder, competition would increase efficiency and all would benefit Service would improve and governments would benefit from corporation tax on profits made etc. However, some argue that private ownership does not guarantee efficiency and attempts should be made to improve competition within the sector. It is argued that without effective government control BT, as a monopolistic supplier, could increase prices, exploit profits and operate against the public interest by cutting loss-making services (lines) it no longer has a responsibility to maintain. Following the work of Prof. Baumol who discussed "contestable" circumstances as a more important criteria than market structure, it is argued that BT should have to compete with other communication suppliers and private ownership merely maintains a monopolistic order (in much the same way as British Gas in 1986) and does nothing to improve efficiency or reduce the likelihood of consumer exploitation. Indeed research shows B.T. to be one of the least efficient Telecoms organisations when compared to her European counterparts.

Note: Figs. 1/2/3 illustrate the economics of price discrimination. Fig.1 shows what happens when all pay the same price, whilst Figs. 2/3 show peak and off-peak pricing respectively. Costs are the same in both markets but by charging P_2 and P_3, profits in both markets are in excess of the single market price of P_1.

170 Supply-Theory of The Firm

PRICE DISCRIMINATION AND TELEPHONE CALLS
— THE THEORETICAL MODEL

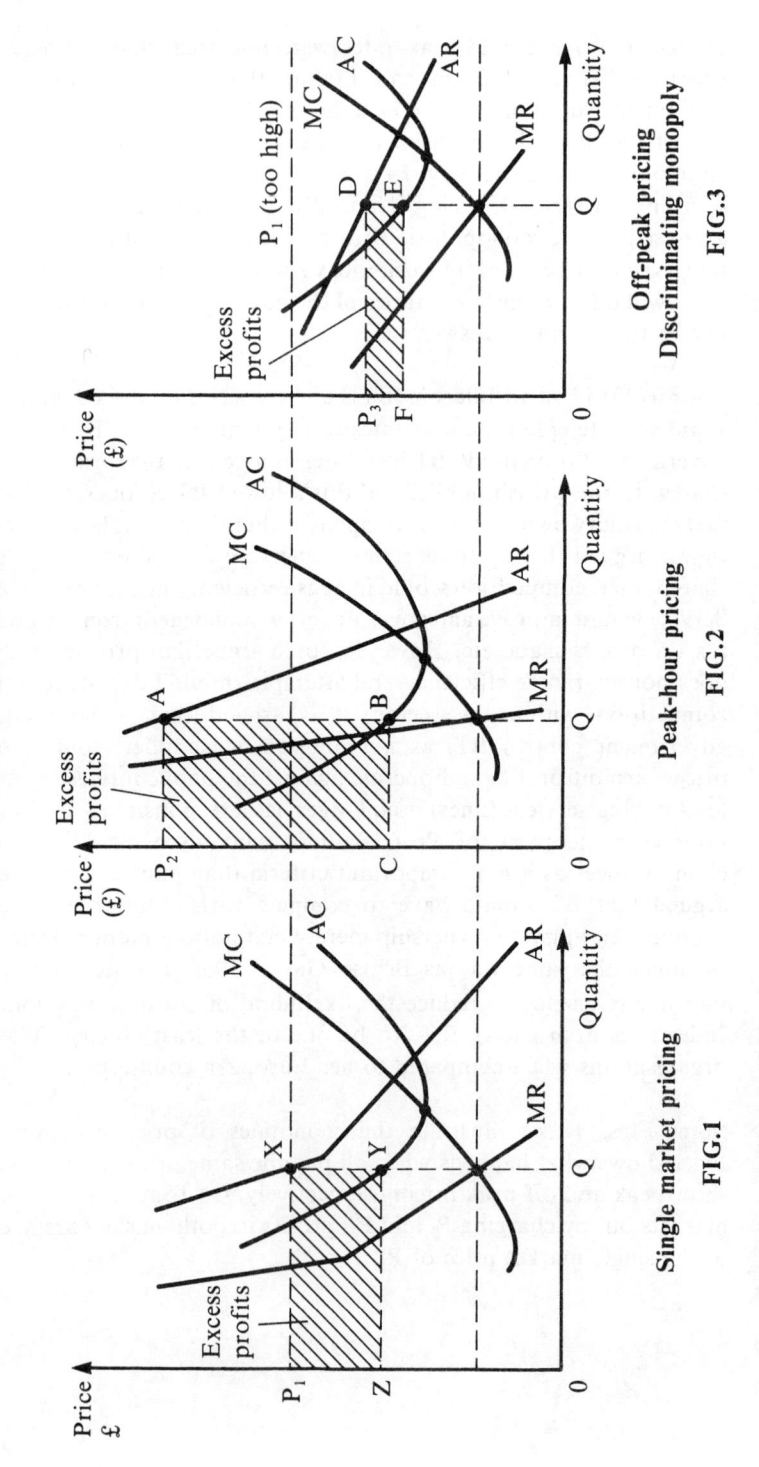

FIG.1 Single market pricing

FIG.2 Peak-hour pricing

FIG.3 Off-peak pricing / Discriminating monopoly

COMBINED COSTS/REVENUE

INDEPENDENT COSTS/REVENUE

FULL COST OR MARGINAL COST PRICING

ANSWER
Method/Calculations
In order to provide a complete answer, the total cost and revenue situation for each producer should be calculated on the basis of how much of a contribution to fixed costs each one makes. This is shown below.

	£'s	A	B	C	Total
So	Direct Materials	42,000	104,000	61,200	207,200
	Labour	54,000	80,000	91,800	225,800
	Variable O/heads	86,400	128,000	146,880	361,280
	Variable Direct	182,400	312,000	299,880	794,280
	Sales	235,500	322,000	363,600	921,100
So	Contribution to fixed costs =	+53,100	+10,000	+63,720 =	126,820
			less fixed O/heads		90,320
			= Profit		36,500

Total Fixed O/h
£'s
A = 21,600
B = 32,000
C = 36,720
      90,320

The above costing emphasises the contribution each product makes to fixed costs which anyway have to be paid at least in the short term. Thus on this basis there is a total profit of £36,500 and although B makes a loss of £22,000 if fixed overheads are allocated to each product (full or absorption costing) it still makes a positive contribution of £10,000 towards fixed overheads for all products, and hence should be maintained. If Product B was scrapped the fixed overheads of £90,320 would still remain and would have to be borne by Products A and C; so profits of the two would reduce by £10,000 to a total of £26,500. In terms of the original full cost data Product B is a loss maker and should be discontinued, but on the basis of contribution costing the opposite is true.

PRICE DISCRIMINATION AND THE MONOPOLIST

ANSWERS

(1) From the Cost and Demand schedules etc., the following (Table 1) regarding Revenue and Costs can be calculated.

TABLE 1

Price		Quantity	Total Revenue			Total Cost	Profit TR − TC		
(a)	(b)		(a)	(b)	(c)	(Fixed + Variable)	(a)	(b)	(c)
70	60	1	70	60	60	150	−80	−90	−90
65	55	2	130	110	115	195	−65	−85	−80
60	50	3	180	150	165	230	−50	−80	−65
55	45	4	220	180	210	250	−30	−70	−40
50	40	5	250	200	250	255	−5	−55	−5
*45−	35	−6*	270	210	285	260	*+10	−50	+25
40	30	7	280	210	315	285	*−5	−75	+30
35	25	8	280	200	340	370	−90	−170	−30

The monopolist will set a price and output level so that profits are maximised — in equilibrium — and from the table this will be at output level 6 and price 45. See Price, Profit and Total Revenue (a). At all other levels, losses are made.

(2) If less is now demanded at all prices, new total revenues and hence profits — see (b) in the table — have to be calculated. In the new circumstances, the profit maximising, loss minimising monopolist, will sell at the same price 6, minimising the loss to 50.

(3) If the monopolist could engage in perfect price discrimination he could charge prices from 60 to 25, i.e. along the demand schedule. Total Revenue (c) is now calculated cumulatively, e.g. 60, 115, etc. Since the monopolist can segment the market at each price. From the table it can be seen that prices can be charged from 60 to 30 and up to seven units will be supplied each at a different price to the consumer. Profit is maximised, i.e. 30, with up to seven different prices being charged, 60 to 30.

(4) In order for the above policy (c) to succeed, the monopolist must be able to physically segment each market and stop reselling taking place between those buying at the low price of say 30 and those who will purchase at the higher prices, i.e. above 30 etc. In terms of economic theory, each consumer has a different elasticity for the product, i.e. those purchasing at 60 and 55 have an inelastic demand, whilst those

purchasing at 30 will only do so when the price falls, i.e. elasticity is greater than one. Lastly, for the policy to succeed, the monopolist must be able to stop new entrants coming in and also convince the government that consumers are not being exploited for excessive profits.

THE MONOPOLIST AND COMPETITION

SHORT ANSWERS

(a) Calculate total costs/revenue for each price level so that a maximum profit is shown at a price of 14 for the monopolist. Demand is 50 and profit per unit is 2.5 or 75 in all. See Table 1.

TABLE 1

To Calculate Profit etc.

	Price	Demand (q)	T.R.	VC+	FC	= TC	Profit = (TR−TC)
	20	20	400	260	200	460	−60
	18	30	540	370	200	570	−20
	16	40	640	460	200	660	−20
monopolistic →	14	50	700	425	200	625	75
	12	60	720	460	200	660	60
competitive/imported →	10	70	700	500	200	700	0
	8	80	640	680	200	880	−240

(b) The competitive industries' long term equilibrium is where total costs and revenue are equal, i.e. ac=ar. This is when price is 10, demand 70, so total revenue/cost is 700: AR=p=AC=10. Assuming AC includes normal profit.

(c) Under perfect competition output expands to the lowest long run average cost optimum capacity, see (b). Each firm attempts to maximise profits and with free entry average cost falls. However, there is a possibility that unit costs could increase later as diseconomies of scale set in.

(d) (i) If a world price of 10 existed and the monopolist insisted on a price of 14 demand would fall. However, if the monopolist reduced price to 10 and left output at 50 with average unit costs of 12.5 there would be a **loss** of 2.5 per unit or 125 in total.
(ii) If the monopolist changed its marketing policy and set a price in line with the imported price, it would mean an increase in output from 50 to 70 and thus lead to normal profits being earned, as price = AC = 10. However, the monopolist could rationalise, cut cost and earn above normal profits. If it engaged in advertising and product differentiation,

174 Supply-Theory of The Firm

it could distinguish its product from the imported one and hence revert to the price/output outlined in answer (a) above.

Diagrammatically, the Monopolistic/competitive situation can be seen in Fig.1.

FIG.1

The Monopolist and Changing Market Conditions

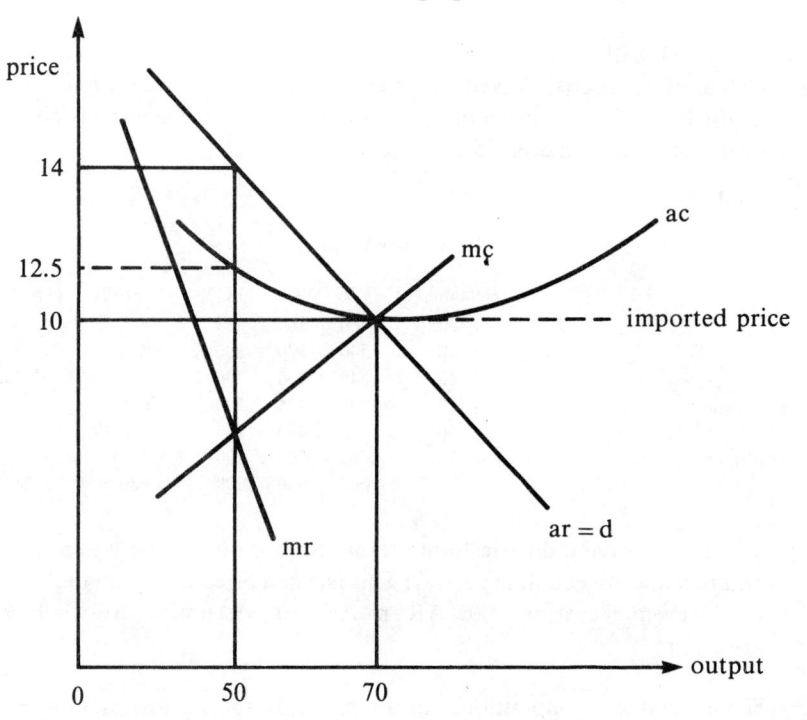

THE PUBLISHER AS MONOPOLIST

ANSWER
Draw up the Table using the information in the data.

(a)/(b) Price	Revenue	Royalty	Net Revenue	Variable Cost	Contribution to fixed costs	
1.00	60,000	(6,000)	54,000	60,000	− 6,000	(Author)
1.25	50,000	5,000	45,000	40,000	5,000	
1.50	52,500	5,250	47,250	35,000	(12,250)	(Publisher)
1.75	35,000	3,500	31,500	20,000	11,500	
2.00	20,000	2,000	18,000	10,000	8,000	

(d) Price	Demand increases by 20% Net revenue	Variable Cost	Contribution to fixed costs	NOTE: Net revenue = Total Sales less royalty
1.00	64,800	90,000	−25,200	
1.25	54,000	60,000	− 6,000	
1.50	56,700	52,500	4,200	
1.75	37,800	30,000	7,800	(Colour)
2.00	21,600	15,000	6,600	

SHORT ANSWERS

(a) Calculate total revenue less royalty, i.e. net revenue at each price. Deduct variable costs from net revenue to give maximum contribution to fixed costs. This maximises profits at £1.50 a copy, i.e. Profits are £12,250 − £10,000 = £2,250.

(b) The author's royalty is maximised at the largest sales revenue, i.e. 10% of £60,000 or at a price of £1. (This implies a conflict between author and publisher over price/output levels).

(c) The variable costs of producing four books equals 4 × £1 = £4 plus the royalty on 3 books sold of 45p so cost = £4.45. The marginal revenue is 3 × £1.50 = £4.50. Therefore one free copy increases profits by £4.50 − £4.45 = 5p. Although a profit of 5p is made, this would hardly cover postage and so the publisher would advise the author to reduce his list. Perhaps the publisher could use more cost-effective publicity, e.g. Advertising.

(d) If the publisher decides to print in colour, given the conditions, the contribution to the fixed costs of £10,000 are maximised at a price of £1.75 but even here there will be a loss of £2,200 — the smallest loss — but nevertheless enough to deter the publisher from going ahead!

176 Supply-Theory of The Firm

THE SIZE OF THE CITY — "CIVIS"

ANSWERS

1. As the city grows in size the marginal cost of production falls due to internal and external economies of scale. Since overall city size increases demand rises and so the overall scale of production increases and so bigger producing units can exploit production, marketing and capital economies etc. At the same time, the increasing size of the city means there is a readily available and possibly trained and skilled labour force and other commercial and financial related services which develop alongside the factories etc. These latter influences are external economies of scale and further increase efficiency thus lowering unit and marginal costs. Around the output level of oq_2 these economies are maximised and MCP starts to level out. Whilst production can benefit from manufacturing and capital intensive methods transport, by its very nature, tends to be a service occupation and overall labour intensive and limited in how far economies of scale can be exploited. As the city grows in size, these gains from capital intensive use are quickly exploited and soon diminishing returns set in as labour and other associated social costs begin to rise. **Note:** The same analysis applies in other service activities such as schools and hospitals where scale soon brings about diseconomies because of the organisational problems associated with labour intensive personal services.

2. The analysis regarding the size of "Civis" is similar to that for the individual competitive firm and overall market equilibrium. If the market price of the product "Civis" specialises in is at op_2 then the city will increase in size until $MC=p_2$ at a size of oq_2; even though marginal transport costs are high at this output level. Any change in the price of the product will bring about a different city size which will be dependent upon the city's overall marginal cost curve. At oq_2 the size of the city will not be at its lowest average cost or its optimum scale of production.

3. If cheap imports occur at a price of op_1, then these will underprice the "Civis" product price of op_2. The city will be forced to cut back production, and hence the size of the city, until its costs fall to op_1, at an output of oq_1. This will lead to an equivalent reduction in output, jobs and an under-utilisation of dwellings, factories and roads etc. of oq_2-oq_1. In the real world this flexible adjustment process may not happen, as the theory predicts, because inhabitants of a city do not necessarily work in one specific industry or firm or indeed within the city. For example, householders commute to other industries or other adjacent towns so the size of the city, in terms of houses etc, could remain at oq_2 even with the imported price of op_1. In this case oq_2-oq_1 would represent commuters

or those engaged in other sectors of the economy. Moreover, if cheap imports disappeared, there is no reason to suppose, in the absence of commuters etc, that the city could increase in size to oq_2. This is because it takes time for planning permissions to enable businessmen to invest in new plant, machinery, factories, and even houses etc. In other words, the above analysis requires a degree of competition and mobility which is not apparent in real world industry, markets or regions etc.

RESOURCE ALLOCATION IN OLIGOPOLISTIC INDUSTRIAL MARKETS

ANSWERS

(a) The economic problem is one of allocating scarce resources between alternative ends. Using the market, the price mechanism is normally supposed to function to help overcome the economic problem and help allocate according to ability to pay and choice rather than need, which is the criteria adopted by the State. Specifically the price system reflects consumer choice and demand patterns and as these change producers vary what and how much they produce in response, i.e. profits or losses are signals to the producer. At the same time, the producer employs resources and factor markets allocate land, labour, capital and enterprise according to profits and demand. Wages, rent, profits and interest are the factor prices and again are subject to demand and supply, i.e. market forces, as are product prices. This leads to resources moving between occupations and industries in order to obtain the best return and factor incomes are the information signals motivating resource movement. In effect the price system helps the consumer, producer and factor income earner decide how, where, when and what to spend, produce and earn so resources are moved speedily and efficiently. According to Galbraith industrial markets are not free competitive markets, assumed in the above analysis, and are unresponsive to demand and cost changes because industrial prices are fixed for considerable periods of time and so prices will not reflect true demand or resource costs. Hence these prices will not be able to communicate accurate information about what and how much to produce and both consumers and income earners will be misled because the signals of prices, costs, profits, etc. are not valid. In the long term, industrial markets will thus become inefficient.

(b) Neo-classical economic theory presumes that monopolies and oligopolies exist to maximise profits, often at the expense of the consumer. This means that prices will be set above marginal costs, output will be less than under competitive conditions and profits will be above normal, i.e. the behaviour could be against the public interest. Galbraith's analysis means that stable pricing could exist at other than profit maximising levels. Indeed in terms of the typical monopolistic diagram price could be stable at the lowest point on the average cost curve (the optimum) at competitive output levels, if industrial oligopolistic or monopolistic producers so desired. This may be in order to maximise market share, sales, normal profit levels or generally improve public relations, etc. This "satisficing" behaviour could mean that the public benefits with lower costs, more output, etc. even though such monopolists or oligopolists fix price and do not compete on price. It could also be argued that the markets described by Galbraith are generally oligopolistic and subject to co-operative price cartel arrangements aimed at satisfactory profit levels, etc. This means, as above, short term price could be lower than profit maximising and not against the public interest. Of course in the long term industrial producers seeking long term survival could set price to maximise profits at the expense of the consumer (public).

(c) Profit maximising behaviour is the prediction of the neo-classical theory of the firm and it depends upon monopolists setting output to marginal cost and marginal revenue and thence price to demand. The implications are obvious. These are that firms wish solely to maximise profits, that marginal revenue and marginal cost are known, that firms are independent of other firms' behaviour and that there are no constraints placed on their behaviour such as Governmental anti-monopoly legislation, etc. In the short term at least, industrial firms may not accord with these behavioural assumptions and hence Galbraith's assertion regarding other goals may be valid. Corporations are owned by shareholders and run by managers and so there is a divorce of ownership and control which allows the employed managers to pursue a variety of corporate objectives. Of course a profit has to be made, viz capital employed, that is satisfactory for raising new investment and making dividend payments to shareholders but modern corporations often attempt to maximise sales revenue, market share, employee happiness, governmental approval, etc. Furthermore, management may not be aware of marginal revenue or costs so price setting may be in line with industry costs and include an average profit mark up. This may result in standard stable industrial prices, especially if labour and capital costs are common. In oligopolistic markets where standard profit and costs apply and where raw material markets change little, i.e. are mature, e.g. chemicals, stable pricing behaviour is predicted on the basis of the "kinked demand curve". This theory suggests price cutting in industrial oligopolistic markets will be followed by other firms so market share remains constant but revenue falls. Any corporation that increases price finds the others not following suit so overall stable prices would be the best policy in oligopolistic markets. Thus stable prices in these markets would be the rational behaviour of firms not wishing to maximise short term profits at the expense of long term survival. Lastly, it is reasonable to expect that corporations subject to government scrutiny will not seek always to exploit the consumer to make maximum profits. Many industries are subject to direct government control, e.g. Nationalised, and even those that are not are subject to Monopolies Commission investigation, so they may play down profit maximisation in order to improve Public Relations. Nevertheless, in times of depression, financial markets will insist upon long term capital returns (profit) consistent with overall market yields, e.g. interest rates. In pursuing this objective, companies may pursue non-profit maximising behaviour in order to ensure survival, but ultimately long term profit maximising would seem to be the main aim.

SUPPLY COSTS

SHORT ANSWERS
(a) Firm A's cost behaves as a typical 'U' shaped cost curve subject to diminishing returns whilst C's illustrates the 'L' shaped behaviour of output economies to scale. Firm A is likely to be a small scale, competitive service sector firm with a high variable cost input which reaches its optimum at low output levels. Firm C is likely to be a large scale, capital intensive manufacturing unit, possibly a monopolist, which advertises in order to increase output to exploit economies of scale and maximise profits. Firm A is likely to be a "price taker" whilst C could be a "price maker".

(b) Efficiency can be interpreted in terms of the optimum or lowest average total cost as it can be seen in terms of the lowest ATC over the whole output range. In the case of the former firm B is the most efficient but thereafter unit costs rise at a faster rate than firm A's. However, firm A experiences a slightly higher optimum cost than B but thereafter manages to keep costs from rising as fast as B's so in this sense firm A may be seen as the most efficient, i.e. its marginal cost rises less fast than B's.

Chapter 22
STRUCTURE OF INDUSTRY, SCALE and LOCATION

THE NATIONAL BUS COMPANY — A PROBLEM OF FINANCE

ANSWERS

(a) Private and Public Commercial Companies usually structure their capital liabilities to include a mixture of loan debt (mortgage) and share or risk capital; sometimes known as equity. The precise nature of the mix is indicated by the company in its Balance Sheet. Loan or debt capital receives an interest whilst ordinary share capital receives a dividend from the earnings after interest has been paid. If there is no dividend to pay because of a recession it is sometimes possible, in the case of cumulative preference shares, to delay this payment until times are better. In the case of N.C.B. its entire capital is composed of debt, so it has a large interest commitment every year which means it could be vulnerable to a recession or to high interest rates. The extent of these debt interest payments were £10m in 1981 which, it is alleged, are unreasonable and uncommercial because other commercial companies do not maintain a 100% debt form of capital, i.e. they are never "geared" so highly and hence so committed financially to interest payments. Furthermore, because NCB maintained uneconomic services, at the government's request, it also has another £4m in debts which it would not have had if it had been free to operate as a Commercial Company. It alleges the insistence of the government that these debts be paid is unreasonable. The effect of that is that because it **has** to pay out such a large amount of interest it is unable to retain some of its earnings in order to provide for future investment, which could enable it to improve its service and overall efficiency levels.

(b) Nationalised Bus Companies have to operate to achieve a variety of objectives which often conflict. As a Nationalised Company, politicians may insist it maintains uneconomic social services and this means it may be subject to political pressures. At the same time, it must try to operate in a commercially efficient manner so that it can break-even and provide for future investment. However, commercially efficient operations may mean cutting out socially required services which may lead to public criticism. Also Nationalised Bus Services have to use the income from profit making services to subsidise loss making, socially needed services which reduces its ability to invest in equipment, e.g. new buses. At the end of the day the general public may not feel they have an efficient bus operator and the quality of services suffer because they have to stretch their bus operating resources too thinly. If, at the same time the government allows private companies to compete then the problems of the Nationalised Bus Companies worsen.

The objectives of a private bus operator will be primarily to make a profit in order to satisfy its shareholders. This means it is unlikely to be subject to political pressures but it will most likely have to compete with others; this may not be the case with a Nationalised bus operator who may well be given a local monopoly by the government. The problem of the private operator will then be one of maintaining a competitive service which generates enough income to provide an acceptable market rate of return on capital invested. If this return on capital is not forthcoming it will be difficult for the company to maintain future investment since it will not be able to rely upon government subsidies or capital grants etc. Again, the private bus operator will most likely have to compete with other operators for its routes and market share and though not necessarily subject to governmental and political scrutiny, it will still have to satisfy customers, investors and other financiers that it is worth investing in.

U.K. REGIONAL LIVING STANDARDS 1975, 1985

ANSWERS
1. The overall regional distribution of income pattern in the UK is heavily concentrated in favour of three areas: Greater London, the South East and East Anglia. Otherwise the rest of the UK have average incomes per head below the average, i.e. less than 100. Since 1975 the West Midlands has declined and East Anglia has developed to become the average region, i.e. around 100.

2. (i) The lowest GDP per head 1985 is N. Ireland with an average GDP per head 25.9% less than average, i.e. 100 — 74.1.
   (ii) The highest GDP per head 1985 is Greater London with an average GDP per head 25.7% above average, i.e. 100 — 125.7.
   (iii) Fastest annual decline in growth of GDP per head between 1975-85 was the West Midlands, i.e. So $\frac{92.3-100}{10} = \frac{7.7}{10} = .77$
   (iv) Fastest annual growth in GDP per head 1975-85 was

   East Anglia ie. $\frac{100.7-92.8}{10} = \frac{7.2}{10} = +.72$

3. Regional variations in GDP per head reflect overall patterns of income, population, investment, market and employment growth and govern-

ment policy. For the most part overall investment, income and spending levels have been high in the South East over this period, as new 'high-tech', commercial and financial service industries have grown faster than the working population. In the rest of the economy overall manufacturing output and investment in the older staple industries, e.g. coal, shipbuilding, cars, etc. have declined due to world recession, world competition and because since the late 1970's the government has tended to allow market forces to shift resources and expenditure towards the South East and Europe. As overall income levels reduced in the North, etc. the income 'multiplier' effect further reduced regional GDP levels. When account is taken of the general drift of the working population to the South East overall GDP has fallen faster in the North than the figures indicate. Furthermore, account should also be taken of regional variations in unemployment rates. In the main, high employment and low vacancy rates in, e.g. The South East, tend to attract industries because of the size of the market and overall spending power. Income levels in the North, etc. are low since the industries located there tend to produce low net value added output and the lower average earnings reflect this fact and so high unemployment rates keep earnings low. The fall in GDP in Northern Ireland is to some extent explained by civil disturbances and the political problem.

4. Since the Second World War governments of all complexions have attempted to reduce regional variations in GDP by providing financial inducements to firms moving to the depressed areas and by discouraging those wishing to set up in the prosperous areas, e.g. The South. These policies were implemented through the Development Area schemes which aimed at attracting capital and hence work to the unemployed in the North etc. On the whole, these policies did little to change the overall "league positions" and it is arguable whether GDP per head variations would have worsened without this government assistance. However, this is difficult to measure precisely without considering how much financial support has been provided over the period since the War. Nevertheless, in 1986 there would be two extreme views presented based on these figures. Extreme right wing free market views would argue that regional variations in GDP per head indicate the natural growth and decline of areas and this process should be allowed to continue unhindered. This is so resources, e.g. labour etc., then move to the high growth areas until the costs of living and investing in the S.E. become so high compared to the rest of the country that entrepreneuers will once more be attracted to low cost, low GDP areas such as the West Midlands etc. To try to stop this natural drift of resources and hence reduce regional income disparities will, according to their view, be self defeating and unnecessarily expensive. On the other hand, "Labour" party policies might argue that such regional disparities in income cannot be allowed or encouraged

because markets may not work to reverse the trend and because the social problems of falling regional income levels have become too expensive. They could also argue that without the financial help given through the Development Areas policies, both home and foreign investment levels might have been lower and so per capita differences would have been greater than they are today. Unemployment tends to be higher in the lowest GDP per head areas because overall income levels are low. It is not always possible for the unemployed to move to obtain work elsewhere because housing costs vary and because the local income multiplier will result in yet more job losses as work moves to other areas. From this point of view it may be argued that positive government investment and business encouragement should be given, on a regional basis, to provide work and income in an attempt to reduce the high regional variations in income per head as indicated, by the table. However, since many believe it costs up to £45,000 per head in government grants to provide for a job in the depressed regions, it may be argued that it is too high a price to pay. Some economists maintain that "Development Areas" policies created 15% of UK employment in the 1960's and 1970's.

THE CHANGING PATTERN OF ALCOHOL SALES

SHORT ANSWERS
(a) The level of sales has risen due to: price inflation, greater real disposable income, greater availability of outlets, more population above the age limit, more TV advertisements (sponsorship), social trends, lower relative prices due to lower alcohol tax etc.

(b) **Pubs' share declined due to** 1) high 'pub' prices due to oligopolistic practices; 2) reduction in number of pub outlets; 3) social trends towards other forms of drinking at home etc. and **away** from "pubs". **Off-Licences' and Supermarkets' share has risen** due to 1) cheaper relative prices in these outlets because of competition; 2) greater availability and choice of alcohol in supermarkets, e.g. in multiples such as Marks & Spencer, Sainsbury's own brands etc.; 3) more wine bought in off-licences etc. because of increase in drinking at home, dinner parties, cheaper wine etc.

THE BOOK PUBLISHING INDUSTRY —
COMPETITIVE STRUCTURES

SHORT ANSWERS
1. Book clubs operated by major publishers and booksellers, attempt by price discrimination to reach a wider market and so exploit economies of

scale in production. They use direct mail methods of promotion to reach a wider consuming public who might otherwise never visit a bookshop.

2. "Authors" appear to be in a very competitive market of sellers with free entry. "Publishers" protected by copyright operate as competitive (i.e. relative freedom of entry) monopolists because of copyright barriers. In the non-fiction rights market the "BCA" appears as a powerful monopolistic buyer whilst "booksellers", though numerous and independent, sell at a standard net price and hence operate a price cartel.

3. The impact on **authors** is that unit royalty reduces (though total revenue may increase as unit sales rise). However, the lack of competition in buying their original manuscripts may reduce future opportunities. **Publishers** seem to gain economies of scale and increase unit profit on standard editions. **Booksellers,** whilst appreciating overall reading habits may increase, fear a loss of market control and also industry revenue. Ultimately the **consumer** may suffer as choice of authors, outlets and material diminishes because book clubs dominate and only pick the most popular works and saleable books.

PRIVATISATION AND NATIONALISED INDUSTRIES

ANSWERS

1. The nationalisation of monopolies enables the community to gain technical efficiency via the exploitation of economies of scale and using pricing/output policies reduce the allocative inefficiencies usually associated with private monopolies, e.g. price above marginal cost etc. Also nationalisation avoids the waste of competition due to duplication of effort and advertising etc. The passage argues in favour of one unit production in order to gain these advantages as well as serving national needs etc. Industries mentioned in Quadrant A could help to reduce price because of scale economies subject to adequate consumer safeguards being made. Those industries mentioned in Quadrant B, if privatised, could reduce services and increase unemployment. If they remained nationalised, adequate safeguards might be made regarding the level of service and jobs.

2. Since competition would be missing in those industries privatised in Quadrants A and B, other controls that could be used to safeguard the public interest are (1) limiting profits to a certain level; (2) the setting up of investigative and regulatory authority; (3) operating a system to outlaw the worst abuses of monopoly power; (4) encourage foreign competition.

Structure of Industry, Scale and Location 185

3. The original article placed the industries in the following quadrants: the NCB and CEGB in C, the others in D. The overall arguments revolved around demand prospects, scope for competition and similarities with existing and comparable privatised industries. The problems which might result from privatisation could be job losses due to reduction in overall service and an increase in foreign competition etc. Also excessive monopoly profits may still be made, e.g. British Telecom (1986) and relative inefficiency could still exist.

CHANGING MARKETS AND THE BREWING INDUSTRY

ANSWERS
1. The amalgamation of the industry proceeded in order to exploit distribution, marketing, capital and technical economies of scale. The result was overall, a concentrated oligopolistic market structure with, price stability. The brewing industry now operates as a price cartel.

2. The main market conditions have been (a) changing consumers' taste towards real ale and local brews and (b) rising costs of distribution which for the large brewer have reduced the gains from plant size. These factors have allowed the small brewer to grow and compete, i.e. "specialisation is limited by the extent of the market". However, the major brewers have retaliated by (i) developing their own new local brews/brand names, (ii) extensive advertising campaigns, promotions and (iii) selective price cutting designed to compete with the small brewer and the overall impact of falling incomes due to the recession, (iv) the large breweries have also diversified into Hotels and Leisure as well as seeking to expand output by increasing their sales to off-licences and supermarkets.

3. The overall market structure is oligopolistic viz. Public houses and some hotels with some regional monopolies, e.g. "Courage" in the Thames Valley. There has been little price competition and there is evidence of a collusive price cartel. However, competition exists in new product development, e.g. New Ales/Lagers, and in advertising. Many managed tied outlets buy spirits from the Brewer at above "off-license" prices. This is evidence of price discrimination and monopoly profits accruing to tied houses owned by the large monopolistic brewers. The fact that beer "pub" prices vary according to regions whilst off-licence beer prices do not is symptomatic of an oligopolistic brewing industry able to maintain regional price discrimination in pubs but unable to do so in off-licences because of competition. The Monopolies Commission is currently (Jan. 1987) investigating high 'pub' prices for beer in the face of declining national sales.

THE U.K. WOOLLEN AND WORSTED AND ELECTRICAL MACHINERY INDUSTRIES — A CASE STUDY IN INDUSTRIAL STRUCTURES

ANSWERS

(a) (i) In terms of output the Electrical Machinery industry (EM) produces £935.8m of output compared to the £428.0m of the Woollen and Worsted (WW), making the output of the electrical industry over twice that of the woollen and worsted. In employment terms there are 140.9 thousand and 84.9 thousand in the electrical machinery and woollen and worsted industries respectively, a disproportionately larger number in woollen and worsted when compared to output. However, for both industries, the small unit establishment employing 1-199 dominates, accounting for 84% of all establishments in electrical and 78% in woollen and worsted.

(ii) In the electrical machinery industry the major share of both output and employment is provided by those large establishments employing 4,000 and over. These establishments provide 45% employment and 52% output of the whole industry. Indeed, these figures correspond to those for the five largest in the industry. In the woollen and worsted the overall establishment size is smaller since the two largest classes are 1500-1999 and 2000 and over, compared to 1500-3999 and 4000 and over for the EM. In the WW the corresponding employment and output figures for the largest units, expressed as percentages of the total industry figure, are 28 and 28, so the largest account for a smaller percentage of the total. In other words, the smaller units provide both more output and employment, e.g. the smallest (1-199) provides 27% of employment and 26% of output. For the EM industry the small scale 1-199 only provides 15% employment and 13% output. Looked at another way in EM the largest 11 enterprises representing less than 10% of the total enterprises and 7% of the establishments supplied 62% of both the jobs and output in the industry. In conclusion, in the EM the share of output and jobs is concentrated in the largest units whilst for the WW output and employment is more widely dispersed over the large, medium and small scale unit. Note: In both EM and WW as the size of the enterprise increases it controls more establishments (plants). Note: 'The Lorenz Curve', described in the Statistical Section, could be used to illustrate the above, viz. the "Concentration ratio".

(b) The average wage of "operatives" and "others" in EM is £3,084 and £3,771, whilst for WW the figures are £2,483 and £3,483 respectively. Explanations of such wage differences would be as follows. The productivity of the workforce could be higher in EM due to economies of scale and plant capital investment, which is reflected in the overall larger unit scale of production. Furthermore, unionisation of EM could be further advanced than in the WW industry so wage negotiations could favour the EM worker. Overall the prices of the EM output could be higher, due to more monopolistic conditions, so marginal revenue product could be larger. In the WW industry competition within the industry and the fear of cheap imports may have resulted in more competitive woollen and worsted products and hence a lower marginal revenue product per worker.

(c) Economies of scale will be reflected in the fact that output per head rises as the scale of production increases. In this case the scale of production will be represented by the size of the establishment viz its employment. In EM output per head of £7355 is highest in those establishments employing 4000 and over. In the WW output per head is stable over the range of enterprise sizes and certainly not greatest in the largest units. In fact, output per head is similar at all levels of output, indeed the smallest unit size compares favourably with the largest. Furthermore, the evidence of capital expenditure by management on plant suggests that they recognise this fact because whilst net capital expenditure, a source of economies of scale, is concentrated in the largest units for EM, it is dispersed over all unit sizes for WW.

(d) (i) The degree of concentration of market power can be measured by calculating the percentage employment, output and net capital expenditure for the largest enterprises. In EM these figures for the five largest enterprises, representing .45% of all enterprises, were 47%, 52% and 50%. Similar figures for the five largest enterprises in the WW industry, representing .63% of all enterprises, were 28%, 26% and 18%; much lower figures. Thus the market power lies with the largest enterprises in the EM industry, and the biggest in the WW have, by comparison, far less power.

(ii) The **actual** market power of the largest enterprises in an industry may not always correspond to the extent of their concentration ratios. As Prof. Baumol claims, the actual market power can be measured in terms of "contestable" pressures (ease of entry and exit from a market) and high concentration ratios can exist alongside low profit rates, thus indicating relatively low market power. The actual market power of the largest enterprises in each industry would be affected by the following. Government control of monopoly power is exercised through the Monopolies Commission which would be able to investigate any misuse of such power in terms of excessive price or profits, etc. The existence of large units is often accompanied by strong, well organised trade unions which can counterbalance the negotiating power of the largest enterprises. At the same time the existence of large oligopolistic markets at the raw material stage for the EM and WW can reduce the market power of large scale enterprises. Overall the degree of competition, e.g. freedom of entry or exist, could mean the large enterprises in the EM could be forced to seek efficient methods and the largest five units may engage in fierce competition, i.e. they may not operate cartel price arrangements. On the other hand, the WW industry, though widely dispersed in terms of output, may operate a cartel to control price and output so it may reduce the actual market power of the leaders who fix output and price levels for the whole industry. Import control could either increase or reduce competition in both industries so the actual market power of the largest enterprises could be irrelevant. Finally, changing demand forces could mean the largest enterprises in both industries could produce unwanted goods and so have little influence over the market. Indeed, research has shown that in many industries which are subject to demand pressures, highest profit levels are gained by firms who can fulfil new demands quickest, regardless of scale, size or nominal market power.

TAKEOVERS: WHO BENEFITS?

ANSWERS
1. The economic case for mergers depends upon the type of merger and both the cost and market conditions which result. Economic theory identifies horizontal, vertical and lateral merger structures though increasingly financial considerations such as risk spreading and improving financial results (profitability) seem to be the main motives for mergers. Horizontal mergers stress economies of scale which reduce cost and improve market control performance. Vertical mergers again stress risk spreading and the ability to control both input costs and output outlets. Generally lateral mergers stress the "managerial" economies which result when a proven Board of Directors are able to use their expertise to rejuvenate an ailing company. The large conglomerate often has a sound financial base and an overseas marketing set-up which can help exploit marketing and capital economies. If the merger presumes all these economic factors which are supposed to reduce costs, improve revenue and hence profit (efficiency), then this may also help improve overall output in the industry, etc. Thus economies of scale are exploited and market control is increased.

2. As a large, successful conglomerate BTR would presumably be able to gain from having a larger marketing base and also would be able to exploit managerial and administrative economies of scale, e.g. improved financial management, since the Board of Directors already have a proven record of profit making. BTR's large capital base could be used to increase investment in R & D on a global scale in order to compete with

French and German firms, etc. As a large conglomerate BTR could also use its industrial power by imposing more efficient practices on Pilkington with respect to manpower (unions) and overall management behaviour. Lastly, since Pilkingtons is a monopoly in U.K. glass production, BTR could be expected to use this power to increase prices and future profits within this sector.

3. The author argues that mergers may not always be successful because (a) academic research on the subject is inconclusive and (b) the German and Japanese experience of successful industrial companies has been achieved without mergers, etc.

4. a) Short term economic efficiency is reflected in high profits and share prices. In order to achieve this, future long term investment and expense in R & D often has to be reduced. Overall management strategy is sometimes to sacrifice maximum short term profits in order to provide for long term survival, growth and overall long term maximum profits. It is argued that if Pilkingtons cuts back long term R & D to boost short term profits and share prices, its overall long term efficiency will be impaired as its product efficiency will fall because R & D costs are reduced.
b) Small competitive firms, according to economic theory, are managed and owned by one person. Therefore there is no conflict between ownership and control. Large public companies do not experience this because there is a divorce of ownership (shareholders) from control (management). Management can therefore pursue a strategy of takeovers which do not necessarily increase profits because shareholders are unable to effectively curtail management's merger activities. Takeovers can be costly in both money and time for both management in the company making the bid and in the company fighting the bid. This can reduce overall profit and shareholders could suffer; usually shareholders of the company threatened with takeover find their share price increases. In all, short term profit can be the main motive rather than long term industrial and economic development.

5. At the moment any takeover of assets exceeding £5m can be referred to the Monopolies Commission who investigate and advise the Secretary of State for Industry. The criteria the Monopolies Commission use is whether the takeover bid is against the "public interest". This can mean with respect to loss of jobs, choice, or overall public standards, etc. If the takeover is not against the public interest, the bid can usually go ahead. However, some now argue (1987) that because of the present spate of takeovers, the predatory company should have to show the bid was actually in the "public interest", which may be more difficult to prove than merely not being against the public interest.

190 Structure of Industry, Scale and Location

BRITISH RAIL AND TRANSPORT RESOURCES

ANSWERS

(1) (i) The Income account shows total outgoings of £1,982m and income of £1,988m for British Rail in 1978. This gives a net surplus of £1,988m less £1,982, i.e. £6m profit.

(ii) Profitability levels are normally analysed in terms of capital employed. This indicates the yield on the invested capital. It is also useful to measure the profit earned to capital employed over a time period in order to see whether capital use is becoming more efficient. Another measure of efficiency, namely profit to sales, indicates, in the case of British Rail, a return of £6m on £1,988m turnover, a low percentage return of .3%.

(iii) The closure of "uneconomic lines" would still leave substantial overheads to be paid for. Labour/staff costs are considerable and unlikely to be reduced by much if uneconomic or loss-making lines closed. Materials, fuel and power would reduce but interest and depreciation are fixed costs and would still have to be borne. In fact, the variable costs of fuel and power and (some) material costs make up a relatively small proportion of the total outgoings.

(2) In the case of Hotels, e.g. "Gleneagles" (prior to its being sold off to private enterprise) it represented a diversification into the expanding field of tourism/leisure. This enabled B.R. to spread its financial risk, improve profitability and reduce its loss. In the case of shipping, e.g. "Sealink" ferries (before they were sold off) it enabled B.R. to provide a complete freight and passenger service to the Continent and Ireland and hence allowed administrative and market economies to be exploited. Furthermore, Shipping/Containers provided volume economies of scale to be improved since much of the service used excess rail capacity.

(3) (i) The expenditure of B.R. in 1978 indicates staff costs of £1,113m were about 56% of all outgoings and/or income. In order to meet this large wages bill, labour must increase its productivity so income (output) is increased to match outgoings (wages).

(ii) It may be difficult to increase labour productivity because labour may be regarded as a fixed factor for many of British Rail activities in the sense that it is difficult to substitute capital for labour. Whilst it may be possible to raise productivity by using "one-man" trains, who drive and act as the guard, many functions such as ticket sales, etc. are labour intensive. At the same time, strong Trade Unionism in B.R. may curtail productivity deals which reduce employment. If uneconomic lines are allowed to survive, perhaps because of political pressures, overall labour productivity will be low and as rail is generally a declining industry overall income will be difficult to boost in the face of road competition.

(4) (i) Expenditure on private and business motoring would include the cost of the road fund tax and petrol expenditure, inclusive of V.A.T., etc. The actual resource cost of transport would include the cost of road improvements, new road building and maintenance, etc. Since motorists do not pay directly for resources used but pay indirectly, via road fund and petrol tax etc., there is likely to be a difference which can boost the Chancellor's income. The excess cost of motoring may be a deliberate attempt by the government to tax the motorist by an amount equal to the "social cost" imposed so overall road use reduces.

(ii) The same argument as (d)(i) can be applied to buses and coaches except in this case they are paying less in tax than the cost they impose on the roads. In effect they are partly subsidised by the private motorist. This may be because coach tax rates are set deliberately low to encourage bus and coach use and provide an effective competition to B.R. It may also be because the bus and coach lobby in parliament is strong or persuasive in making its case, or it may be because in generating coach and bus use, by subsidising coach road use, the government wish to transfer travellers from cars to buses, etc. Thus the social costs of pollution and congestion, brought about by car use, are reduced to a socially optimum level.

(5) The support payment of £434 to British Rail in Table 1 explains the difference between expenditure by users and actual resource costs used. Such support payments are argued on the basis that B.R. provides a national network of transport and in so doing helps provide a "service" to the community. This service means uneconomic lines should be kept open so that remote communities can survive and employment can be generated. Without such subsidies many of the poor, who do not own a car, could not travel to obtain work and without an adequate bus transport system no other transport is available. It is also argued as in (d)(ii) that by subsidising train users you discourage car use which reduces overall social costs of pollution, police use, ambulance services, etc., and so improves social efficiency. Also a severely restricted B.R. service, as would happen if uneconomic lines close, would reduce the economies of scale in transporting goods which B.R. can exploit. Unit costs would rise above the long run marginal cost which indicates efficient resource use. Lastly, the support payments guarantee rail jobs and without them unemployment would rise. Many of these workers could not obtain alternative work, i.e. they have a zero opportunity cost, so it may be cheaper to subsidise their work on B.R. rather than pay them unemployment benefit.

UK CEMENT INDUSTRY RESTRAINED BY IMPORTS

ANSWERS

1. At the time (1983) cheap imported cement posed a serious threat to home cement producers. However, the fall in the value of sterling effectively made cement imports dearer and exports cheaper. This had the effect of raising the imported sterling price of cement and hence gave some relief to home producers as well as making their product more competitive in overseas export markets.

2. In terms of economic theory the UK cement manufacturers' market would be **oligopolistic** in structure; though according to UK Legislation Blue Circle Industries (BCI) would be a monopolist since it controls more than 25% of the home market. This oligopolistic market structure does not compete on price since it has formed a non-competing price cartel which controls both output and price. There were also agreed standardised prices according to areas. It is also likely that the non-competing cartel is likely to have its price set by the market leader (BCI) which is also able to influence market output because it has 55% of the market. Again, the existence of this cartel, controlling price and output, possibly led to "barriers to entry" being erected against new home producers and cheap overseas competition. The economic rationale for the existence of the cement cartel was argued by the Industry on the basis that it (i) provided local and national continuity of output for the Construction Industry; (ii) was necessary for stable capital investment and job opportunities in the cement industry, and lastly; (iii) the cement cartel, by controlling new entrants into the market, was able to provide a high quality product together with expensive technical support and back up services to the Construction Industry.

3. The importation of cement would disrupt the cartel because existing members would have to reduce their price to match the cheaper imported product. This would undermine the operation of the cartel and each member would find revenue falling. As the industry faces high fixed energy costs, the reduction in output would reduce efficiency levels, raise unit costs and so reduce profits. In such a situation producers may be tempted to undercut the cartel price and hence the industry would become competitive; price would fall but market share would not increase. Only profits would suffer. Thus outside competition would undermine and disrupt the cartel and make it more competitive.

4. The West German cement manufacturers operate a dual pricing policy for home and export markets. They may, as with UK producers, have

surplus capacity so they keep export prices down in order to generate overall efficient levels of production. This may help them keep down their costs and so keep up profit margins. Economic theory could explain cheap export prices as an attempt to cover variable costs and provide some contribution to the heavy fixed costs, e.g. energy. At the same time, they are establishing a foothold in the UK market which could be developed if UK producers lost market share. Again, if West German producers maintain a cartel they may operate the dual pricing system to maintain high profits at home and generate overall output levels which maintain minimum scales of efficiency in production. If they themselves have a home cement cartel they will not wish to compete on price and so their operations are akin to UK practices.

5. The impact of the disruption of the cement cartel can be analysed in terms of short and long term factors. As mentioned above, if UK producers reduced price, to match imports, short term profit margins would suffer and the cartel could possibly break up. This could lead to the smaller, weaker producers going out of business; and BCI may then end up with an even larger market share and possibly able to exploit greater scale economies. At the same time, users and consumers in the Construction Industry would benefit from lower prices. In the long term it might encourage new entrants and a more competitive environment, e.g. more imported cement. However, if BCI gained greater control of the market and was able to exploit economies of scale, it might resort to monopolistic pricing practices which could lead to consumer exploitation; especially if cheap imported cement could be eventually curtailed. At the same time, the disruption of the cartel, in the long term, could lead to attempts to reduce costs by reducing quality, standards and further Research and Development which could ultimately adversely affect the consumer of cement. Lastly it could, by reducing cement costs, reduce overall construction costs and lead to cement structures becoming cheaper to produce than traditional brick or timber buildings.

Note: In February 1987 the 53-year-old cement makers cartel broke up. This led to lower cement prices and regional prices for ready mix concrete which reflected true transport costs.

U.K. MOTOR CAR DEALER OUTLETS AND MARKET SHARES (1984)

ANSWERS

1. a) **Manufacturer** — These are the major U.K. and overseas producers of volume motor cars. They essentially design, assemble components and then distribute to private and commercial users.

    Dealer outlets — These represent the wholesaling and retailing functions and are the middlemen between consumer and manufacturer. They are often allowed exclusive or monopoly privileges to sell a particular model in a specific area and they provide promotion, advertising, after sales servicing facilities, etc.

    Market share — This indicates the percentage of annual new car sales taken by a specified manufacturer and is of vital importance for those engaged in volume car production as it determines the extent to which manufacturing scale economies can be exploited.

    Outlets per 1% share — This indicates how many outlets are required for a 1% share of the U.K. new car market and reflects overall efficiency in the distribution of cars.

    b) Import penetration ratios serve as a useful and quick guide as to how far imported goods supply the home market. In the case of motor cars they aggregate to 26.5% of the 1984 U.K. market. However, many of the components going into G.M. U.K. (Vauxhall) and Ford U.K. are produced overseas and even Ford/G.M. produce specific models in Germany and France, etc. for sale in the U.K. market. Therefore crude import penetration figures based upon the origin of the manufacturer can be misleading and understate true importation figures.

2. Economic theory would identify the U.K. new motor car market as being oligopolistic in structure. This is because there are a few similar sized producers who are selling into the same markets with very similarly priced cars. Even though foreign manufacturers have a small U.K. share, in European terms, their overall global market share would compare very favourably with the largest U.K. market share holders. One of the predictions of the oligopolistic model is price stability, and a similarity of overall pricing structure (see the KINKED DEMAND CURVE) together with heavy advertising and little or no price competition. These predictions are to some extent confirmed in the U.K. where there is heavy product advertising, but overall a stable pricing structure between companies and models.

3. G.M./Vauxhall and Ford seem to be most efficient in their dealer networks because they need fewer outlets per market share. Indeed

compared to Fiat, G.M./Vauxhall need around three times fewer dealers per 1% share of the market. This indicates that these two manufacturers are selling more units through each dealer and to some extent this is confirmed by noting that they hold the first and third largest market shares. British Leyland with 17.8% of the U.K. market require twice as many dealers as G.M./Vauxhall to sell roughly the same number of cars! Calculations indicate that 50 outlets only are required to support a 1% increase in market share, so only around 5,000 outlets are needed. If this is the case only Ford and G.M. achieved this level in 1984. The Economies of Scale which are at work in dealer outlets are essentially buying and selling in bulk. In other words, car manufacturers, such as Ford and G.M. selling to "fleet" buyers, e.g. companies or hire-cars, etc., are able to sell in bulk via their dealers and so require fewer dealers. The "fleet" market accounts for about 60% of all new car sales so it benefits manufacturers and dealers alike. Furthermore, sales "know-how" and managerial economics mean specialised market knowledge of the bulk car sales market and so improve efficiency. The ability to stock a narrow specialised range of models, spare parts and provide other ancilliary services also helps to explain why, for example, Godfrey Davies is a large scale Ford dealer with substantial market share. Smaller dealers dispersed over the whole country catering for the private new car market are unable to offer the marketing services, etc. and hence are much less efficient. This means that dealer discounts have to be maintained for the less efficient dealer networks, e.g. Fiat, Renault, and this reduces the profitability of those car manufacturers, at least in the U.K. Though to some extent this has been alleviated by the extra high U.K. car prices compared to European new car pricing practices.

4. Overall dealer outlet efficiency could be improved if dealers amalgamated into bigger units so the economies of horizontal scale integration could be exploited, e.g. buying and selling in bulk. Otherwise it is suggested that improved efficiency could be attained by dealers moving from expensive city sites to less expensive locations where a full range of showroom and back-up services could be provided. Furthermore, more car manufacturers could attempt to supply into the fleet car market and indeed they could possibly by-pass the dealer by selling direct to the company buying for fleet purposes or the personal buyer. Lastly, some have suggested the major share of new car sales will be conducted by out of town car hypermarkets who are offshoots of the large chain multiples able to gain by buying in bulk from the manufacturers. Certainly foreign car importers may see this as a more efficient way of distributing cars rather than remaining with the expensive and small scale existing networks.

196 Structure of Industry, Scale and Location

UK REGIONAL EMPLOYMENT AND OUTPUT PATTERNS

ANSWERS

(a) (i) Food, drink and tobacco is the least concentrated industry geographically. This can be shown by comparing the percentage figures for employment and net output for the industry. As can be seen, for each region the employment and output figures are roughly the same, e.g. for the North the percentage figures are 4.8% and 4.5% respectively. The fact that the industry is widely dispersed could be explained because (1) Food production is widely dispersed so reflecting the overall distribution of the population; (2) Economies of scale are limited since although production economies **would** centralise and concentrate production, distribution costs are high because of the low value, high volume nature of the business. This means production is localised to minimise distribution costs.

(ii) Following the above analysis it can be seen that Instrument Engineering is the most highly concentrated geographically with around half its workforce and output in the S. East region. Though for other areas it does tend to be more widely dispersed when compared to metal manufacturing. Instrument Engineering reflects the growing tendency of high value low volume products to be located near the largest and richest markets, in this case the S. East and even Europe. At the same time, electrical power, supplied through the National Grid, has meant many industries which rely on power are "footloose" and no longer depend upon locating near their prime power source. **Note:** It is difficult to conclude anything about the size of the producing unit since there may be many small or medium sized units in the S.E.

(b) (i) Production of the final product can be achieved successively through different industries. This means the gross value of output of one industry will include the output of the previous industry in its output. In order to distinguish the output or value added at a specific stage, Economists use net output to indicate the additional unit of output produced at that stage of production. Gross output therefore includes all the previous cumulated output and so "double counts" output produced earlier. In this case the total net output column shows the added value of each industry over the whole country and thus avoids the problems that would occur with gross output accounting.

(ii) Calculation to estimate the labour used to produce one thousand pound's worth of annual net output in the Food, Drink and Tobacco Industry (UK)

Structure of Industry, Scale and Location 197

$$\frac{\text{Total UK workforce of Food, Drink \& Tobacco}}{\text{Total UK output (net) of Food, Drink \& Tobacco. £m}} \text{ in UK}$$

$= \dfrac{762.3 \text{ th.}}{£6576.0\text{m}}$ or .11 workers are needed for every £1,000 worth of output.

For Instrument Engineering, similar calculations give .16 workers.

(iii) The degree of labour intensity in an industry, as shown in (b)(ii) will depend upon such economic factors as the technology and capital usage of the industry, the nature of the output and the extent to which standardisation can exploit economies of scale and the scale and size of demand of the market. In this case Food, Drink & Tobacco may require less labour because it can use capital intensive methods of production, whilst Instrument Engineering may be subject to small production runs which are to order and hence more labour intensive, i.e. similar to the service sector where non-standardised products are purchased. Lastly, it may be that the variety of instrument engineering output, compared to food etc., means the scale of production is smaller and hence less able to exploit mass production methods.

(c) Wage rates, according to marginal revenue product theory, will reflect the value of output produced per head. Thus by comparing the value of output per head in manufacturing in the S. East and N. Ireland, it is possible to confirm this prediction.

So in the S.E. Total Output is $\dfrac{£14{,}223.2\text{m}}{1828.3\text{th}} = £7{,}779$ per head
In Manufacturing, Total Employment is net output

and in N. Ireland the figures are $= \dfrac{810.1\text{m}}{143.9\text{th}} = \dfrac{£5{,}630 \text{ per}}{\text{head net output}}$

Thus output per head differences would predict higher wages in the S.E. than in N. Ireland.

(ii) It is possible that the S.E. has a higher concentration of high net output (value) industries such as Instrument Engineering which N. Ireland does not have. This would bias the figures in favour of the S. East which would then attract these industries because of the high wages and incomes in the area. Also net output per head could be lower overall in Northern Ireland because of poor management, insufficient capital investment, due to a lack of overall spending, political disturbances etc. At the same time, lower wages in N. Ireland may be due to increased labour supply caused by unemployment or lower living costs or even weaker trade union negotiations.

(d) When reaching a decision about industrial location, the Japanese manufacturer should assess 1) Existing comparative geographical net output per head figures for Instrument Engineering. This will possibly indicate where a trained and productive labour force is located. 2) If an area is heavily concentrated geographically in Instrument Engineering, it will also indicate where "external" economies of scale are to be found which would help improve overall efficiency and lower unit costs. In this case the S. East indicates a heavy concentration and hence likely external economies of scale. 3) Government grants are available today in Enterprise Zones etc. for those firms wishing to invest in manufacturing capacity. In particular, substantial local and government financial assistance is available where unemployment levels are high and the Japanese manufacturer would be advised to investigate all regional alternatives. 4) Lastly, a thorough investigation of market potential, transport facilities, housing etc., would also have to be undertaken before a final decision could be arrived at.

STRUCTURE OF UK GROCERY TRADE

ANSWERS

(a) The main trends in grocery retailing were:—

(1) The overall number of both multiples and other shops declined by about 50% with multiples showing the greater loss in numbers.

(2) Multiples doubled their market share of the grocery trade with other retail outlets suffering a dramatic decline.

(3) Fewer "multiple" shop units, e.g. Tescos, Sainsburys, Fine Fare etc., have larger grocery sales per retail unit and the other retail units have lost market share in rough proportion to the decline in shop units so the overall shop size remains the same, i.e. small scale.

(b) (i) Economies of operation available would be:—

(1) Buying in bulk and selling (merchandising) in bulk to the consumer with national TV advertising campaigns to promote sales for the multiples.

(2) Own Brand selling techniques, e.g. St. Michael and Marks & Spencers.

(3) Larger shops with self service check out facilities increases sales yield per square metre of shopping space.

(4) Wholesaling operations and own packaging facilities together with **own** distribution networks thus reducing unit transport costs.

(5) Specialist management economies such as Buyers/Merchandisers, Credit Management etc.

(ii) Social/Economic changes could be:—

(1) The growth of the motor car and hence ease of large bulk shopping.

(2) Large new housing estates with purpose built hypermarkets and car parks.

(3) The rise of women's occupations and the preference of once a week, bulk "shops".

(4) The advent of freezers, credit and cheque facilities have made bulk buying easier to finance and store, e.g. frozen foods.

(5) The abolition of Resale Price Maintenance led to the demise of the small shopkeeper and the growth of the large bulk buying multiples able to undercut on retail price and so only the large multiples with financial back-up have been able to survive.

(6) The small independent unit is able to survive because they provide a service "open all hours", a local convenient shop for the immobile and elderly and often a friendlier atmosphere.

Chapter 23
INTERNATIONAL TRADE-DEVELOPMENT ECONOMICS

PRINCIPAL MANUFACTURING STATISTICS IN SINGAPORE (1971-1981)

ANSWERS

(a) (i) Real labour productivity would be calculated by taking output per worker figures and deflating them by the GDP deflator which measures inflation. The corrected real labour productivity figures would then show real output based upon 1968=100 rather than current dollar output values.

(ii) The increase in gross domestic capital formation would explain real productivity gains to labour and clearly the increase in real gross domestic capital formation net of inflation has been positive and considerable.

Note: Calculations to show real percentage gains in labour and capital productivity 1968=100.

Labour output per worker 1968=100. Gains.

$1971 = \$ 36{,}137 \times \dfrac{100}{109} = \$33{,}153$

$1981 = \$131{,}158 \times \dfrac{100}{186} = \$70{,}515$

A real gain between 1971-81 of 112.7% or **10.2%** p.a.

Capital formation (m) 1968=100.

$1971 = \$ 2{,}744 \times \dfrac{100}{109} = \$2{,}517$

$1981 = \$11{,}553 \times \dfrac{100}{186} = \$6{,}211$

A real gain between 1971-81 of 147% or **13.4%** p.a.

(iii) Apart from capital accumulation real gains in labour productivity could come about from better management of labour and production, better labour training and working practices or improved corporate organisation and structure, which could increase size and hence economies of scale.

(b) (i) International competitiveness could be reflected in the growth of export markets and clearly as exports increase, compared to output, more production is being channelled to overseas markets, perhaps because of cost advantages caused by gains in international competitiveness. The column of the ratio of direct exports to output increases from 44.7 to 60.3 percent over the period, so showing that productivity gains have improved the international competitiveness of firms in Singapore.
(ii) The international competitiveness of firms in Singapore could also be due to a) a fall in the value of the Singapore $ in terms of overseas currencies, having the effect of reducing export prices and making them more competitive, at least in the short term. b) At the same time, Singapore may have become more competitive because other countries have become less so due to cost increases or overvalued currencies.
(iii) As well as output per worker increases helping Singapore's competitiveness, actual labour cost figures may have fallen due to wage levels reducing. This may be due to an abundance of labour supply which may act to depress the wage rate paid. The table shows competitiveness will have risen due to output per worker rises, capital investment increases and falling wages to output, i.e. wage costs have gone down in respect of output.

(c) In 1971, 1972 and 1973 wages took around 10% of output. Between 1971 and 1981 real output per worker increased by around a factor of two. In crude terms the size of the "cake", the National Income, has doubled: see 'real output per worker' in (a)(i). Of this increased 'cake' the wages to output ratio has fallen to around 7.7% so the wage share has fallen in percentage terms but not necessarily in overall wage terms. It is true that real productivity gains average 10% per annum per worker, i.e. 112.7 — 11 years, but the ratio of wages to output has fallen slightly from 9.9% in 1971 to 7.7% in 1981. However, it is difficult to say exactly whether the employees have received all productivity gains. Clearly, with a stable workforce, wages have not kept pace with productivity gains across the economy, though for some this may not be true. If however the workforce reduced by two or three percent, then wages may match labour productivity gains even though in relative terms wages fell when compared to output. If as seems likely the workforce has expanded, then the productivity gains of 10% p.a. per worker are not reflected in similar wage increases as the ratio of wages to output has fallen. Nevertheless, the slight fall in the wages to output ratio and a stable population would imply that some of the gains in productivity would have been distributed to employees in the form of higher real wages. As capital formation increased over 1971-81, much of the output increase could have gone to capital in the form of profit and interest.

ECONOMIC PERFORMANCE IN SELECTED ASIAN ECONOMIES

ANSWERS

1. India — GNP per head (US dollars) is an indicator of living standards and this was lowest of all those countries in the table.

2. False. Sri-Lanka has roughly the same GNP per head in 1980 as India but has experienced a higher growth rate (2.4% p.a.) as opposed to (1.4% p.a.) for India. Hence the initial GNP in 1960 must have been lower in Sri-Lanka than in India.

3. Malaysia: Because both are expected to have the same growth rate of GNP per head 1980-90 (either high or low forecast) but Malaysia is expected to experience a faster population growth rate than Singapore, i.e. Population is expected to double in 36 years in Malaysia and to take 59 years in Singapore. If GNP per head in both countries is expected to be the same, then GNP must grow faster in Malaysia than in Singapore in order to offset the faster population increase.

GLOBAL INCOME DISTRIBUTION

ANSWERS

(a) The distribution of the world's income and population clearly illustrates a high degree of inequality between rich and poor countries. If total world GNP output is compared to total world population and percentage figures are calculated, it can be estimated that North America, Oceania, Japan and Europe, with around 10% of the world's population, take around 70% of the world's output and income. On the other hand, less developed areas of Asia and Africa with around 50% of the world's population, only account for about 10% of all output and hence income. These figures are corroborated by GNP per capita figures showing North American, etc. where income per head at 7,880 U.S. dollars is far in excess of per capita figures for Africa and Asia. In terms of economic analysis "Lorenz" curve diagrams would clearly show this up in terms of cumulative percentage terms and the curve itself would be bowed to reflect world inequality of income. As such inequality exists, it obviously means that in poor countries, poverty and inadequate health provision will prevail and attempts to improve overall income levels must rely on richer nations providing aid and trade to less developed countries, as well as understanding the overall problems of inequality.

POSTSCRIPT 1986/7 African famine
The gap between rich and poor countries is widening and less developed countries, with large overseas debts, are unable to increase exports to developed countries who have low demand income elasticities for their goods. The increasing debt interest of the poorer countries reduces their ability to invest and provide for future development. At the same time, increasing population pressures in less developed countries have led to poverty and starvation as internal policies in Africa have moved populations from the rural to the urban areas. This is because the poor rural and urban worker has found real incomes falling but food prices rising and hence their ability to buy food has fallen and so poverty has resulted.

(b) Comparisons of international living standards often use "per capita" basis with some international currency, the dollar, acting as the financial yardstick. Nevertheless, when making crude comparisons, various factors must be borne in mind, namely:
1) GNP per capita does not refer to average earnings or income but only to a hypothetical figure estimated by dividing total population into total income per country.
2) Accounting definitions and practices vary between India and the U.K. so that it is possible that some income is ignored and is miscalculated so that actual per capita figures may not be accurate.
3) Exchange rate variations between the U.S. dollar, the pound, and the Indian rupee can distort actual per capita figures, though in this case the overall conclusions re living standards still stand.
4) Living standards depend upon other than hypothetical income per head figures. They should also refer to health, education and social provisions. They should include the overall state of housing and shelter provision. These will not be reflected in crude per capita figures.
5) The actual distribution of GNP in each country will depend upon the level of government spending on such things as defence, taxation policies

and overall market distribution of income in each country. If inequality of post-tax income is greater in India than in the U.K., then the general living standards of each householder will be even worse than the statistics indicate.

6) Living standards cannot always be indicated by economic statistics. The degree of freedom, environmental pollution and general lifestyle, etc. will all contribute to living standards, but these will not show up in GNP statistics.

7) Living standards will have to be related to the real costs of living, not just earnings, e.g. per capita income. Essentially per capita income does not indicate the cost of goods, which can be distorted by both internal inflation and taxation rates.

8) Living standards will depend on personal assets previously acquired or purchased, e.g. books, T.V's, cars, etc. These will not be shown up in current per capita figures.

Therefore, in view of the above factors, it is clear that whilst per capita figures indicate in broad terms that the U.K. experiences a far higher living standard than India (thirty times), precise indications of actual living standards must also reflect the above considerations.

THE EUROPEAN MONETARY SYSTEM (EMS)

ANSWERS
1. Between 1945-71 Western economic development existed alongside a fixed exchange rate system, i.e. The Bretton Woods System. From 1971 to date the U.K. has remained on a generally flexible or free exchange rate system though, in an effort to promote greater economic unity, other member countries of the EEC have joined to become part of a fixed exchange rate system known as the European Monetary System (EMS). Since the majority of individual trade takes place between member states of the EEC, such a fixed exchange rate system was thought appropriate because it provides: (i) an internal financial and monetary discipline on participating countries; (ii) reduces uncertainty about future exchange rates and thus helps promote stable trade and; (iii) reduces the destabilisation impact of speculation which could result from free and floating rates. If a fixed rate is established for a member country it does mean, as in the case of France 1984/5, that if internal inflation increases the authorities have to take steps to deflate in order to bring internal prices back into line with the externally established fixed currency values. This can reduce uncertainty amongst traders and investors who know the government have to act to stabilise not only the internal but also external value of the currency. If at the same time member states trade as much as

70% of GNP between themselves, as in the case of Holland and Belgium, then a stable currency is almost essential for day to day workings of the Economic union, i.e. the EEC.

2. Although fixed exchange rates have many advantages, one of the reasons why the 'Bretton Woods System' of fixed rates collapsed was because of the costs of such a system. A fixed system depends upon an adequate supply of an international money form, in this case the U.S. Dollar, Sterling and gold. Furthermore, for the fixed rate system to work, countries with Balance of Payments deficits should deflate their economy or devalue their currency, e.g. U.S.A., U.K., whilst those with surpluses, e.g. Japan and Germany, should reflate their economies or revalue their currency. In the event neither course of action was followed so costly attempts were made to create new forms of international liquidity for deficit countries and at the same time ways had to be provided for countries to artificially boost the value of their own currency, e.g. the U.K. This involved setting up expensive and bureaucratic systems, e.g. IMF loans, etc. and also led to the implementation of unnecessarily draconion deflationary measures. U.K. experience during the 1960's was costly in terms of lost jobs and output because of such deflationary policies.

3. Between both countries and regions within the EMS (EEC) there is, and will be, disparity with respect to economic growth and so income variations will exist, e.g. North and Southern England and between W. Germany and the U.K. If this happens there will be trade deficits and surpluses on a regional and country basis which will be exaggerated in the capital and investment market where free mobility could result in capital moving to the more prosperous areas, e.g. South of England from the North, or from the U.K. to West Germany. In order to overcome this problem, funds will have to be made available from the EEC budget to subsidise these low income regions in order to stop the drift of investment, output, jobs and opportunities to more prosperous areas such as West Germany. These subsidies could take the form of investment grants or other suitable financial or economic incentives.

4. If member states of the EEC operate within a fixed exchange rate system, they would hope to maintain Balance of Payments equilibrium amongst themselves, i.e. imports and exports of goods, services and capital should roughly balance. This will only be possible if internal prices, output, costs and overall efficiency (economic performance) are the same. In order for this to happen, the overall economic framework, policies and systems encouraged by local and central government should be similar. If economic performances diverge, for example, the U.K.

might experience high rates of inflation compared to West Germany, then she will experience problems with her balance of payments as imports rise and West Germany could find exports rise and her Balance of Payments will strengthen. This will weaken the pound and strengthen the Deutch Mark, which will put the fixed rate EMS under pressure. This will mean that unless the U.K. maintains industrial policies and performance in line with W. Germany, she will revert back to successive policies of 'stop-go' so reminiscent of U.K. economic history between 1945-71 when she was on the Bretton Woods fixed exchange rate system.

SELECTED ITEMS FROM THE UK BALANCE OF PAYMENTS — THE VALUE OF THE POUND

ANSWERS

(a) The behaviour of the U.K. Current Account 1979 to 1983 shows that from a deficit of £653m in 1979 the account moved into a surplus of £3235m in 1980, rising to £6547m in 1981 and thereafter decreasing to a positive surplus of £2049m in 1983. The initial deficit was due to major imports of oil and visibles, e.g. manufactured goods and raw materials, outweighing the surplus on invisibles such as financial services and tourism, etc. Thereafter the export of North Sea oil improved our current account and pushed up sterling exchange rates. However, our export of visible manufactured goods worsened due to high interest and exchange rates and this worked to reduce our current account balance by 1983. By 1983 export oil revenues were outweighed by imports of manufactured goods etc., and it is only the surplus on invisibles which provides the now greatly reduced current account surplus.

(b) The U.K. trades and competes worldwide with all major developed countries, including Japan, Germany, France, U.S.A., Italy, etc. In the main, it competes with these countries in the highly competitive market for manufactured goods and financial services. Whilst trade with the U.S.A. is important, trade with EEC countries and Japan, etc. is of more importance and an indication of overall trade balances and U.K. competitiveness is measured by the "effective trade weighted index". This index is calculated by including all the currencies of our trading partners on a trade weighted basis, and then averaging them against the pound. This index is more accurate then in reflecting our present and future overall trade position. The U.S.A. dollar rate tends to be used as a psychological indicator and is of more importance in the financial and capital markets in assessment of our performance on such things as interest rates, etc. Indeed if the U.K. and U.S.A. maintained similar economic performances the pound would remain stable to the dollar, but it could fall when compared to the trade weighted effective exchange rate if our major trading partners experienced improved economic export performance and this index of performance would have a greater significance for U.K. decision makers and politicians, etc.

(c) (i) As can be seen, as the current account moves into a surplus, the capital account shows a net outflow. In effect what is happening is that the oil revenues generated by N. Sea oil are being invested abroad in foreign stocks and shares, or fixed capital formation. This was allowed to happen originally to keep the balance of payments in balance and hence keep the value of the pound down. The surplus on current account is greater in 1981 as is the capital outflow. Eventually, it is argued, the capital outflow will generate a flow of profits and dividends back to the U.K. and this will swell the invisible trade account so that eventually capital outflows will relate to the current account. However, it should be noted that there is now a stable relationship between the two so that in 1983 the current account surplus was less than that in 1982 but the capital outflow was nearly three times more in 1983 than 1982. This means that capital outflows will reflect not only current account behaviour but also speculative factors which may be influenced by the overseas interest and exchange rates. Thus if the speculators foresee a fall in the value of the pound, they will draw out capital and put it into stronger currencies so that they can then bring the money back into London at advantageous exchange rates regardless of balance of payments behaviour.

(ii) The overall Balance of Payments should have an impact on overall exchange rates because as the Balance of Payments worsens, e.g. imports increase faster than exports, the exchange rate falls and vice versa. Calculations for the actual Balance of Payments are shown and generally, apart from 1981, are positive, so predicting stable or even rising exchange rates. In effect both rates peaked in 1980 and thereafter fell. What happened was that the rising oil revenues and capital accumulation of 1981 onwards were predicted ahead in 1980 and the pound rose accordingly. Thereafter the underlying weakness of our manufacturing goods sector and its declining trade balance were forecast and so the £ fell against both rates, i.e. it was discounted in advance. The reason it fell more against the trade weighted index than against the U.S. dollar was that the U.S.A. was experiencing a growing deficit on **its** Balance of Payments so it was thought to be itself a weak currency. On the other hand, our major trade competitors and trade partners were becoming more competitive with less inflation so the £ fell to the trade weighted index in anticipation of our poor export behaviour. Furthermore, government economic and interest rate policy imposed itself upon Balance of Payments factors and indeed they may have engineered an overall decline in the value of the pound in order to improve short term export competitiveness and create output and job opportunities within the U.K.

SUMMARY OF THE UK's BALANCE OF PAYMENTS IN 1974 AND 1981

SHORT ANSWERS
1. (i) Investment transactions, which appear in the Balance of Payments, are often split into two forms; namely portfolio investment and direct investment. The former includes transactions in foreign securities by large institutional investors such as pension funds and also by individuals. Direct investment is that carried on by companies in their business when they purchase shares in subsidiary companies or when they build new factories or offices. An individual buying a villa overseas would also come into this category.

   (ii) These refer to government investment and borrowing transactions which affect the management of official reserves. Government borrowing overseas can be from the IMF, foreign banks or from overseas capital markets. These assets can take the form of gold or short dated securities in either US dollars or other stable and respected currencies. The movement of these reserves can be affected by governments selling these securities and converting to sterling or it can build up reserves by buying gold or US dollars on the open market which may then be used for future international debt settlement.

2. Calculations for 1974, all in (£bn) (i) Visible trade exports = $-21.7 + x = -5.4, x = +21.7$; (ii) Invisible trade payments (imports) = $10.5 + (-x) = 2.1$, $x = -8.4$; (iii) Official financing: her foreign currency borrowing = $x + (-.1) = 1.6$, $x = +1.7$ (increase).

3. Calculations for 1981, all in (£bn):
   (i) Invisible Balance = $+ 51.0 + (-48.0) = \underline{+ 3.0}$
   (ii) Visible Balance = $+ 29.7 + (-26.2) = \underline{+ 3.5}$
   (iii) Current Account Balance = $+ 3.0 + 3.5 = \underline{+ 6.5}$
   (iv) Capital Account Balance = $\underline{+ 6.5,}$ check = Current Account Balance.

WORLD TRADE PATTERNS

ANSWERS

1. Base materials provide the raw material inputs for industrial products so when demand for manufactured industrial products increases or decreases this affects the market price of commodities; demand for which may be relatively inelastic in the short term.

2. The cause for concern arises from the fact that the prices of raw materials, after 1971, seems far more sensitive to variations in world industrial output, i.e. nearly three times as much. This instability will mean investment and output of raw materials will become uncertain and hence manufacturing input and output will be subject to bottlenecks and uncertainty of supply. This will eventually affect industrial activity, world output and employment.

3. An institution could be invented which would coordinate world production of raw materials and industrial output along the lines of the IMF viz world banking, etc. This institution could provide for buying up excess output of raw materials so preventing price falls and future output contractions, i.e. a Buffer Stock Agency.

4. Essentially the market for commodities is one characterised by many buyers and sellers, i.e. competitive (except for a few exceptions, oil etc.) whilst the industrial market output is increasingly characterised by oligopolistic or monopolistic tendencies. The implication is that adjustment in the raw material markets is affected via the price mechanism (and hence supply) whilst oligopolistic markets, characterised by stable controlled prices adjust via the building up or running down of stocks of raw material inputs and finished products. This further worsens the ability for both sectors to co-ordinate their activities.

FREE TRADE & THE JAPANESE CASE

ANSWERS

1. The theory of comparative costs, as stated by Ricardo, predicts that countries should specialise and trade in goods and services where they have a cost advantage and hence can produce at the cheapest price. This idea was developed by Heschker and Ohlin who tried to explain why production possibilities varied between countries. They stressed that different countries possess different factor endowments of land, labour,

capital and enterprise, etc. and trade is worthwhile as it allows countries to take advantage of these differences. Thus if Japan has an abundance of labour it should, according to the theory, specialise in labour intensive products rather than capital intensive high technology products.

2. The simple theory of trade fails to include the role of demand within its framework. Thus a large home demand, e.g. Japan, allows a country to build up and exploit economies of scale in the manufacturing sector. Furthermore, world demand for manufactured goods is income elastic and world income was predicted to grow in the 1960's, etc. Advantage in the manufacture of high technology goods has to be built up and the industrial history of Japan points to a natural endowment of enterprise and commercial expertise, i.e. the assumption of homogeneity of labour is unrealistic. Lastly, the theory of trade assumes technological advances cannot be lost to others — again highly unrealistic as technology developed in one country has been commercially exploited in Japan; a country with few endogenous natural resources and so dependant upon foreign trade.

THE PROBLEM OF FLOATING EXCHANGE RATES

ANSWERS
1. In those countries with overvalued currencies, export prices will be forced up whilst import costs will be less than they would be according to supply and demand. Hence consumers will buy in cheap imports at the expense of home manufacturing and so investment will fall in home industries as their exports suffer and home markets contract. If the currency were not overvalued, increased consumer demand would lead to more investment (capital formation) in home production as prices and profit rise.

2. Overvalued currencies means internal purchasing power is artificially high by the extent that the prices of imported goods are underpriced by high exchange rates. This represents an increase in real wages not matched by internal productivity, which is protected by workers in wage bargaining so that when exchange rates fall and imported consumer goods rise, compensatory rises in money wages are sought in order to maintain real living standards. This pumps up cost push inflation.

3. If exchange rates move against a country artificially, it will distort comparative cost advantages and reduce the national gains from trade which countries experience. If countries see this occurring they will

protect home industries against unfair price advantages, due perhaps to cheap imports because of unwarranted currency appreciation, by imposing tariffs or other forms of protection to increase the price of imported goods.

WHY DID THE SYSTEM OF FIXED PARITIES BREAK DOWN?

ANSWERS
1. Exchange rates, in theory, should reflect long term relative cost advantages between countries and even fixed exchange rates should adjust to reflect long term changes in world cost and demand conditions. However, countries such as Japan and Germany often refused to revalue their currencies because to have done so would have removed their export price competitiveness which they established and which they valued because it meant their economies were able to benefit from export led growth. Thus their currencies were held down by artificial means, e.g. marking up their export prices in dollars, etc. and so gradually their balance of payments surplus increased as did their foreign currency holdings. Eventually these policies led to surplus and deficit countries, namely Japan, Germany, U.K. and U.S.A. respectively, with over and under valued currencies. Severe pressures were put on the fixed exchange rate system since the surplus countries refused to inflate and the deficit countries refused to deflate; as postulated by the fixed rate system. Ultimately these fixed rates became unrealistic and speculative pressures undermined the whole system.

2. Briefly, the three main reasons for the collapse of the system were (i.e. disadvantages of the fixed rate system):—
   (i) An overvalued $ compared to the convertible price of gold, hence the international hoarding of $'s and gold.
   (ii) Differing rates of inflation led to currency instability, i.e. real rates diverged from fixed rates.
   (iii) Disruptive speculation against weak and strong currencies caused capital market instability and hence uncertainty over investment and capital building projects, etc.

THE VALUE OF THE POUND

ANSWERS

(a) The equilibrium price for sterling will be at **12.10 francs to the £,** with **£20m** of sterling being supplied and demanded.

(b) If a trade deficit is experienced, the new foreign exchange conditions become:—

Price of Sterling (in francs)	11.50	**11.80**	12.10	13.00
Sterling demanded (£ million)	20	**17**	15	12
Sterling supplied (£ million)	15	**17**	20	22

Hence the new equilibrium price for sterling will be at **11.80** francs to the £ with **£17m** of sterling being supplied and demanded.

(c) In order to peg the exchange rate at 12.10 French Francs to the pound the government could, in the short term, raise **interest rates** to attract foreign capital and/or **purchase sterling (£5m)** in the foreign currency markets by using up its gold and dollar reserves. It could also **borrow** from foreign banks or the IMF in order to provide support to the pound. If the UK were in the EMS France could help the UK by **selling French Francs** in the market to weaken its own currency.

At the same time, short term measures to reduce French **imports** by £5m could be undertaken. This would reduce the supply of sterling in exchange for French Francs and could take a variety of forms. These might include **restricting the amount of French Francs which could be bought** for trade or tourist purposes, e.g. currency controls. **Medium term schemes** to reduce imports could also be introduced, e.g. tariffs, voluntary import restraint schemes, import deposit schemes, etc.

(d) If financial techniques were used to either artificially restrict supply or increase demand for sterling, then clearly this would not be a natural equilibrium price for sterling viz a viz francs, hence **overvaluation** of sterling is implied by the government action.

FREE TRADE AND THE DETERMINATION OF PRICE

ANSWERS

(a) If no trade occurs the **equilibrium price in A** will be **£6** per unit for x (where quantity demand/supplied are equal at **60 units**). **In B the price** will be £2 per unit (quantity demanded/supplied will be equal at **70** units).

(b) If trade occurred with no transport costs the **world demand and supply quantities** will be: (adding supply and demand for each country at each price).

Price of x per unit (£)	7	6	5	**4**	3	2
Total Supply	210	180	150	**135**	110	70
Total Demand	90	105	120	**135**	150	170

Hence world price is £4 in equilibrium with 135 units being bought and sold.

(c) At this world price of £4 country A would be supplying 45 units but consuming only 80 thus **importing the difference**, i.e. **35 units**.

On the other hand, country B would be supplying 90 units and consuming 55 (i.e. **exporting 35** units).

(d) If country A imposes a £1 tariff per unit the **price in A will increase to £5** (ignore elasticity). This means A will **import** only **20** units as at £5 demand is 70 and home production is 50. Country B will find demand for its exports to A cut from 100 to 80 and so its internal price will fall to £3, i.e. at £3 supply is 80 and the demand is 60, a difference to export of 20.

(e) A comparison of the before and after tariff position will show that the **government** in A will benefit with £20 of tariff revenue, **producers** in A will be able to sell more at the higher internal price of £5 and **consumers** in B will also be able to consume at the lower price of £3 per unit as against £4 which was the previous world price. These three groups will gain in **economic welfare** from the imposition of the £1 tariff in A.

BRAZIL AND INTERNATIONAL SUGAR PRICES

ANSWERS
(a) (i) Many developing countries borrowed heavily in the seventies to finance internal growth. Along with borrowing goes paying off the interest on the debt, the principal or sum borrowed. Initially the payments would have been sensible and in line with current interest rates. However, the sharp rise in world interest rates in the 1980's means that the cost of paying these debts amounts to huge sums of money. In

effect some countries are paying interest on debt which itself is increasing due to previously unpaid interest charges. In the case of Brazil, as interest rates rise, this debt increases the burden on taxpayers and the economy generally.

(ii) The terms of trade measure the overall value of exports to imports. Initially a base year is chosen and valued at 100. In the case of Brazil it was 1980. Based on 1980, 1979 export values were clearly higher than import values by around 14% (114-100). However, by 1982 export prices had fallen by around 16% (100-84) to import prices when compared to 1980 figures, and when compared to 1979 this fall was around (114 less 84), i.e. 30 percent. In effect to buy the same imports in 1982, as in 1979, cost around 16% more in terms of exports sold.

(b) The theory of comparative advantage suggests that 'specialisation and world trade will take place if relative costs vary between countries'. In other words, countries with specific factor endowments will experience relatively low cost conditions and they will specialise and trade so long as the terms of trade reflect the internal opportunity cost ratio. Brazil is a huge country with many national advantages in the production of sugar. This should imply that its costs are low by international standards so it should specialise and export sugar. The extract supports the theory of comparative advantage since it shows that Brazil has the lowest sugar costs in the world at 7-9 U.S. cents per pound and is also the world's biggest producer and third biggest exporter.

(c) In the E.E.C. farmers are guaranteed target support prices for their sugar, normally in excess of production costs and well over world market price. This has led to expensive overproduction in excess of demand and huge amounts of sugar are stored and then dumped overseas at artificially low prices, (calculated in 1986 at $\frac{1}{3}$ of world prices). Thus excess EEC sugar capacity has led to price cuts below cost in order to generate sugar sales in non-EEC countries. These sales provide revenue to offset the subsidies given for sugar production and other associated storage costs.

Chapter 24
MONEY AND BANKING

U.K. MONETARY AGGREGATE AND GDP

SHORT ANSWERS

1. (a) M3 is the monetary aggregate used by the Bank of England to control money supply. It includes notes, coins, sight deposits of the UK private and public sector in interest and non-interest bearing forms plus time deposits of the private and public sector. UK residents can hold these deposits in sterling £M3 and additionally in other currencies which gives the full M3 money stock figure. The figures in the table are Sterling £M3 ones.

   (b) GDP is Gross Domestic Product. It is the value added sum of all output produced internally and includes all capital formation before wear & tear (depreciation).

2. Calculations:—
   (i) Real GDP in 1985 (1983 = 100)
   $= £306bn \times \frac{100}{110} = £278.2bn$

   (ii) Velocity of Circulation $= \frac{\text{Money GDP}}{£M3}$

   $1983 = \frac{225.6bn}{64bn} = \times 3.5$ This fall in V can be due to falling GDP and/or rising £M3.
   $1985 = \frac{306}{125.4} = \times 2.4$

3. Allowing for inflation £M3 can increase when time deposits rise because interest rates are attractive due to new forms of deposits induced by competition and financial innovation. Otherwise, if people and institutions decide to hold their assets in money form and prefer money balances or liquidity preference, then £M3 would increase.

4. Keynesians would see the change in V as confirming their views regarding liquidity preference and demand for money being the main influence on money supply. If V depends upon liquidity preference it will be subject to speculative and psychological pressures and subject to change, i.e. unstable. Monetarists may view the figures with scepticism and suggest that annual average figures might show a more stable value for V which is assumed in the Fisher equation of MV=PT. Thus if V and T are constants then the rise in M (£M3) causes inflation (P) etc.

MONETARISM AND THE MEDIUM TERM FINANCIAL STRATEGY: A STATEMENT

ANSWERS

1. The MTFS was designed by the 'monetarist' Conservative governments of 1979 and 1983 as a medium term plan, over four to five years, to reduce overall levels of money supply in the economy so that overall inflation levels would fall. The plan sought to limit Public Sector Borrowing in line with published Monetary Supply Aggregates such as M0, M_1, M_2, M_3 etc. The economic reasoning behind limiting the growth of the PSBR was twofold. Firstly, by limiting the PSBR to some agreed percentage of GDP, government borrowing needs especially from the Banking Sector would be reduced. This would limit bank lending and hence the money multiplier process would be controlled. Thus bank deposits would not increase too fast and since bank deposits indicated money stock, this would reduce overall money supply and inflation; assuming the velocity of circulation remained constant.

   The second part of limiting the PSBR was an attempt to switch resources back to the private sector which would be more willing to invest and compete in overseas markets if it was convinced that government policy was determined to reduce inflation and costs. As well as controlling the supply of money the MTFS complemented an Industrial Strategy which the government believed would increase competition and private initiative. This strategy sought to improve labour mobility, reduce the power of the Trades Unions, and increase competition by the privatisation of state-run nationalised monopolies such as British Telecom, etc.

2. As a 'monetarist' government the 1979 Conservative Government believed inflation was a monetary phenomenon and as indicated above, assumed the overall validity of the Quantity Theory of Money, i.e. $MV = PT$. In this, the monetarist assumptions are that in the long term both V and T are stable and there is a causal relationship between M, money supply and P, prices. Thus as the second paragraph states "to reduce inflation further ... the Government continues reducing the rates of monetary growth." Firm financial policies would refer to controlling PSBR, money supply and hence inflation so the assumed link is that money supply directly causes inflation. Keynesian analysis, on the other hand, would argue that the fall in inflation during the period 1980-85 was due to simple demand deflationary measures. They would point to the fact that the cutback in the PSBR was no more than a reduction in the budget deficit, and a cutback in Government spending, even more drastic than that undertaken during the Great Depression of the 1930s.

216 Money and Banking

Furthermore, they would argue inflation fell because of falling world commodity prices and lower overall levels of output which reduced the demand for money and therefore its supply.

3. As the level of the Public Sector Borrowing falls, this has a supposedly twofold impact on interest rates. As mentioned above, as the PSBR reduces, this slows the growth of money supply and inflation. This tends to strengthen the value of the pound and nominal interest rates fall as compensation to overseas investors adjusts downwards because of a stronger sterling currency. If at the same time expectations regarding inflation become more realistic then it is argued real rates also fall because nominal rates fall faster than inflation. This process is reinforced because as government borrowing reduces this takes the pressure off interest rates. However, if private demand for borrowing increases, as government borrowing reduces, then this will now allow interest rates to fall. Similarly from 1985 as the PSBR fell as a percentage of GDP UK real and nominal interest rates continued to rise because of the fall in the value of the pound to most major trading currencies and because of the uncertainty regarding the 1987 Election and whether the UK would join the European Monetary System.

WHY GOLD STILL GLITTERS

ANSWERS
1. To operate effectively, modern money forms have to perform certain identifiable functions and possess certain characteristics. Money has to be regarded as a medium of exchange, a standard of value, a store of value and a method of deferring payment (credit). Money in cash form should also be divisible, durable, portable and generally acceptable in settlement of a debt. The writer considers gold a suitable store of value over the long term but because of volatile price changes in terms of its value to other currencies, he does not consider it performs as a monetary **standard** of value. This means that whilst you can relate the price of goods to a pound note, even though it might fall in value, it is impossible to relate the price of these goods to gold because it does not have a stable nominal value, i.e. a £1 coin. On the other hand, gold has been seen as a basis for the stock of money and because of relatively slow growth of output it could be viewed as stable and a rough equivalent to the growth of output, trade and exchange, i.e. it could be a reliable medium of exchange. However, this fails to appreciate that whilst gold could be matched, even convertible in terms of paper money, the growth of borrowing and deposit money could not conceivably be planned in line

with the output of gold. The growth of deposit money in Great Britain in the nineteenth century, when we were a gold standard, far outstripped the increase in gold held at the Bank of England. In terms of money characteristics gold is certainly acceptable, because of its scarcity, and generally is divisible, malleable, and of a standard quality but because of its heavy weight is not always portable. Nevertheless today many countries are willing to accept gold in settlement of debt, on an international basis, so it does perform increasingly as a monetary form.

2. The annual increase of gold is relatively limited and stable being produced by only a handful of countries. The existing stock of gold, at any time, far exceeds the flow of new gold output and overall the market for gold will be influenced by a variety of factors. The main influence will be the demand for gold for speculative purposes, i.e. to act as a hedge against world inflation and the uncertain values of major world currencies. Indeed speculators can buy either the U.S. dollar, sterling, D.Marks, etc. or gold as a store of value and by moving into gold they force up its value and, at the same time, reduce the value of other currencies. Indeed, such is the scale of world speculative capital movements that gold prices can move up or down merely on the whim of a major trader. Monetarists who believe that excessive money supply leads to inflation would argue that the rise in the U.S. dollar value of gold merely indicates that U.S. inflation is high due to rising money supply and gold **should** rise in value accordingly. Whilst this is true it understates the role of the speculator as initiator and moreover a money system based on gold immediately gives an unfair advantage in world trade terms to those countries either producing or storing gold.

A small proportion of gold is bought for industrial and cosmetic (jewellery) purposes but this demand has a minor role to play in influencing the price of gold. Essentially the choice is between the U.S. dollar and gold and any uncertainty over future values of the U.S. dollar or U.S. Balance of Payments has a direct impact on the demand for gold and hence its value.

3. The underlying economic rationale behind the concern of the Central Bankers lies in the assumed relationship between gold reserves and internal money supply and hence inflation. If the dollar value of gold rises then those countries with large gold reserves will see the value of these reserves rise and thus their ability to settle debt internationally also rises. This, it is assumed, may encourage countries to reflate, even if this leads to inflation and balance of payments problems, because any deficit can be easily met from the increasing value of their gold reserves. In effect the whole process could create "irresponsible" reflation which on a world scale could be destabilising, i.e. "the rise in the gold price weakens

anti-inflationary resolve." In essence the assumption is that the increase in gold values increases money supply and hence inflation. However, many would argue that inflation may be a non-monetary phenomenon caused by cost-push pressures and if countries reflate then the output increase may help dampen down inflationary forces because rising productivity could increase faster than spending. At the same time it is assumed that those countries with productive potential may not reflate, as they should, because they have little or no gold reserves and so fear Balance of Payments problems which may result from increasing internal demand. However, this assumes that such decisions depend upon purely financial factors and not "real" economic forces such as productive potential development and efficiency. In the real world, the rate of a country's inflation, output or money supply growth often bears little resemblance to its holdings of gold reserves and so the concern of Central Bankers may be unfounded as it rests upon somewhat dubious assumptions.

FOREIGN EXCHANGE AND MONEY MARKETS

ANSWERS
1. a) **Sterling: Spot and Forward.** The spot rate for sterling is the **current** (23rd April 1986) rate at which sterling can be bought in terms of other currencies, e.g. F. Francs or U.S. Dollars. Forward rates are those quoted when traders wish to buy ahead, e.g. one month, at a predetermined rate, estimated in this case, on the 23rd April 1986. The premium quoted shows the dollar is becoming cheaper in terms of the pound when trading is projected forward. The **actual** spot rate for the pound viz the dollar or the F. Franc may be more or less than the forward rate quoted. Sterling can also be expressed in terms of a basket of other currencies valued to the pound. This average in index form, 1975=100, is the effective exchange rate, and shows a truer picture of the sterling movement in world markets.

b) **Treasury Bills.** These are short term forms of debt issued by the government. They are sold new, usually for 91 days, but can be traded up to redemption date in the money market. The difference between their face value and their market cost is equivalent to a discount or interest rate and this is quoted and dependant on the time period to redemption.

c) **Certificates of Deposit.** Again these are short term loan forms issued by large companies in sterling (£) or other currency denominations. They enable companies to raise loan finance and are similar to Treasury Bills in so far as their market price depends upon the discount or market interest rate, i.e. current supply and demand for funds. They originally developed as a secondary or parallel form of loan finance to the main money market.

d) **Interbank Market.** A large amount of day to day borrowing and lending takes place between the large city banks. This is the interbank or wholesale market as opposed to the retail market which is between High Street banks and their customers. The interbank market enables banks with large money inflows to lend and hence helps finance working capital needs.

e) **Clearing Banks Base Rate.** This is the interest rate determined in the "money market" and established by the High Street clearing banks as the basis on which they calculate lending and borrowing interest rates. It is influenced by money market movements and is the keyrate for retail lending and borrowing for the small borrower, etc. It also tends to influence mortgage rates, bank lending rates and credit card rates, etc.

2. Spot exchange rates indicate current market rates for the pound whilst the term rates of one and three months shows what the forward contract prices for buying the pound were in US dollars and Fr francs in New York and Paris on the 23rd April 1986. To take the US dollar as an example. In New York the buyer of sterling, on the 23rd April 1986, would pay a spot rate of $1.5285 and the bank bought sterling at $1.5165. In New York the one and three month "premium" means that the value of the pound is rising viz the dollar based on future expectations, i.e. the U.S. bank sells sterling ahead at $1.5165 + .53%, i.e. $1.5695, and sells dollars at $1.5285 + 150%, i.e. $1.5785. If a London trader bought ahead one month on 23rd April the forward exchange rate in London would be $1.5285 less one month premium .50%, i.e. $1.4785. This could be used to calculate a dollar export order which he may wish to sell ahead on the 23rd April. Alternatively a "discount" percentage is deducted from the spot rate to calculate the value of dollars to sterling. The above analysis equally applies to the case of Fr Francs etc.

3. The overall structure of money market rates will reflect a variety of factors such as (a) **the time period:** Normally as the time of the loan increases the interest rate increases to compensate the borrower for giving up money. In the Table, interest rates reduce as the time increases. This may be due to U.S. investors marking down the pound further than the interest rates so relatively high dollar yields on 3 month securities mean lower actual interest rates paid. It may reflect falling inflation rates in 2 or 3 months' time so "real" yields in the future are still higher than the current yield. (b) The range of money market rates reflect the **security of the issuer.** The government is the most secure issuer and would normally

pay less interest (lower discount rate) than commercial borrowers who issue Trades Bills which carry a greater risk than government issued stock, etc. (c) **Buying and selling rates.** In most cases the debt form, e.g. prime bank bills, quotes a buying and selling price with the difference equal to costs of operation plus profits. Often the margin is very small, e.g. $10^{13}/_{32}$ less $10^{11}/_{32}$ so only $^2/_{32}$ of a percent is cost plus profit. However, on millions of pounds turnover this can often represent substantial amounts.

U.K. FINANCIAL BALANCES, 1985

ANSWERS

1. As the Table shows, the 'financial balance' is the difference between a sector's savings and its capital spending. In the case of the personal sector there is a net surplus of £10.5bn, so savings far exceed any expenditure on capital goods such as houses, T.V.'s, cars, etc. Interestingly the public sector shows a roughly similar deficit, £10.3bn, which is the overall Budget deficit on government spending less taxation, otherwise known as the Public Sector Borrowing Requirement (PSBR).

2. Whilst personal savings equate with public borrowing, the Corporate Sector shows a net surplus of 6.2 plus 1.2 or £7.4bn. Much of this goes into overseas investment with £4.6bn being a statistical residual error, i.e. uncertain destination. The size of this figure does throw some doubt on the overall reliability of the Table. Nevertheless, it would seem much Corporate saving (profit) is being sent abroad.

3. Personal savings behaviour is very difficult to explain and the savings ratio is subject to a number of conflicting influences such as inflation, speculation, consumption and overall income levels, etc. Perhaps because of the recession in 1984, overall uncertainty about the future regarding prices and poor Income and Employment prospects have encouraged people to save, rather than spend out on capital goods, etc., so the personal sector has put more money aside for a 'rainy day' and savings have risen.

4. Capital outflows (imports) from the U.K. are generally related to U.K. companies investing in speculative and capital ventures abroad. Profits from trading (North Sea Oil revenues, etc.) were channelled overseas in the early 1980's, giving rise to arguments that future investment and employment prospects in the U.K. were being jeopardised and lost to overseas firms and workers. Some Economists have calculated this to be

worth 2% p.a. of GNP or equivalent to half a million jobs lost overseas. In view of this, some politicians have threatened to curb these capital movements. On the other hand, free market economists argue that the outflow of funds is indicative of poor U.K. profits and companies are entitled to send their money to invest in more profitable enterprises overseas. Furthermore, in due time this overseas investment will generate a flow of dividends and profits back to the U.K. They also argue that capital outflows keep the value of the pound low and help to create more competitive exports. Lastly, it is argued that restrictions on overseas capital flows will lead to reductions in investment in the U.K. by overseas businesses, e.g. multinationals. Therefore, the solution is not to reduce capital outflows but to improve the efficiency and profitability of U.K. industry, and at the same time reduce interest rates globally and U.K. inflation rates in particular, so that U.K. investment generates higher yields on capital.

THE QUANTITY THEORY OF MONEY — COST-PUSH INFLATION

ANSWERS

(a) The association between the annual change in money supply (M3) and the velocity of circulation (V) appears, in broad terms, to be an inverse relationship. That is to say as M3 rises in the early 1970's V falls, in fact becomes negative for 1972/3. As M3 reduces between 1974-6 V becomes positive. However, whilst this association is in broad terms there is no precise relationship between the two with respect to actual values.

(b) The Quantity Theory of Money, i.e. MV=PT, is one explanation of the overall relationship in (a). In this equation M (Money Stock) times V (Velocity of Circulation) represents the supply of money and this equals P (Prices) times T (Real GDP) which is the demand for money. Monetarists believe that by rearranging the formula to $\frac{M}{P} = \frac{T}{V}$ the left hand side represents real money supply and the right hand real money demand. If, as happened in the early 1970's, M3 increased real money supply and T remained roughly constant, the value of V fell to preserve the equation. V, the velocity of circulation, according to Friedman, is a mirror image of the demand to hold money balances and as this rose, V fell. As real money supply fell for 1974/5, due to stringent credit controls and high interest rates, real money demand fell to restore the balance, so pushing up the number of times money changed hands, i.e. V increased to 14.6%. According to Friedman, if Real Money Supply is stabilised by the authorities then long term V will also stabilise, reflecting the communities' demand for money for transactions purposes. In fact, during this period, control of money stock (M3) was erratic and unplanned which meant the communities' demand for money balances was erratic and this influenced V in the short run.

On the other hand, a Keynesian interpretation of the relationship between M3 and V would stress liquidity preference. To Keynesians liquidity preference depends upon speculative motives for holding money such as inflation rates, expected bond prices and likely interest rate trends and profit taking. The amount of money people and institutions wish to hold (money demand) determines money deposits and hence money supply (M3). In this model the lower the proportion of people's real income held in money the higher the velocity of circulation and vice versa. Therefore V is influenced by liquidity preference and inherently unstable since money can be substituted for any financial or physical asset. In the table money demand and supply (M3) increased in the early 1970's because of the possibility of speculative gain from high yield investments in for example property, even though interest rates rose, V fell reflecting real money holdings were expensive. As this potential for profit disappeared after 1974 money demand and supply, M3 fell and V rose to reflect the lower opportunity cost of holding money balances.

Quantity Theory liquidity preference is $\frac{1}{V}$ so as liquidity preference increases, V increases so the fraction ($\frac{1}{V}$) becomes smaller and V has to increase to enable a smaller money stock to facilitate transactions in the economy. In this model $\frac{1}{V}$ is influenced by speculative pressures, interest rates and overall money GDP. If prices and/or interest rates rise then $\frac{1}{V}$ would decrease as liquidity preference rose and V rose. As money demand increases it would lead to greater bank borrowing and lending which would push up money supply M3 accordingly. In other words, the association found in (a) is not a necessary or strict relationship but the end result of money demand and liquidity preference which will be influenced by speculative factors such as interest rates etc.

(c) As the 1970's opened the initial fall in real GDP was matched by an upturn in unemployment which dipped slightly in 1972, by .4%, as the economy grew by around 4.3%. As this growth continued in 1973 unemployment fell. However, 1974 and 1975 saw the growth of the real economy falter and unemployment rose again. Thus by 1976 there does not seem to be any relationship between real GDP and unemployment as the former increased by 4.2% but unemployment rose to 5.5%. However, it might be there is time lag between the two so that the 1973/4 downturn of the economy fed through into the labour market in 1975/6. Again this might explain the 1972/3 upturn in the economy and its impact on the labour market in 1973/4.

(d) Many economists believe that cost push factors are important in explaining inflation rates. These factors relate to wage and material increases as well as higher rents and interest rates. According to this view, a sudden upsurge, in say wages, above output, will lead to a rise in wholesale and then retail prices. Many believe this is more important than money supply in explaining inflation in the U.K. in the early 1970's. Statistically between 1970-76 import prices rose by nearly 40% due to a fall in the value of the pound and more expensive oil and commodity prices. It is usual for import prices to take a year or so to work through into higher internal retail prices and this seems to be so with respect to the data. Wage and salary earnings rose throughout this period and seem to have directly affected the Retail Price Index. It therefore seems that cost-push factors played a major part in inflation in the U.K. 1970-76. On the other hand, in the early 1970's Money Supply (M3) rose to 28.8% p.a. and no doubt monetarists would explain the increase in the RPI, which reached 25.3% in 1975, as having been directly caused by this factor.

UNEMPLOYMENT AND INFLATION

ANSWERS
(a) The diagram relating the rate of change of prices to unemployment is the "**Phillips Curve**" which shows an inverse relationship between the two variables. This indicates, to some economists, the trade-off between unemployment and inflation and, for example, indicates the opportunity cost of less unemployment in terms of increased inflation. At zero stable price inflation the unemployment rate is also determined and referred to currently as the Non-Accelerating Inflation Rate of Unemployment (N.A.I.R.U.). Since the curve is non linear it also indicates that reductions to unemployment will only be possible with disproportionate increases in inflation and vice versa. As the inflation rate becomes vertical the economy approaches full employment of resources and so bottlenecks appear in the labour, capital and land markets which push up inflation as maximum aggregate demand is attained. Professor Phillips never claimed the curve necessarily proved a causal relationship but merely indicated how inflation could rise as demand pressures in the economy increased, i.e. unemployment falls. Cost push pressures also build up at low levels of unemployment as

trade unions bid up wages and high interest and import prices fuel inflation.

(b) Apart from the 1973/4 unemployment figures the data seems to show both unemployment and inflation rising and so the Phillips Curve relationship may no longer hold, i.e. the UK economy suffered from "slumpflation", high unemployment (low growth) and inflation. Interpretations of these figures vary. Some economists hold that the Phillips Curve has merely shifted to the right due to (i) higher import prices as the UK devalued sterling in the early 1970's after a stable period when the UK was on the fixed exchange rates; (ii) substantial energy price rises, e.g. coal/oil; (iii) increasing labour militancy and rising wages; (iv) multinationals increasing UK prices in line with other overseas subsidiaries; (v) higher real unemployment benefits which reduced the willingness of many to obtain work so voluntary unemployment rose. On the other hand, **Monetarists** interpreted the figures differently. They deny the existence of the Phillips Curve and stress that long term unemployment is dependant upon the efficiency of the producer and factor markets. Trade Unions and others can increase wages and prices but unemployment will, in the short term, be independent of these actions. However, if labour bargainers **expect** inflation to rise they will build this into their next wage demands and so there will be a price wages spiral. If at the same time the government finances increased monetary demand, this will further push up prices so making UK labour and goods uncompetitive which will increase medium term unemployment. To cure the inflation problem monetarists argue wage-price expectations must reduce helped by government reduction of the money supply and so unemployment can only fall if wages fall and UK prices become more competitive. Thereafter the long run natural level of unemployment, in the diagram a vertical line drawn perpendicular from the unemployment axis where the Phillips curve cuts, can only move to the left as UK labour costs fall and labour demand rises. This view was clearly expressed in 1976 by the then Prime Minister, Mr Callaghan, in his speech to the Labour Party Conference, when he said: 'We used to think that we could just spend our way out of a recession, and increase employment by cutting taxes and boosting government spending. I tell you, in all candour, that that option no longer exists, and that, in so far as it ever did exist, it worked by injecting inflation into the economy. And each time that happened, the average level of unemployment has risen. Higher inflation, followed by higher unemployment. That is the history of the last 20 years.'

Chapter 25
MACRO-ECONOMICS, NATIONAL INCOME ACCOUNTS

FREEWHORN — NATIONAL INCOME ACCOUNTS

ANSWERS

(a) Production of (i) Cattle   (ii) Grain (tonnes)

Opening stock	300	**Consumption**	2500
Production	200	Input for cattle	2500
	500	Total	5000
Less consumption	200		
Closing stock	300		

Gross Domestic Product (note no external trade)

Personal Consumption
  Cattle   200
  Grain   2500

So GDP at factor cost = 200 cattle + 2500 grain, less capital consumption = 0, so GDP = NDP, so Net Domestic Product (National Income) = **200 cattle + 2500 grain. EXPENDITURE BASED.**

(b) If the economists receive an income this will be added to the present Net Domestic product at factor costs as above. Thus in strict terms National Income will increase by the extent of their incomes. If they are paid a high income it will increase overall NDP so average or per capita incomes will rise in terms of goods and services consumed. However, if the amount of cattle and grain remain unchanged then there will be less physical output of cattle and grain per head. Thus in one sense living standards have increased due to the services of the economists, which hopefully will increase future output, but in a physical sense since the island's inhabitants have to share their output between more people, living standards could decline. As National Income Accounts values services in the same way as physical output, problems of measuring living standards can arise, as this case illustrates.

Note: This question is used to illustrate economic theory and may not be biologically accurate!

GDP EXPENDITURE BASED 1981-85

ANSWERS

(i) £m 301 052 less (taxes/subsidies etc.) £42 780 = **£258 272m.**

(ii) Total domestic expenditure for 1981 of £246 704m less sum of expenditure components = **−£2,810m** (destocking).

(iii) Total Final Expenditure £450 170m less import equals GDP at market prices £351 567m so imports equal **£98,603m.**

(iv) Total domestic expenditure £225 100m less the sum of the known components equals consumers' expenditure of **£137,234m.**

(v) Total domestic expenditure for 1983 is the sum of all known components of expenditure = **£298,235m.**

(vi) GDP for 1984 at market prices is the sum of known components = **£320,168m.**

(vii) (a) Consumers' expenditure represented 47.4% and (b) General government expenditure represented 16.4% of total final expenditure in 1985 compared with 1960-75 averages of 52.4% and 14.5% respectively. Consumers' expenditure has slightly fallen as export expenditure has increased and general government expenditure has risen compared to 1960-75, as unemployment has pushed up social security payments.

(viii) $\dfrac{\text{GDP at market prices for 1982}}{\text{GDP at market prices for 1980}} \times \dfrac{100}{1} = \dfrac{276\,155}{230\,329} \times \dfrac{100}{1} = \mathbf{119.9}$

(ix) (a) MPC = $\dfrac{\text{\% Change in Consumption 1984/5}}{\text{\% Change in Income (GDP at market prices 1984/5)}}$

$= \dfrac{(213\,208 - 195\,711) \div 195\,711 = +8.9\%}{(351\,567 - 320\,168) \div 320\,168 = +9.8\%} = +.91$ of gross not disposable income

(b) MPM = $\dfrac{\text{\% Change in Imports 1984/5}}{\text{\% Change in Income (GDP 1984/5)}}$

$\dfrac{(-98\,603 - -92\,390) \div 92\,390}{(351\,567 - 320\,168) \div 320\,168} = \dfrac{+6.7\%}{+9.8\%} = +.68$

A MACRO-ECONOMIC PROBLEM

ANSWERS
(a) Equilibrium Income is where:—
$Y = C + I + G - te + X - M$
i.e. Where $C = 0.8$ of disposable income and disposable income $= 0.5 Y$
So $C = 0.4Y$ with no indirect taxes or subsidies.

Therefore:—
$Y = 0.4Y + 260 + 400 + 300 - 0.2Y$
which solves to $Y = \mathbf{1200}$.

(b) Total spending/income increases by 600 so the change in income $(\Delta Y) = 600$.

So $\Delta Y = 600 = \Delta C + \Delta G - \Delta M$ with no changes in I or X.

So $C = 0.4 \times 600 = 240$
$M = 0.2 \times 600 = 120$
So $600 = 240 + \Delta G - 120$
$G = \mathbf{480}$

(i) The budgetary position of the government changes from the initial position of
$\quad\quad G = 400 \quad$ given
$\quad\quad T = 600 \quad$ (0.5 of 1200)
$\quad$ Surplus $= 200$
$\quad$ to $G = 880 \quad$ (400 + 480)
$\quad\quad T = 900 \quad$ (0.5 of (1200 + 600))
$\quad$ Surplus $= \mathbf{180}$

Thus the **budget surplus falls from 200 to 180.**

(ii) The Balance of Payments position was
$\quad$ Initially $\quad X = 300 \quad\quad$ given
$\quad\quad\quad\quad\quad M = \underline{240}$
$\quad\quad\quad\quad\quad\quad\quad +60 \quad$ (surplus)
This changes to $X = 300 \quad$ no change
$\quad\quad\quad\quad\quad M = \underline{360} \quad$ (0.2 of 1800Y)
$\quad\quad\quad\quad\quad\quad\quad -60 \quad$ (deficit)

Thus the balance of payments moves from a **surplus of 60 to a deficit of 60.**

FIG.1

Expenditure (E)

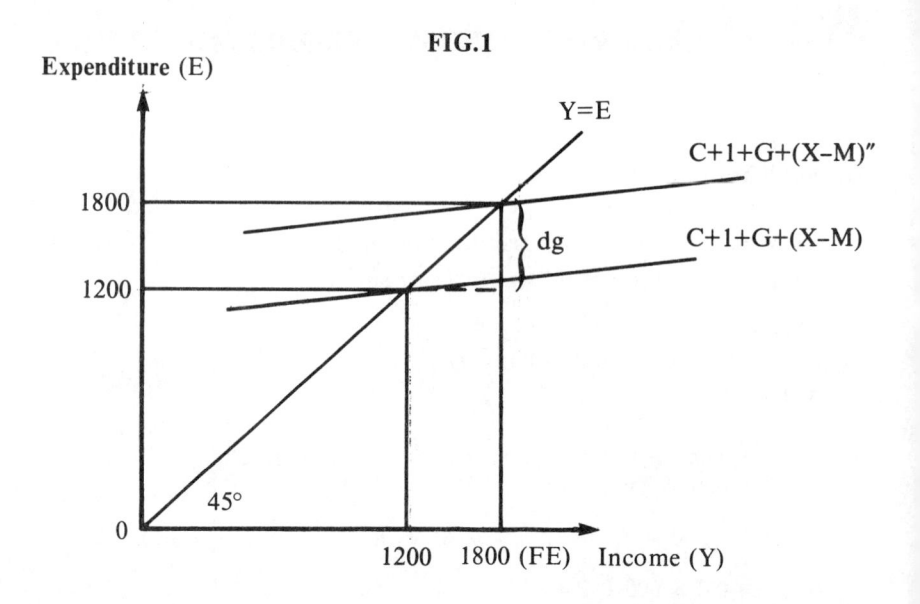

- 1800 ────────────────── Y=E
- C+1+G+(X−M)″
- dg
- 1200 ────── C+1+G+(X−M)
- 45°
- 0   1200 1800 (FE)   Income (Y)

From Fig.1 the dg (deflationary gap) is the lack of spending (i.e. 600 in the above example which is necessary for full employment equilibrium to be achieved at 1800. In the above example, an initial injection of 480 by the government will, via the multiplier of (×1.25), increase to 600 which is the amount of spending necessary to bring about full employment of the existing resources. If 1200 had been the full employment equilibrium, the extra 480 of government spending would, via the multiplier, have created an extra 600 of income which would have been inflationary so the diagram illustrating the deflationary gap would have shown an inflationary gap.

UK OUTPUT AND EXPENDITURE, 1984-87

ANSWERS

1. The chart shows the indexed, 1984=100, changes in consumers' expenditure, GDP (output), and manufacturing output and because these variables are composed differently and influenced by a variety of economic factors, it is quite possible for divergences to occur between each one. The GDP output measure comprises all domestic output and includes not only manufacturing, a fast declining sector, but also financial, leisure, personal and commercial services, energy output, construction, retailing, and other industries which may be experiencing strong economic growth. Manufacturing output relates to

specific sectors and itself experienced a dramatic downturn from 1979-83 so whilst the index shows an increase based on 1984=100, this does not necessarily imply we are back to pre 1979 output levels in manufacturing. Manufacturing output has been subject to influences which the rest of the UK output sectors may be immune from. It has experienced fierce overseas competition which was not helped by high interest rates and at times an overvalued pound. It has also suffered from small home markets, a low level of labour productivity and a consuming public who often prefer to buy imported manufacturing goods. Consumers' expenditure refers to disposable income and this element comprises the largest component, 53% of all domestic expenditure. Government taxation policies can affect disposable income and consumers themselves can save their income rather than spend it. At the same time, a strong pound can give consumers more buying power than their output deserves and earnings can often rise faster than output; at least for those in work. This means whilst expenditure growth lagged behind output 1984-85, it has subsequently risen at a faster rate from the third quarter of 1985 through 1986. If some of this expenditure goes abroad on imports, then neither GDP nor manufacturing output will be affected and since consumers' expenditure can include income from abroad (GNP), it would not show up in domestic GDP statistics. Therefore, although one would expect the three variables to move broadly together, they often can and do, diverge in the short term.

2. The overall trends in 1986 are for consumers' expenditure to outstrip domestic output and generally for there to be a levelling off in manufacturing output performance. The likely implications of this economic scenario are:— (1) Rising disposable incomes fuelling consumer spending, often on imported goods, alongside (2) disappointing manufacturing performance at home and abroad. For the moment (1985/86), GDP is buoyed up by North Sea Oil output and export earnings but as these decline and home demand pushes up imports (3) the Balance of Payments could come under pressure and the pound may fall. The increase in consumer earnings, boosted by tax cuts, together with high imported costs could push up (4) inflation and to offset this (5) interest rates have to be raised in London to stop an exodus of capital. These high interest rates will (6) prevent an increase in internal manufacturing investments. If global economic recession persists, this will (7) dampen down any growth in the UK Economy and generally usher in a downturn in (8) GDP which will again lead to (9) rising levels of unemployment and (10) cutbacks in the social services.

MACRO-ECONOMIC INDICATORS: LIVING STANDARDS

ANSWERS
1. The average weekly earnings of men in manufacturing (row 8) is a representative figure of earnings — basic wage rates plus overtime and other extras — of those males in manufacturing sectors. These figures, as averages, give a representative figure of overall earnings but say little about actual earnings in a specific sector, firm or region. There are two basic averages used in economics, the mean and the median (see Statistical Section). The "mean" is calculated by dividing the total wage bill in the manufacturing sector by the number of workers whilst the "median" wage would be calculated by listing all wages earned, from lowest to highest, and then identifying the middle wage in the range. In this case the figure would be based on the arithmetic mean and would be gross earnings, i.e. before deductions for tax and National Insurance. In order to obtain comparable figures for earnings over time it is necessary to deflate actual money earnings, by a factor equal to inflation so that 'real' adjusted earnings can be analysed (Row 9). To do this it is usual to select a base year, e.g. 1975 = 100 and then re-calculate the actual money wage by multiplying by the inflation factor — given by the Index of Retail Prices so:—

   a) Actual wage for year, e.g. 1980 $\times \dfrac{1975 = 100 \text{ i.e.}}{\text{Retail Price Index for the year, e.g. 1980}} = \pounds 59.74$

   b) Thus for 1980:—
   $= \pounds 111.64 \times \dfrac{100}{195.6} = \pounds 57.08$

   and for 1985:—
   $= \pounds 170.58 \times \dfrac{100}{276.9} = \pounds 61.60$

   The adjusted figures show 'real' earnings fell between 1975 to 1980 but recovered slightly by 1985; at least for those still at work in manufacturing.

2. The terms of trade relate comparative import and export prices and are given by the formula: $\dfrac{\text{Index of Export Prices}}{\text{Index of Import Prices}} \times \dfrac{100}{1}$

   In order to make a comparison, a sample of import and export prices are selected and both are compared to a base year, e.g. 1975 = 100, which is the representative yardstick of comparison for both import and export prices.

Then for 1985 the formula above applied gives $\frac{281.9}{250.3} \times \frac{100}{1} =$ **112.62**

Since 1975 the terms of trade have moved in favour of the U.K. since they have increased from 1975 = 100 to 114.0 in 1980 and 112.62 in 1985. Essentially changes to the terms of trade mainly occur because relative import and export prices change due supply and demand factors. This can happen for a variety of reasons. If relative demand for exports increases faster than imports or if supply (cost conditions) change, i.e. shortages occur in the production of the exported good, the terms of trade will move favourably for a country. In the case of the U.K. buoyant oil prices, at least until 1986, and stable prices of exported manufactured goods existed alongside lower prices for imported commodity goods, caused by the world depression. Also the value of a currency will also have an impact since an appreciating currency will push up export prices and so reduce import prices. The value of sterling between 1975-85 was kept up by buoyant North Sea oil revenues and high internal interest rates caused by the "Monetarist" experiment. Other factors which influence the terms of trade are artificial changes in export and import prices due to tariffs and internal levels of indirect taxation, e.g. V.A.T. These would not have had a significant impact in the case of the U.K. 1975-85.

3. Living standards will depend upon real earnings so actual earnings have to be corrected for inflation, see Row 9. The Retail Price Index, the usual deflator of actual earnings, is a representative figure based upon a sample of householders' expenditure, both young and old etc., and shows how the prices of the sample of goods in the household budget changes. Clearly row 9 indicates that the real earnings of male employees in manufacturing fell and then rose in general terms. However, the living standards of different groups will differ and for a complete picture other variables have to be considered, see Question 4. Nevertheless, living standards can be seen to have fallen as real earnings fell and then rose between 1975-85. Furthermore, as the terms of trade moved in favour of U.K. imported goods, then for example Japanese cars would have fallen in price and living standards would have risen. Generally speaking, if the terms of trade move in a country's favour, it becomes cheaper for the country, and its workers, to buy imported goods so living standards improve. On the other hand, the price of new houses rose faster than overall retail prices and since for many mortgage costs represent a quarter of all expenditure, then living standards could have fallen; though by the same token, food prices rose less than the Retail Price Index (R.P.I.). Living standards are also influenced by factors such as the quality and provision of social services, the extent of unemployment and job opportunities, the quality of goods consumed and the overall quality of

the environment, etc. Nevertheless, real earnings will give an indication of living standards and consumer purchasing power.

4. The Retail Price Index and hence adjusted earnings (row 9) are simple indicators of living standards but as a general representative figure they have their drawbacks. As mentioned above they fail to provide a comprehensive picture of economic well-being and because they are calculated as an average they do not reflect actual specific figures. Actual individual householder's budgets will not be reflected in the construction of index numbers and if the basket of goods selected in the sample does not change to reflect accurately spending patterns, then their use will diminish. This is because as individual market prices change, some groups will become worse off, e.g. Old Age Pensioners, whilst other high income groups will become better off. This is because the Retail Price Index does not accurately reflect changes affecting specific income or social groups but only shows up **broad** changes. Similarly average weekly earnings do not reflect actual earnings of workers, which can vary greatly according to occupation, industrial sector and region. Indeed indices of retail prices, earnings and hence living standards can be very misleading and of little use, unless interpreted with care. However, they do indicate in a simple way overall trends.

MACRO-ECONOMIC FORECASTS OF THE UK, 1986-87

ANSWERS
1. (a) **The real rate of interest** refers to nominal published rates, as issued by Banks (Base Rates) and Building Societies, corrected by the rate of inflation to real rates. Thus a nominal rate of 10% becomes a real rate of 6% with 4% inflation.

(b) **The savings ratio** refers to the rate of savings in the economy compared to disposable income. It depends on the rate of spending and to some extent refers to the average propensity to save, though whether saving influences consumption or vice versa is difficult to ascertain. In the passage it is assumed that lower inflation levels increase consumption and hence reduce the savings ratio.

(c) **The P.S.B.R. Target** The Public Sector Borrowing Requirement. This is the difference between Public Revenue (taxation) and Expenditure, which the government has to fund by borrowing from banks, individuals and companies at home and abroad. The 1979 UK Monetarist government who aimed to control inflation by regulating money supply, saw the PSBR as an important determinant of money supply and hence set targets for its growth. However, taxation revenue depends upon overall levels of income, spending and, for example, North Sea Oil Tax, and these factors are subject to uncertain influences so the actual PSBR often diverges from its budgeted target.

(d) **Real Personal Disposable Incomes** Personal incomes arise from wage earnings, dividends, rental income, etc. After deductions for Income Tax and National Insurance the personal (Householders) sector is left with personal disposable incomes. However, because of inflation this money income can be distorted and so it has to be deflated to real terms. This is usually done by using an index of inflation, e.g. Retail Price Index and the result is the level of real personal disposable incomes.

(e) **Negative contribution to growth** In terms of Keynesian analysis "leakages" of spending from an economy reduce the value of the multiplier and reduce overall levels of spending, income and economic growth. If imports rise, the leakages from the system increase and reduce overall income levels thus providing a negative contribution to growth of National Income levels. Indications of import levels, etc. can be seen in the Balance of Payments figures.

2. To a large extent movements in interest rates are assumed to be dependent upon the growth of money supply, PSBR, exchange rates, inflation and city expectations, etc. Some monetarists believe U.K. interest rates are aligned with real overseas exchange rates, e.g. U.S. dollar, and these will be influenced by relative inflation rates and the Balance of Payments; which is largely influenced by UK oil exports revenues. Thus if oil export prices are held up at $15 a barrel, if Public Borrowing can be controlled and hence limit money supply and inflation, then interest rates will stabilise viz others or even fall. At the same time, money market expectations in the city, about these factors, will be influenced by electoral uncertainty which will also play a part. These ideas in general terms relate to loanable funds theories of interest rate determination and exclude such concepts as liquidity preference and psychological factors, as elaborated by Keynesian liquidity preference theory. Nevertheless on the basis of the above argument the writer argues for a fall in interest rates to 9% by the end of the year. In actual fact, shortly after this article was published, interest rates rose rather than fell.

3. Total output refers to the sum of value added production in **all** sectors of the economy inclusive of primary, manufacturing and service. Industrial production refers mainly to **manufacturing industrial output.** Whilst the total output of the economy will be influenced by such factors as overall spending by the private, corporate and government sectors, industrial production will be influenced by the state of U.K. manufacturing competitiveness, foreign competition, and overall demand for oil (energy) to fuel industrial production, etc. Though consumer spending

can stimulate overall output of, for example, the service sector, other factors are at work to depress U.K. industrial production, e.g. import penetration to the manufacturing sectors. This is recognised in the last paragraph when forecasts about deficits on current accounts are made.

NATIONAL INCOME CALCULATIONS

ANSWER

Estimation of Gross National Product at Factor Cost

	£m
Consumer expenditure	84,000
Government expenditure	29,000
Capital formation	25,000
Value of physical increase in stocks	1,300
Total domestic expenditure	139,300
Exports	43,000
Total final expenditure	182,300
Less: Imports	42,000
GROSS DOMESTIC PRODUCT (at market prices)	140,300
Net property income from abroad	400
GROSS NATIONAL PRODUCT (at market prices)	140,700
Factor cost adjustment	
Taxes on expenditure	− 20,000
Subsidies	+ 3,000
GROSS NATIONAL PRODUCT (at factor cost)	**£123,700**

U.K. MALE UNEMPLOYMENT BY DURATION, 1970–85

ANSWERS
1. The overall long term trend has been one of rising unemployment though there have been periodic booms and slumps, with 1981 as the start of a sudden upsurge in male unemployment. At the same time, analysing the components of male unemployment, in terms of unemployment duration, shows similar overall trends though recently

long term unemployment has risen as short term unemployment has stabilised. One explanation of this may be that the long term unemployed are losing out to the short term unemployed who are able to offer more recent job experiences when competing for the same job.

2. Economists offer a variety of explanations for the sudden upturn in male U.K. unemployment after 1981. Government policies since 1979 have had a deflationary impact on the economy, coupled with high interest rates and increasing rates of taxation. Government spending has been reduced as the Public Sector Borrowing Requirement has been cut and overseas world demand has been sluggish and foreign competition fierce. This has not been helped by an overvalued pound, at least until 1985, caused by North Sea Oil revenues boosting the pound's value. This had the effect of pricing many U.K. manufactured exports out of world markets. Lastly, some argue the increase in unemployment was a symptom of an inefficient industrial base and an immobile, untrained workforce who had obtained excessive wage rises because of Trade Union power and who were not inclined to obtain new jobs because of over-generous social security provision compared to incomes, i.e. a rising "replacement ratio".

3. Apart from the various types of unemployment identified in textbooks, such as cyclical, structural, frictional and technological etc., there is also the crucial difference between short and long term unemployment; split evenly in the case of the current U.K. situation. This means government policies to reduce unemployment must recognise these two broad types and deal with them accordingly. On the one hand, economists argue that the long term unemployed have no real impact on the current labour market and therefore wage-push inflation will only be influenced by short term labour market pressures. If this is so, reflationary measures could be persued to create jobs for the long term unemployed without fear of cost-push inflation resulting. Since the labour market does not seem to have a place for the long term unemployed, Governments, it is argued, have to initiate planned work creation schemes, e.g. rebuild and rejuvenate depressed inner cities, etc. Furthermore, retraining schemes with guaranteed jobs at the end could, and are, being implemented for the long term unemployed.

In order to bring down both long and short term unemployment levels, the labour market may have to become more mobile and responsive to home and overseas market pressures. There is a need for more labour mobility between occupations and regions and in order that labour does not push up costs, economists such as Prof. R. Layard, propose a tax to be imposed on companies who pay their workers more than an agreed annual norm. This would be a form of Incomes Policy, similar to those tried in the 1970's. Otherwise, Keynesians argue, short term demand deficient unemployment can only be tackled if all Western Economies co-operate with reflationary policies, possibly directed towards re-investment in key manufacturing sectors suffering from structural readjustment problems.

Free market economists argue that the slowing down in the rate of short term unemployment indicates that the free market approach works. Natural market forces have meant that competition has left only the healthy firms and labour has been forced to accept realistic wage levels and move areas to take up work. At the same time, reductions in real Supplementary Benefit payments to the unemployed has meant labour has had to accept lower wages and thus it has 'priced itself' back into work and this is indicated by lower short term unemployment levels gradually falling. In other words, short term unemployment is responsive to competitive pressures which the government should encourage rather than adopt overall reflationary measures. However, some argue that long term unemployment at 4.9% compared with a peak of 3.3% in 1933 — The Great Depression — poses a major social problem and steps should be taken to bring the long term unemployed back into the labour market.

INDEX NUMBERS OF UK OUTPUT AT FACTOR COST

ANSWERS

(a) (i) Estimates of sectoral output are based upon the "weights" which show the relative proportions of each industry to total output produced. These proportions are indicated by each weight and the combined total of each industry's weights will add up to total output or Gross Domestic Product, i.e. 1000.

(ii) The "Service" sector includes personal and financial services output in the economy. In the Table the combined output of Transport and Communications, Distributive Trades and other services totals 88 + 101 + 376, i.e. 565 out of 1000 or a 56.5% share of total output.

(b) (i) The indices of output at factor cost have been based upon 1975 = 100 so comparing the industry figures for 1981 indicates that the fastest growing sector was Agriculture, Forestry and Fishing which increased by 21.7 points over 1975, i.e. (121.7 – 100).

(ii) The contributions of each sector to GDP can be calculated by multiplying the output increase since 1975 by the "weight" which reflects its proportion in the GDP. Thus for Other Services the output growth is + 7.3 × 376 = 2744.8 of a total GDP output growth of

4.5 × 1000 = 4500. Therefore the contribution of Other Services is 2744.8 out of a total increase of 4500, easily the largest contribution, i.e. 61%. Other sectors' contributions can be calculated in the same way and the calculations show as follows:—

Agriculture	28× 21.7 =	607.6 out of 4500 =	13.5%
Total Industrial	407× .3 =	284.9 out of 4500 =	6.3%
Manufacturing	283×−10.3 =	−305.6 out of 4500 =	−6.8%
Transport	88× 7 =	616 out of 4500 =	13.6%
Distribution Trades	101× 4.1 =	414.1 out of 4500 =	9.2%
Other Services	107.3×376 =	2744.8 out of 4500 =	61%

(c) (i) Comparing increases in GDP (output) between 1975 and 1976 shows a rise of 1.8 points which is equivalent to labour productivity. In other words, the same labour force have been able to increase output by 1.8% so no change in employment would have been likely.

(ii) In order to calculate employment changes in each sector it is necessary to estimate output changes between 1975 and 1976. In agriculture, forestry and fishing output reduced by 7.9 points which is likely to mean that unemployment increased, unless the sector was able to keep the same labour force producing less output. This could happen if the volume of output increased by at least 7.9 points. This means that the wages could be afforded with less output and higher final product prices, but this would seem most unlikely. Otherwise Transport and Communications and Distributive Trades both show a fall in output between 1975 and 1976 of more than 1.8 points, so unemployment is unlikely to have occurred in all these sectors.

(d) (i) The level of economic activity would refer to changes in Gross Domestic Product. When compared to changes in GDP total industrial production seems to follow the same trends, though until 1980 booms and slumps which occur in the level of overall activity are matched by greater changes in industrial production. After 1980 the fall in GDP is matched by a disproportionate fall in total industrial production. The output of Other Services from 1972 to 1980 follows a gradual upward trend. Its pattern does not match those of overall output which is more volatile and therefore does not experience any downturn, as GDP figures indicate, at least not until 1981 when it falls from 108 to 107.3. It is interesting to note that until 1979 manufacturing production follows the same path as total industrial production and hence overall output levels in the economy, though from 1979 onwards the level of manufacturing suffers a decline.

(ii) Other Services will include financial and personal services which will be dependant upon personal incomes and the demand for financial services such as banking and insurance. The demand in the economy for these services has grown steadily in the 1970's due to rising incomes in the S.E., the attraction of London as a financial centre, the growth of tourism and general household leisure habits increasing due to rising levels of spare time, etc. Industrial production is a larger element of GDP, i.e. 407/1000 as opposed to Other Services 376/1000, so any change in the GDP will be reflected in GDP. However, there are factors which relate movements of Industrial production closely to GDP. Much industrial production will be of producer or capital goods, in other words investment demand. This investment demand will respond to overall output or capacity levels of the whole economy and will be responsive to changing GDP levels as the "Accelerator theory" would predict. At the same time, industrial production will be more responsive to world trade conditions and international levels of competitiveness, e.g. Exchange Rates. Clearly as world trade fluctuates overall GDP will change and total world demand for industrial production will coincide with changing GDP levels. In a sense as GDP increases in the U.K. the economy could produce a multiplier effect throughout industry and this would have an impact on industrial production in either a positive or negative manner. The significant downturn in industrial production after 1980, greater than the downturn in the GDP, is due to the decline in manufacturing output which comprises 69% of all industrial production and 28.3% GDP output. After 1979 high interest and exchange rates coupled with a loss of internal export markets and foreign competition led to a run down of many manufacturing sectors especially in the North and Midlands. By comparison, "Other Services" demand was cushioned by a strong consumer expenditure and foreign demand patterns, e.g. tourism which moved in its favour. The slight dip in 1981 was due to an overvalued pound which increased overseas holidays at the expense of tourism to the U.K.

U.K. UNEMPLOYMENT AND HOUSE PRICES, 1985

SHORT ANSWERS
1. In broad terms there does seem to be a relationship between regional annual house price inflation and unemployment in 1985. In areas of low unemployment, e.g. the Home Counties, house price inflation is high whilst in high unemployment regions such as the North and Yorks. house price rises are below the level of inflation, i.e. they are negative. Whilst this overall relationship has been true for some years, recently the differences have become more marked, giving rise to the 'North-South Economic divide' debate.

2. This analysis reflects the varying economic strengths of the regions and their likely development. The movement of capital investment and resources to the South has led to a population drift which has put pressure on available land and hence house prices. In effect, the availability of jobs has been accompanied, in the South, by expensive housing. In the North the decline of traditional manufacturing industry together with a lack of investment and overall market income, has meant jobs, wages and overall demand has generally depressed house prices. The key point is that consumers' incomes are very closely related to mortgages and hence house prices and in the North incomes have lagged far behind those of the affluent South. In fact job losses in the South from 1980-86 have been around 6% whilst in the North the figure is around 36% which will reflect different regional GDP per capita figures.

3. The impact of such wide variations in national house prices could be considerable. In the South the overall wealth of those owning their own homes will be increased and the future income stream this represents will provide a form of "golden-handshake" or bonus to those in high price housing. At the same time labour mobility will be impaired. On the one hand, those unemployed in the North or other low housing cost areas will be unable to move South to take up jobs because of high housing prices whilst those in the South will be able to gain profits when moving North but will be unable to move South again because house prices will be too high. This could prevent workers and executives moving from the South to the North.

    At the same time the pressure on land in the South will increase and this will push up land values and increase demands for green belt land to be made available for the building of houses, offices, shops etc. On the other hand, certain high unemployment spots in the regions will be associated with cutbacks in home development and in specific cases the value of individual homes will be lower than the initial mortgage borrowed, thus causing personal hardship. This may lead to home buyers being unable to meet mortgage repayments and therefore finding themselves homeless as the Building Society takes possession. In all, the social implications of the North-South divide could be part of a wider political debate.
    Note: The student may note the similarity of this analysis to the Phillips Curve. However, this Data are cross-sectional whilst the Phillips Curve is historical in nature.

U.K. MANUFACTURING STOCK/OUTPUT RATIOS

ANSWERS

1. (i) Stocks are goods which are for sale at a later date or are used at a later stage in the productive process. In the National Accounts stock-building is classified as part of capital formation. Specifically manufacturer's stocks would cover materials and fuel inputs, work in progress, i.e. partly finished goods and finished goods stocks held by manufacturers, wholesalers or retailers awaiting sale. These could represent a buffer against fluctuations in sales and in the production/distribution process.

   (ii) Stock/output ratios show the statistical relationship between stock levels in each industry or the whole economy to overall output levels in the industry or the economy. They reflect sales, output, stock building and stock levels and they may be subject to wild fluctuations.

2. In the short term, changes in stock levels are often large and reflect changes in the level of sales and expectations about future sales. Firms can meet demand either from production or stock. A rise in demand can be met by increasing production or by drawing on stocks. In the very short term, firms may find it easier to adjust stocks rather than production and so volatile short term stock output ratios can exist.

   Firms hold stocks of materials and fuels and work in progress as part of their normal production schedule. The level of these stocks will vary in response to market conditions. In the long run, the level of stocks will depend on techniques of production or stock control, e.g. innovations in methods of inventory control recently have reduced the need for companies to hold large stocks. Other long term factors would include the cost of purchasing and holding stocks and the expected level and variability of sales. Sales could be affected by overall world or local demand patterns as well as competition and seasonal factors.

3. As the Chart shows, manufacturers' stock output ratios have fallen since 1980. This fall has been observed in other than the manufacturing sector and by the end of 1985 these ratios were at their lowest values for 10 years. The main textbook influences which cause companies to vary their level of stocks are expectations of output, prices and interest rates. The general decline in stock-output ratios since 1982 may now reflect a cautious attitude by companies after the recession of the early eighties. As mentioned, improved stock control methods could also have played a part. Also, higher interest rates and other high costs of stock holding will have contributed to the reduction in stock-output ratio. Specifically the cost of stock holding will reflect interest rates higher than the price of the

stocks held. It becomes expensive to hold stocks. Research indicates that for every 1% rise in the interest rate, there will be a fall of some £300m in the level of manufacturing stocks. Lastly, tax considerations also play a part. Until 1984 stocks held by a company could be partly offset against profits so it was worthwhile building up stocks so that profits reduced and the burden of corporation tax also fell.

4. Statistical analysis indicates that prior to 1980 stock levels were extremely volatile and this could have had a major impact on the economy in much the same way as the "accelerator" theory predicts for capital-output ratios. If businessmen's profit expectations increased in boom times they could raise stock-output levels, increase production and, via the "multiplier" effect, stimulate the overall growth of the economy. Similarly in times of depression they could reduce stock output levels which would reduce overall production and have a similar dampening impact on the economy. The magnitude of the resultant production changes may be much greater than the initial upswing or downturn predicted in the economy. This would make for a de-stabilising impact on investment in other sectors as well as on related labour markets. Economists believe that recently stock-output levels have fallen and have also become more stable, which could help contribute to a more even growth economy.

"WILL U.K. MANUFACTURING RECOVER?"

ANSWERS
1. It is alleged that North Sea Oil revenues have boosted our Balance of Payments and led to high exchange rates, which have made much of U.K. manufacturing industry uncompetitive. The Dutch economy experienced this in the 1960/70's when indigenous gas reserves led to high export earnings, an over-valued currency and an industrial decline. Nevertheless as North Sea Oil production declines the pound will fall in value making our manufacturing exports more competitive. This will lead to a resurgence of industrial production as our manufacturing export prices become cheaper. This is the mechanism by which North Sea Oil values fall and lead to an automatic recovery of the U.K. manufacturing sector i.e. falling sterling values make our exports competitive. It is argued that this may not happen because a) Germany and Japan both experienced a boom in manufacturing export output in the 1970's, though at the time they both maintained highly valued currencies; b) The exchange rate is not just influenced by the "balance of trade" on trade but also by capital movements and speculative pressures

which can distort exchange rates; c) Overseas manufacturing competitiveness depends not only on cheap exports but also the range and quality of the product, competitive substitute alternatives, etc.; d) It takes time and experience to commence manufacturing output from scratch and overseas dealer networks may not be available so even with new cheaper products it may not be possible to sell them abroad. Furthermore, if interest rates are high, manufacturing industry may not be inclined to invest in capital to produce for the new manufacturing competitiveness, i.e. they may be better off leaving their money in banks if U.K. interest yields are high enough.

2. The Balance of Trade traces the flow of imports and exports of visible goods. It is argued that this may not balance because a) the Japanese and U.S.A. balance of trade do not balance even with free exchange rates in operation; b) The U.K., it is assumed, has a high demand for manufactured goods so we must manufacture more goods ourselves otherwise there will be a permanent deficit on the Balance of Payments. However, it is previously argued that manufacturing industry may not make a dramatic recovery and so U.K. output of manufactured goods still may not respond. If U.K. demand for manufactured goods persists in the presence of low home-based output, then the balance of trade could be in a permanent situation as Japanese goods are imported into the U.K. etc.

THE COSTS OF UNEMPLOYMENT

ANSWERS
(a) The cost of each unemployed person to the Government can be calculated by adding foregone taxes and benefits costs and then dividing by those unemployed, i.e. 2.88m.

Thus $\frac{£12,945m}{2.88m}$ = approximately £5,000 per person.

(b) The figures in the Table represent the direct costs of unemployment but in another sense the 2.88m unemployed also represents lost output in the economy. However, the impact of unemployment in reducing output is difficult to calculate. One estimate by the Manpower Services Commission calculates that from a base level of 700,000, each 100,000 extra unemployed people cost £590m of output foregone, i.e. the opportunity cost of unemployed resources. Thus the loss to the national economy of three million unemployed would be in the order of £13.6 billion of output. This roughly doubles the cost to the economy of each unemployed person to around £10,000. It is also argued that unemployment is underestimated because many women made redundant fail to sign on and the young unemployed become students and claim educational grants. If at the same time one includes the extra cost of importing goods we are unable to produce ourselves because of the recession, the real cost of those unemployed may be well over the £26 billion of direct and indirect costs which these figures indicate. It is therefore easy to see why 1986 estimates of job creation schemes calculate that each new job created could cost as much as £40,000 per person.

THE ECONOMY IN EQUILIBRIUM

SHORT ANSWER
(a) The process at work is the negative income multiplier effect. Thus as actual savings rise this leads to a disproportionate fall in the level of income, i.e. savings exceed investment. Firms are left with unsold goods as consumption falls and this leads to less output and income in successive weeks. This is because savings remain at 20%, and exceed investment at 10% and so consumption and output continue to fall until a new equilibrium is reached.

(b) (i) **Assumptions necessary for the equilibrium are:—**
(1) Investment is exogeneous and fixed at 10%.
(2) Savings remain at 20%; that is unlikely in the real world.
(3) There are no other leakages, other than savings, such as taxation or imports.
(4) The Government do nothing to increase income or increase consumption etc.
(5) The process assumes a lagged adjustment to a static equilibrium of 50 which could change.
(ii) The new equilibrium will be reached when leakages (savings) equal injections (planned savings) at a National Income of 50 after "n" weeks. Here National Income (50) equates with Consumption (40) plus Investment (10).

INTERPRETATION OF THE P.S.B.R.

BRIEF ANSWER

The quote requires a definition of the P.S.B.R. as the excess of government expenditure over taxation, and also the economic background to the Monetarist, versus Keynesian interpretation of the management of the Economy. The **Keynesian view,** which the passage reiterates, would see the P.S.B.R. as similar to the Budget Deficit. In times of a slump it would increase to offset unemployment as government spending rises and in a boom period the P.S.B.R. would reduce and cut back overall expenditure in order to reduce inflation and prevent the economy overheating. Thus government expenditure and receipts and therefore the P.S.B.R. automatically adjusts and acts as automatic stabilisers in the economy. If the government sets a P.S.B.R. regardless of the state of the economy it is no longer following Keynesian demand management policies but rather sees the P.S.B.R. in a **Monetarist light. Monetarists** believe a rising P.S.B.R., via bank borrowing, causes an increase in the money multiplier, money supply and hence inflation. At the same time, Monetarists believe overall output, income and employment depend upon supply side policies and free market forces operating along with competitive prices. If the P.S.B.R. rises not only does it cause inflation it also pushes up interest rates and shifts resources from the private to the public sector and this could dampen down any economic recovery. Furthermore, say the Monetarists, unemployment does not depend upon demand management policies but rather depends upon the "natural rate" which is influenced by free market forces. This policy was pursued in the UK from 1979–86. Its success was mixed and critics argued that Monetarism and a fixed P.S.B.R., in the face of fluctuating economic levels of activity, failed to recognise that inflation can be due to cost push pressures and furthermore free market forces do not always work. In support of this critics argue that lower import commodity prices pushed down UK inflation after 1984 and also investment demand may be interest inelastic, immune from lower interest rates, so only by government investment spending will the economy pick up in a recession. Ultimately the argument resolves around whether demand (Keynesian) or supply (Monetarist) pressures motivate the economy and also whether inflation is a monetary phenomenon or due to cost pull pressures.

Chapter 26
PUBLIC FINANCE

THE COMPOSITION OF THE U.K. NATIONAL DEBT

ANSWERS

(a) The National Debt represents the total sum of cumulative borrowing by past and present governments. It is incurred because governments spend more than they receive in taxation so they have to borrow the rest. This debt is funded by issuing a variety of paper securities, e.g. Treasury Bills, in return for interest and these are bought by individuals, companies and banks etc., both internally and externally.

(b) (i) Over the period shown by the data, the amount of short term debt, i.e. Treasury Bills, has been reduced whilst long term forms such as "gilt-edge" securities has increased. Debt bought by the public in the form of National Savings Securities has increased whilst the amount sold to the overseas sector has reduced. Finally, the National Debt represented 64% of GDP in 1970 and only 43.6% in 1982, although the cost of servicing the debt has risen from 2.8% as a percentage of GDP in 1970 to 4.1% in 1982.

(ii) The structure of the National Debt has changed for a variety of reasons. Initially (1971) Treasury Bills were part of the Commercial Banks $12\frac{1}{2}\%$ Reserve Asset Ratio and by selling them to banks the government directly, though unintentionally, encouraged bank lending and hence indirectly the money supply aggregates, which is thought by monetarist economists to be inflationary. The significant fall in Treasury Bill debt occurred after 1978 which is when "monetarism" was first tried under the first Thatcher government of 1979. Again, monetarists believe that a rising Public Sector Borrowing Requirement is inflationary since it requires bank lending, etc., and furthermore they believe in the concept of a Balanced Budget with the commensurate reduction in Public Spending which this implies. These two factors explain why overall National Debt fell between 1978-82 as a percentage of GDP as the Thatcher government reduced public spending and the PSBR. At the same time, by selling debt to the general public, e.g. National Savings Certificates, they have been able to reduce the actual interest rates paid (viz rates paid to the banks) as the general public are willing to accept lower interest rates than the financial institutions. This has helped reduce the burden of servicing the debt and by reducing the amount of debt held overseas the authorities have tried to reduce speculative pressures on the pound. This is because such debt can quickly move into and out of London and so lead to fluctuations on sterling exchange rates and ultimately interest rates, which can have detrimental effects on home investment.

(c) The National Debt is often alleged to be a burden to the nation since interest has to be paid and the cost of servicing can become excessive. To a large extent the National Debt is money owed by the nation to itself and clearly as the public buy more National Savings Certificates and as this form of funding increases, then the National Debt effects a redistribution of income rather than solely representing a debt. Gilt Edge securities etc., are bought by companies, banks and pension funds etc. who themselves are owned and managed on behalf of the general public. Thus all ultimately benefit as holders of National Debt since interest paid by the government to these holders is paid by taxation, often from the self same people. Nevertheless, the National Debt can be seen as a burden to the nation when the cost of servicing the debt rises and when the debt is owned by overseas holders. In the first place, if interest rises faster than the economy's capacity (GDP) to pay off the interest, then clearly resources will be diverted towards paying for past expenditure which will reduce the ability of the economy to provide for future investment, etc. If this happens, then interest itself will be an increasing part of National Debt provision and social provision, etc. will be difficult to afford. At the same time, if debt is increasingly held overseas then it is a burden since the nation will be paying interest overseas. In the case of Mexico, etc. such debts represent significant proportions of National Income and export revenues and taxation revenues, etc. will go overseas rather than help increase indigeneous productive capacity. In the case of the U.K., the data shows that these factors have reduced in importance and as more debt is purchased internally, then the burden to the nation of the National Debt is reducing. On the other hand, ever increasing interest rates over the period means greater redistributive shifts in income so some sectors may find the Debt a burden because of taxation levels increasing, whilst others, e.g. National Debt lenders, will be better off as taxation levels fall and interest income rises. However, although the overall structure of the National Debt indicates a lesser burden to the nation, the answer to (b)(i) indicates that whilst the Debt represented a smaller percentage of GDP over the time period, the cost of servicing the Debt has in fact risen due to increasing interest rates.

THE IMPACT OF TAXATION ON THE POOR

ANSWERS

(a) The marginal rate of taxation is the percentage tax rate levied on the extra portion of income earned. In the U.K. there are increasing bands of income tax as taxable income rises, e.g. 29%, 40%, 45% etc. These bands of income tax are the marginal rates of tax as, for example, illustrated by the Pay As You Earn system.

(b) The U.K. income tax structure has a lower limit under which no income tax is payable and is dependant upon tax allowances given for household circumstances and individual status. However, inflation has pushed up money wages, though not necessarily real wages so many low income earners fall into these low income tax brackets. This situation also applies with National Insurance Contributions so a low income earner will suddenly find income tax levied at 30% (29% as from the 1986 Budget) and National Insurance deducted at a rate of $8^{3}/_{4}\%$ of gross income. This is because neither tax nor National Insurance lower levels have risen in line with inflation. If at the same time subsidies are no longer receivable, as income is now earned, then together these deductions mean that 250,000 low income families could find themselves with a sudden increase in income tax; effectively at a combined marginal rate of 50% in some circumstances. The problem or dilemma this causes to low income groups is known as the 'Poverty Trap' and Fig.1 illustrates graphically how the problem can arise, i.e. section b of the 'old system'.

(c) If the low paid are subject to such a high effective marginal tax rate, they may not enter the labour market because they may receive as much in the form of Supplementary Benefits as they receive in net pay. This will reduce the supply of labour into low paid occupations and vacancy levels will rise. This could threaten the output of certain industries and supply may reduce. It could also be argued that this may lead the business to install capital to improve output and replace labour. At the same time, unemployment levels may rise and government spending may rise so pushing up the Public Sector Borrowing Requirement. On the other hand, if labour supply reduces, entrepreneurs will have to pay higher rates which could increase the average industrial wage rate and threaten to increase cost-push inflation.

As the name implies, when income earners fall into the 'Poverty Trap', family hardship and suffering increases and there are estimates that around 25% of families, living in the North of England, receive an income below the poverty line. Many work rather than live off

Supplementary Benefits whilst others argue that in order to evade such penal tax rates the low paid accept cash payments and are part of the 'Black Economy' of unrecorded output and lost tax revenues. In order to make up this loss of tax revenue the Chancellor has to increase tax rates, lower real allowances or switch to other indirect tax forms such as V.A.T. which overall have a regressive impact and hit the low paid hardest.

FIG.1 THE POVERTY TRAP

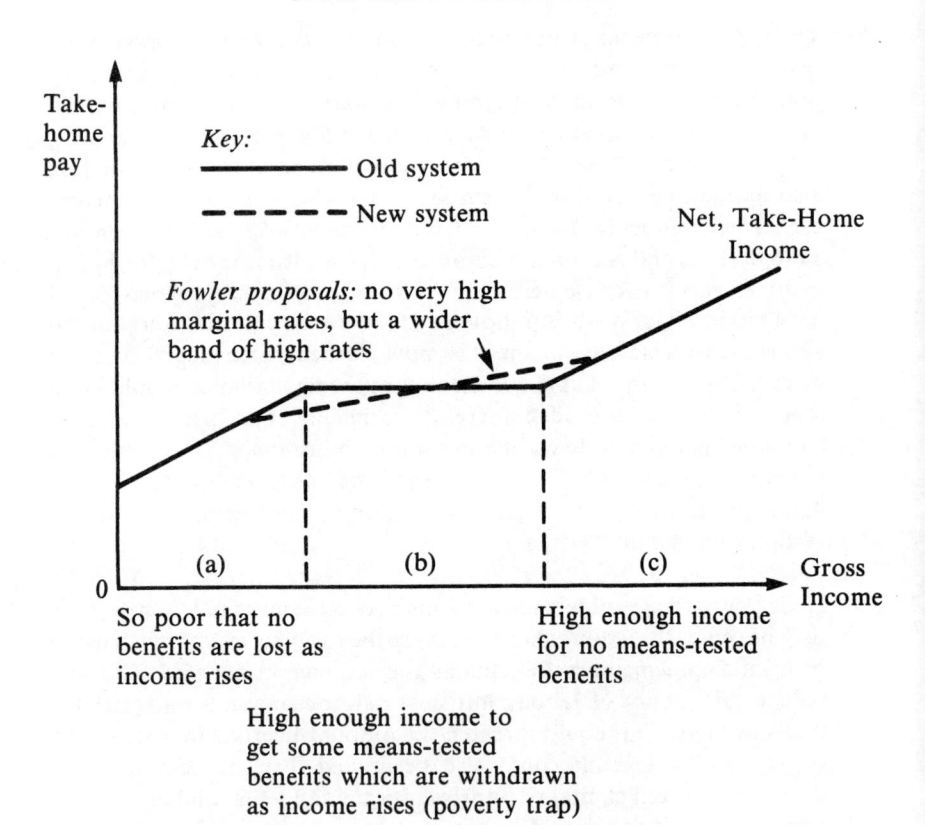

Key:
——— Old system
– – – – New system

Net, Take-Home Income

Fowler proposals: no very high marginal rates, but a wider band of high rates

Take-home pay

Gross Income

(a) So poor that no benefits are lost as income rises

(b) High enough income to get some means-tested benefits which are withdrawn as income rises (poverty trap)

(c) High enough income for no means-tested benefits

(d) In order to eliminate or reduce the problems caused by the 'Poverty Trap' the government could consider a number of reform options such as (1) Raise the minimum income level on which income tax and NI becomes payable in line with the rate of inflation. Alternatively, increase the tax deductible allowances in line with inflation, both reduce the average rate of tax paid. This 'indexation' process known as the Rooker-Wise Amendment sought to protect income earners from losing out when real wages fell but taxable income rose. The problem with the last proposed is that it would not specifically help the low paid since all income earners would be included so perhaps the former proposal would be more effective. (2) Reduce the lower tax rates and National Insurance Contributions in line with real wages received by the low paid so even if the poor fell into the initial low tax bracket it would not be a disincentive to work. The present Minister of Health & Social Security (Fowler), see Fig.1, has proposed a similar scheme whereby marginal rates would be lower than present ones and spread over a wider band of tax rates. This, in terms of Fig.1, provides a positive net of take home pay and overcomes the disincentive effect. It could also incorporate a means tested system of subsidy or Supplementary Benefit provision similar to (3) Abolish the present income tax system and introduce a Negative Income Tax (Tax Credits) scheme. In this sytem the Government would establish a minimum income which the householder receives — initially as a Supplementary Benefit — and thereafter as work is found and income is earned, the subsidies reduce and little or no income tax is paid. At some earned net income level all benefits stop and thereafter income tax is introduced. However, in all cases, after tax income is positive and rises so providing an incentive to work. In effect this Tax Credits System would abolish the distinction between income tax and benefits and effectively amalgamate the functions and operations of the Inland Revenue (Tax) and the Department of Health & Social Security (Supplementary Benefits). This would save on administrative costs but the Treasury may feel such a system could cost Tax Revenue unless it was carefully devised and implemented. (4) Lastly, it has been proposed that in order to overcome the anomalies and disincentive effects of the 'Poverty Trap', all income tax and National Insurance Contributions should be replaced by an indirect tax system, e.g. VAT. This would be regressive in its impact and do little to improve the lot of the low income groups who would possibly find their wages cut as the supply of labour into the market increased.

THE STRUCTURE OF U.K. TAXATION, 1974-81

(a) (i) Direct taxation is levied directly on the householders' income, i.e. on their wages, rent, interest and profit. Personal Income Tax, e.g. PAYE is a direct tax paid to the Inland Revenue.

(ii) Indirect tax is payable indirectly from income by the taxpayer when goods are purchased or when rates are paid, etc. Thus taxes on goods and services, e.g. V.A.T. would be an indirect tax as it is imposed indirectly on the income earner when goods and services are purchased. V.A.T. is collected at the place of sale and is payable to Customs and Excise.

(b) A progressive tax system is one where the percentage of income paid in tax rises faster than income. A regressive tax is one which has the opposite impact to a progressive one and a proportional tax takes a constant percentage of income in tax as incomes change. Personal Income Tax and National Insurance are progressive taxes and these totalled 50.5% of total taxation in 1974 and 49.1% in 1981, thus indicating a slight reduction in the progressiveness of the tax system. However, National Insurance is less progressive than taxes on personal income since the upper rate of N.I. contribution occurs at a relatively low level of income and to that extent the reduction in taxes on personal income from 33.4% to 29.3% could indicate a reduction in the progressiveness of the tax system. Otherwise both tax percentages on goods and services and rates rose so reducing the overall progressiveness in the system.

(c) The major tax changes shown in the Table are as follows:—
(1) Overall taxes on personal income have reduced whilst those on goods and services have increased. This has meant overall taxes on individuals have become more regressive thus widening income differentials and worsening the plight of the poor. This increase in taxation on goods and services will have an uncertain impact and incidence on individual industries output and profit and on central government tax revenues. On the other hand, it could be argued that the reduction in personal income tax and corporate income tax (on company profits) could improve the incentive to work and invest and thus help increase output.

(2) Increases in indirect taxes on goods and services, e.g. (VAT) immediately increase the rate of inflation and can lead to Trade Unions pushing up wages and hence costs. VAT also distorts the true marginal cost of factor use so prices no longer relate marginal utility and marginal cost. At the same time, National Insurance is seen by many as a payroll tax on labour employment and by increasing this tax employers may be deterred from taking on labour or they may find their wages bill increasing, because of National Insurance costs, so helping increase "cost push" inflation.

(3) Overall taxes on property (rates, etc.) have increased and again many argue that this is regressive since the ability to pay rates is not

related to income bu the rateable value of property. This may reduce mobility of labour as people are deterred from moving because of high rates, and since rates increase as the size and value of the house increases, it has been argued that rates are a tax on home improvements and hence investment in the condition of the housing stock reduces. Rates imposed on non-domestic property, e.g. factories, can act as a deterrent to businessmen setting up in an area and this could lead to potential job and income losses.